Personal
Equation

BOOKS BY ALBERT GUÉRARD

PERSONAL EQUATION

REFLECTIONS ON THE NAPOLEONIC LEGEND

PREFACE TO WORLD LITERATURE

THE FRANCE OF TOMORROW

NAPOLEON III: AN INTERPRETATION

EUROPE FREE AND UNITED

FRANCE: A SHORT HISTORY

ALBERT GUÉRARD

Personal
Equation

W · W · NORTON & COMPANY · INC ·
NEW YORK

921
Q92

First Edition

PRINTED IN THE UNITED STATES OF AMERICA
FOR THE PUBLISHERS BY THE VAIL-BALLOU PRESS

26702

TO

MACLIN CATHERINE COLLOT

Born with This Book

Animula vagula blandula. . . .

Contents

Preface

Le peuple n'a guère d'esprit, et
les grands n'ont point d'âme. . . .
Faut-il opter? Je ne balance pas,
Je veux être peuple.
LA BRUYÈRE, Caractères.

═══════════════════════════════

THIS IS not an autobiography in the usual sense. Happy men, like happy nations, have no history. I have lived in Utopia: free from want and free from fear, with no responsibilities beyond my strength, with no desires beyond my reach. So this book does not record the outward events of my life, which has been placid. It records the evolution of my thought. Thinking has been my pleasure, my business and my dignity. America has made it possible for me to think: in acknowledgement of this great privilege, I am submitting an account of my forty-year stewardship. I have long looked forward to this tranquil hour—yes, tranquil amid the tragic turmoil of the world.

If I am to present a candid report of my ideas, I must carefully discount the accidents which have affected them. I must measure the "aberration" of the instrument, my own mind. I must define, in order to guard my readers and myself against them, the prejudices and influences which have colored my thought. This is what I mean by "Personal Equation."

This is a book about myself; but my conception of Self is the reverse of that held by the glamorous ones, Romantics, dictators, debutantes and other self-idolaters. I believe that the Self is unique indeed, but so unique as to be incommunicable. What *they* call Self and obtrude upon the world is but *persona,* script, trappings, limelight, for the enjoyment of the performers and the audience. To me, the visible Self is but a flaw. In these pages, I appear as an individual only in order to be a more reliable witness. My testimony anticipates its own cross-examination.

No two readers would agree as to what is relevant to the main purpose of such a story. I have been unable to keep strictly separate my daily life, my thoughts, and the historical background. Cities, poets, events, have not merely been my teachers: they have become part of my Self. I am a detached bit of Paris, a fragment of Victor Hugo, a super in the Dreyfus drama, a cog in the monstrous war machine. I am conscious of inner change through these seven decades. But *growth* would not suffice to define the process. There is no element in my mature mind that was not present, and conscious, in my adolescence. The progress, if I dare to use that question-begging term, has not been an extension, but a deepening; not a discovery, but a more harmonious perspective. I should have called this book my *Education,* if Henry Adams had not pre-empted the name; or my *Americanization,* if Edward Bok had not stolen my thunder; perhaps my *Humanization,* if the haughty shade of Irving Babbitt would allow me to call myself human. But the aptest title would be: *I Accept Democracy.*

This was no sudden revelation, but a gradual focusing. As a young man with a ravenous appetite, I absorbed more facts and ideas than I could assimilate. I was barely conscious of contradictions: they appealed equally to various sides of my nature. This complexity was not irremediable chaos. I left Europe with an adult mind, whose firmness, such as it was, resulted from antagonistic stresses. These have not disappeared; to the present day, my Self is their equilibrium. It would be suicidal for me to cut loose from any of them. I have an experimental spirit coupled with a conservative taste. I had in early youth, and have retained almost unimpaired, a deep love for long-rooted things, for mellow books, quaint old streets, ancient creeds. I felt also, and I am still able to feel, the exhilaration of the unexplored, the eternal *Invitation au Voyage;* I am ready, at a moment's notice, to embark for Utopia—with a return ticket. But the Tory and the Radical within me are on the friendliest terms. I have read Ecclesiastes in a four-mile-a-minute airplane, and enjoyed both flights without any sense of incongruity. Why not admit it? *I am not a divided soul.* My frontiers may be pretty far apart, but there is no danger of secession. It is perfectly true that the dull have not enough selfhood to be split. But to be rent asunder is no sign of profundity. After all, the flimsy tears more easily than the tough. Strange epoch, in which a man has to apologize for being incurably sane; just as if a nation were ashamed of not being in a state of civil war.

I came to America a Tory and an anarchist; just a trifle proud of each paradoxical attitude, and of their still more paradoxical coexistence. I was a democrat in an obvious, barely conscious, and, I might have thought, superficial way; a democrat like "the man in the street," then a vague figure to me, ignored rather than despised. Democracy, to my mind, was like common speech; Toryism and anarchism were *styles*, and their combination was *my* style, that is to say myself. Today, my perspective is totally altered. Democracy is the core of my thought; the rest is but accident or ornament.

I need hardly say that democracy never meant for me our peculiar political machinery, and still less economic *laissez faire*. I am fond of quoting the very wise words of Lord Tweedsmuir (John Buchan): "I could imagine a democracy which economically was largely socialist and which had not our constitutional pattern." [1] I share Washington's contempt for parties or "factions." I never believed in the absurdity that men were created equal. I have no superstitious awe for our Constitution. Indeed it seems to me the highest proof of our national sanity and vitality that we have been able to do so well with such a creaking and cumbrous instrument. To cap all my heresies, I consider voting merely as a clumsy make-shift. Voting becomes meaningless whenever there is an intelligent way of reaching the truth. No one thinks of submitting the theories of Einstein to a popular referendum. Voting is simply homeopathic civil war. Undoubtedly it is better to count heads than to break them, and ballots at their worst are less harmful than bullets. But, on the battlefield or at the polls, there is no proof that God is on the side of the big battalions. *Vox populi* is not *vox Dei*. It takes an individual to articulate a thought. The masses can only grunt approval or growl dissent.

What do I mean by democracy then? Simply the regime that will place the least obstacles in the path of justice. And the obstacles to justice are *privileges*. I might go further, and rally to Michelet's conception: Democracy is the regime that will place the least obstacles in the path of love. The two ideas are linked; for it is privileges that breed hatred; and there can be no fraternity without liberty and equality of status. In so far as democracy does not hamper justice (the will that truth shall prevail), it joins hands with science, which is the quest of truth. In so far as democracy does not hinder love, it opens a free field for religion, which is the rule of love.

[1] Lord Tweedsmuir, *Pilgrim's Way* (New York, 1940), p. 222.

Democracy therefore, modestly and negatively defined, is
the denial of privilege. It combats all special interests that
attempt to raise themselves above justice. Naturally, since
the privileged, as a rule, are minorities, and since the "underprivileged" or "unprivileged" are the many, democracy champions the cause of the masses. So it may be defined as the
government of the people, by the people and for the people.
But it is not based on the divine right of the majority to do
wrong. Jaurès taught me that the defense of a single man,
the militarist and capitalist Dreyfus, could be a democratic
cause. Democracy does not imply that the "common man"
is a noble savage, unspoilt, closer to our pristine innocence
than the alleged elite. I have met admirable characters among
the well born, the wealthy and the wise; and I take it there
must be no lack of fools and scoundrels among the masses.
But "Charity . . . vaunteth not itself, is not puffed up, . . .
seeketh not her own." The elite, by asserting privilege, do
those very things.

In 1906, I came into a country that had rejected old-world
privileges. The most radical democracy then could be, not a
remote Utopia, but a way of life! As my transplanted roots
drew nourishment from the rich American soil, my latent
democracy grew strong and bore fruit. I realized that I had
been a democrat all my life, and not merely an anti-Royalist.
Without being fully aware of it, I, like La Bruyère over two
centuries before, had taken my stand: "The masses have no
wit, and the privileged have no soul.[2] If it comes to a choice,
I do not hesitate: I want to be with the common people."

That is why, as an American in the spirit, my work has
been and is directed against all the supercilious elites, the
exclusive aristocracies, the embattled professionals, the exquisite connoisseurs, the esoteric cliques, the special interests,
the Pharisees in every domain, so deeply thankful that they

_____

[2] I.e., "no conscience when their privileges are concerned."

are not as other men are, so damnably clever in defending their little fortresses of ivory or gold. Any privilege that refuses to stand the test of reason and justice is a superstition and must be challenged. If anyone should claim that America constitutes an elite among the nations, and as such is entitled to peculiar rights and immunities, I should denounce such a claim as un-American. This constant protest against *assumed* superiority is probably the chief factor in my personal equation.

Descartes said: "Of all things in this world, good sense is the most evenly distributed." This is radical democracy indeed, and I am too cautious to endorse such a statement. I should like to amend it as follows: "Good sense is not automatically improved by subtlety or erudition. Good sense is common sense. Exact truth is refined truth; but good crude thought is more sound than perverted thought, just as good plain fare is more wholesome than elaborate poison. And the pride of belonging to the Chosen Few is an intellectual and moral poison."

Repeatedly I have found that ordinary people, the common folk, were more receptive to simple and daring ideas than the sophisticates. I trust John Doe in preference to Charles Maurras or T. S. Eliot. In Europe, "democracy" was long considered uncouth, while conservatism of the Burke–de Maistre type was cultured. The connoisseurs are at last rediscovering Victor Hugo. But they sneered at him for fifty years. The people *knew* all the time. In the Dreyfus Case, the workers saw the light before the members of the Academy. We had similar affairs of our own: the common people flocked to meetings of protest; it was those learned in the law who found complicated reasons why justice should not be done.

Scholars, scientists and philosophers of note have rallied to the idea of an international language; but, for generations, how they had scorned the ignoramuses who took it seriously! In 1919, John Doe knew the right answer: the aristocrat, the scholar, the statesman Henry Cabot Lodge did not. During the Second World War, the professionals of the State Department and their appointed experts put their trust in Pétain, Weygand, Giraud, and refused to understand what De Gaulle stood for.[3] Again the people knew: Giraud had to be smuggled hurriedly through New York, and De Gaulle was acclaimed. The plain man knew that he wanted world peace through world organization: it is John Doe in his hundreds of thousands who bought *One World* and *The Anatomy of Peace*. The experts had to promise what John Doe wanted— but with tongue in their cheek. When the end was in sight, those "in the know" smiled contemptuously at such a naïve ideal. "We must be realistic! We must not be perfectionists!" And the splendid momentum that had carried us to victory was broken; and the nations resumed that elaborate game of power politics and secret diplomacy which, inexorably, "realistically," must end in Armageddon.

There are two ways of despising the people. The worse is to court popularity; Renan chose the other. An aristocrat in thought, he poured upon the vulgar herd his "transcendantal disdain." But, after forty years, he had to confess that his epigraphy, his philology, his philosophy, his theology, had led him to the conclusions of the man in the street. This admission took great courage, although he veiled it with a deprecatory smile. For all his subtleties and ironies, Renan had a strong, honest mind. But how much stronger he would have been, if he had spurned the vanity of the Elect, if he had not

[3] Whatever happens to De Gaulle, his place in the Resistance movement is secure.

tried so long and so hard to keep aloof from the people! Between Renan and Lincoln, there is a difference in moral stature.

I am not Lincoln, I am not Renan, I am I. And this is my testimony.

Albert Guérard

STANFORD UNIVERSITY
CALIFORNIA

PART ONE

My Europe

CHAPTER ONE

My Paris:
River, Streets and Churches

=================

I AM A water rat. The river Seine was my swimming hole, my playground, my first teacher. I still have its gentle confidential plashing in my ears, its soft pewter gleam in my eyes, its faint intimate odor in my nostrils. Whenever I find myself again on the lower quays of the Seine, Time is abolished: I am the eager and dreamy gamin of years before the flood, under President Jules Grévy and Sadi Carnot, when automobiles, airships, movies, existed only in the teeming brains of Jules Verne, when even that wizard had not dreamt of X rays, the radio, or atomic energy.

For some twenty years, until 1901, we lived not a hundred yards from the Seine, in the placid, provincial and rather melancholy rue de Lille. The Quai d'Orsay Railway Terminal did not cumber the left bank of the river until the very end of that period. I still feel its presence as an intrusion in the Faubourg St.-Germain, that aristocratic quarter moated and battlemented in its old-world prejudices and its Catholic traditions. From the first, I was amused and annoyed by its heavy *beaux-arts* ornamentation, like costume jewelry on an overripe bosom: in architecture, 1900 is a particularly bad vintage. My grudge has lost its bitterness: we have tolerated each other for nearly half a century. Time has tempered the glare of the nine arches, and of the three majestic ladies seated on pseudoclassical odds and ends. I suppose that if the poor old thing, with its tarnished stone frippery, were to be removed, my relief would be tinged with regret. An inveterate nuisance grows insidious roots; pull it out, and its vacant place is a scar. I shed a tear, with the proper blend of irony and pity, over the Palace of Industry and the paunchy old Trocadero.

In my childhood, there stood between our house and the Seine two contiguous barracks: Dragoons on the quay, Municipal Guards on the rue de Lille, so that my days were punctuated with bugle calls, and the silvery tones of cavalry trumpets. These barracks were commonplace and decrepit. They had to be heavily shored up before they were abandoned. But next to them rose in gloomy magnificence one of the vanished wonders of my Paris, the ruins of the Cour des Comptes.

It was a massive palace in the Roman style—round arches separated by engaged columns, as in the Colosseum; Tuscan for the lower story, Ionic for the second. Until 1871, it had housed the Council of State and the Chamber of Accounts. When new, it was robust, unimaginative, dignified: a worthy home for Napoleonic bureaucrats, their heads stiff with high collars and starched neckbands. In the last throes of the Commune, it went up in flames, as did the Tuileries, the city hall, and many other public buildings. The charred walls were not pulled down until a quarter of a century later.

The magic of fire had purified and sublimated that morose citadel of administrative routine. Gone were floors and rafters; the arches stood out, vigorous and yet aerial, on the changing sky. The grayness of aging stone was touched with richer hues: ochre, sienna, umber, with patches of angry red. In early childhood, I was fond of Victor Hugo's weird drawings; but, although I was entranced by their romantic charm, they depicted a familiar reality, the Cour des Comptes. Later on, I discovered that the ghostly palace, somber and defiant, had been my gallery of Piranesi etchings: in certain moods, the nightmarish mysteries of "The Dungeons," at other times the grandeur and melancholy of "The Antiquities."

As in Piranesi's visions, the mighty and tragic ruins could wear a smile. They were overgrown with wild flowers, creepers, brambles, that rank vegetation which thrives on crumbling walls, and spreads its mantle over rubble; it astounded and delighted London after the Blitz. The rigid classical features were fantastically festooned. On the terrace along the Seine, and in the Court of Honor, a jungle had sprung up; trees, with gentle tenacity, had wrenched apart the heavy flagstones. Life had reconquered the ruins, now that the dead accounts and official reports had turned into impalpable ashes. Innumerable pigeons dwelt in the crannies. The ground floor was a vast asylum for strayed and decayed cats; the devout old maids of the neighborhood brought them the leftovers of their frugal meals. Once a year, in autumn, migratory birds would gather at the Cour des Comptes. For days, they actually practiced flight formations. Suddenly, they were gone.

The walls had been well and truly built; although unbraced, they stood the storms and the rains. Yet they were treacherous, and the ruins were not open to the public. As my nurse and I were passing by, a huge block hurtled down from a third-story cornice and crashed within ten feet of us; soon afterwards, a hoarding was put up around the whole edifice. I used to look up with proud proprietary interest at the white scar left by the fallen stone. I felt that there my personal enemy had lurked. I am no Dr. Pangloss, and I do not believe in the universal benevolence of men and things; still, I never had again that sense of inscrutable malignancy. That stone had been my Moby Dick; and it had spent its rage in vain.

In architecture, there are three ascending stages: newness, with its smooth and banal perfection; age, which means decay; and death. This is almost Baudelairian doctrine; yet, out of sheer perversity, I suppose, I refuse to acknowledge myself an orthodox Baudelairian. Next to the Quai d'Orsay Station stands the charming little Palace of the Legion of Honor. It has lived for nearly two centuries; it is full of wrinkles, patches and blotches—doors and windows which mar its exquisite purity, wooden shutters that break its classic lines. Compare it with its improved, its perfect replica in San Francisco, grandly overlooking the Golden Gate; in the Californian version, there is not a single blemish; but the smiling little edifice has been turned into a mausoleum. Years confer upon a building the grace of life; but death is the supreme artist. Is there a mansion, a castle, a church, a palace, that a conflagration would not improve? This is no incitement to arson: I am a practical man, and like a roof over my head. But Europe, in all likelihood, is going to erect brand new monuments to the heroes of the Great War. Let her preserve ruins instead: the symbol will be deeper, and beauty will be better served.

Now we leave behind us the ghost of the Cour des Comptes and the incubus of the Gare du Quai d'Orsay; and we are at last in view of the river. Let us descend to the water level. Others, my neighbor Anatole France best of all, have sung the upper quays with their unique riches, the bookstalls on the parapets, the antique shops, the stately buildings. I was to be slowly initiated into their beauty; but my first fascination was for the river itself, the water's edge, *la berge*. No one fully understands the Seine who views it only from the upper level; no balcony reveals a street as does the sidewalk. I played by the hour, usually alone, on the huge piles of sand, gravel and building stones that were stored in front of the Cour des Comptes. I ventured on derricks when there were no watchmen around. I should have been drowned, had not a higher fate awaited me; for that was a long time before I could swim. But I never had any fear of the water. We felt that the river was a friend—an indiscreet friend at times, which, every winter, paid an unwelcome visit to our cellar.

So my earliest recollections are not of our modest home, of our streets, of the quays, but of the glaucous flowing water and of its changing temper: placid as a rule and, in the early hours of a summer day, almost as still as a canal; striated and rippling with the wake of many boats, a blurred shimmering mirror to the mottled sky; pitted by the rain; almost angry in floodtime, its brownish yellow waves lapping first the feet, then the knees, then the breast of André, the great stone Zouave guarding the Alma Bridge.[1] Almost every winter, it carried ice floes; and as you watched them rush by, barely ten feet below, from the parapet of a bridge, it was the solid arch itself that seemed to run upstream in a smooth, swift, uncanny motion. Once at least within my experience, it was frozen over.

The architecture of Paris assumes a richer perspective when viewed from the river below. The quay walls form a basement in miraculous harmony with the buildings. A bridge, for the man who crosses it, is a mere convenience; from a boat, it is an encumbrance, and a thing of beauty. Most of the bridges in Paris are honorable; a few are a caress to the soul. Even the Pont Alexandre III has a robust elegance, veiled but not destroyed by its baroque 1900 ornamentation. The Auteuil Viaduct is a worthy descendant of the Pont du Gard: it blends austerity and grace in the best tradition of

---

[1] The greatest flood of all, that of 1910, I missed. The Seine oddly reappeared in former beds forgotten for centuries; in front of St. Lazare Station, for instance.

imperial Rome. There is only one bridge in Paris which is cynically, irremediably hideous, the Pont des Arts. Fate and the stupidity of engineers have placed it in the most perfect of urban landscapes, just below the point of the *Cité*, the prow of a fabulous vessel anchored in midstream. There is one extenuating circumstance: it is so slight that it can easily be overlooked. Foreign visitors often think that it is temporary: it is now among the antiques, and, in Paris, the very earliest example of iron construction. It was built under Napoleon I, and the Emperor was furious when he saw it. But he was too economical or too busy to have it removed. No regime has had the courage to pull it down; and with the obstinacy of the dull, it refuses to commit suicide.

Of all the bridges, my favorites were the oldest, the Pont Neuf and the Pont Royal. The primacy of the Pont Neuf is undisputed. But the plainer Pont Royal appealed to me more deeply. Perhaps because it has a hump: a flat bridge still seems to me unimaginative and utilitarian. Obscurely, I thought of the Pont Royal as a kindly Titan allowing pigmies to cross the river over his back.

The lower quays have a life of their own. They had, in my days at any rate, their local industries: floating washhouses, hot baths, swimming baths, carding the wool (and it was wool) of old mattresses. Everyone was familiar with that philosophical figure, symbolic of much that is eternal in France, the "compleat" and ever-frustrated angler. Paris began as a fishing village, and has not lost touch with its origins. Behind the fisherman stands the *badaud*, the still more philosophical idler, who says admiringly: "What marvelous patience! I have been watching him for hours, and he hasn't caught anything yet!"

Just below the Pont Solférino, there was a man who clipped, shampooed and bathed dogs; and clipping a poodle in true Parisian fashion was a work of art: lion's mane, body closely shorn, a tuft at the tip of the tail, a ruffle above each foot. I can't vouch for the following scene, which I have from Jules Moinaux, but it is quite in the spirit of the quays. *Dog Beautician:* "That dog needs a clipping." *Man:* "Just what I was thinking." *Beautician:* "Lion Style?" *Man:* "That would be nice." *Beautician:* "What about a bath?" *Man:* "As you like." The performance completed, the man looks critically at the dog, and nods approval. *Beautician:* "Forty sous." *Man:* "That's very reasonable." A pause. *Beautician:* "Well, aren't you going to pay me?" *Man:* "Why should I? I don't know the pooch."

River life had its sordid side: the down-and-out found shelter under the arches of the bridges. It had its tragedies. When I went to Notre Dame (a frequent pilgrimage), I invariably pushed on to the Morgue, then just behind the apse of the cathedral. The place was freely open, even to irresponsible gamins such as I. We flattened our little noses against the glass cases, and peered with equable curiosity at the bloated forms, which through some mysterious semantic quirk were known as *Macchabees.* I felt no horror, and therefore no fascination: I told you I was not a Baudelairian. Robert Browning devoted a poem to the "Doric little Morgue"; [2] apparently, it was "threatened" as early as 1863. But it clung to its site for another third of a century. Now, in a less conspicuous location, it is very proper and sanitary under the dignified name: Institut Médico-Légal. I regret, not the macabre (or "macchabean") show, but the frank and familiar name. Our official vocabulary is getting painfully sensible. The city pawnshop used to be called Mont-de-Piété; this gave a pious fragrance to an otherwise sordid transaction. Now, as Caisse du Crédit Municipal, it is irreproachable and

[2] *Apparent Failure,* in *Dramatis Personae.*

dull. Someday, the Marché aux Puces (Flea Market) may be rebaptized Bourse des Vêtements Usagés (Worn Apparel Exchange), or, in modern American, W.A.E.

Naturally, the life of the river meant first of all the shipping. I knew every one of the hundred and five little passenger steamers which plied the Seine in those days. They took you all the way from Austerlitz to Auteuil for two cents, the magic gondolas of a greater Venice, the enchanted yachts of the poor. They turned the plainest business trip into a marvelous excursion. They gave the river a friendly animation which is now a memory. Although they were built in three or four series, I could tell almost every individual one by some slight peculiarity. As soon as I could descry them, I could name all the tugs and the steam barges: I recognized them by their silhouettes, or by the symbols on their funnels. Their sirens were the voices of friends—shrill and triumphant, hoarse and grumbling, some with a long wail in which, with Jehan Rictus, I could feel obscurely the giant agony of the world. I had a more tepid interest in the passive towboats—the flat-nosed *péniches* from Flanders, with their scrupulously neat house amidship, the home of the whole family who served as the crew, and the larger, more shapely *chalands* of the Lower Seine. But the prizes were the seagoing vessels that moored at the Port Saint Nicolas, in the shadow of the Louvre.

It was, of course, highly incongruous to have a miniature seaport at the foot of the great historic palace; but it was one of those absurdities which endear themselves to the true Parisian. I remember them all: the four Bennett "liners" from London; a couple from Manchester; one from Glasgow, with the romantic name of *Kenilworth;* two or three which plied the Atlantic coast, Brest, Nantes, Bordeaux and northern Spain. To me, one and all, they were THE SHIP, the eternal symbol, Argo, the caravels. They illustrated my Jules

Verne; they evoked the North Pole of Captain Hatteras, and the Mysterious Island. When laden, they would lower their masts and funnels, fold back the davits, and even the railing of the boathouse, so as to creep under the low bridges. In that state, they gave me a tragic vision of crippled vessels, raked by the mighty storms or by enemy fire. And when they moved slowly into midstream, I waved my *béret*, as though, carrying all I held most dear, they were about to defy the multitudinous sea.

The romance of the Port Saint Nicolas went out suddenly, after my first trip to London in 1896. Thereafter I saw those little boats with realistic eyes: humble seagoing barges, of some 500-ton burthen, squat and submissive. They did not bring the gold of Ophir, the spices of Celebes and the Moluccas, the nameless subtle treasures of Cipango and Cathay; they carried mostly sanitary ware from the Doulton factory in Battersea. I even wrote a dirge on my dying dream: "When I was small, how great was the world! O Death, old Captain! It is time: let us weigh anchor. This land is boring us; O Death! Let us set sail." Who knows but the ghostly ship with the dread shade at the helm, as soon as we have found our berth, deck chair and table seat, will not seem as commonplace as my steamers of the Bennett Line? If the voyage beyond our bourns of space and time were but to lead to another Battersea! [3]

I must confess that my artistic education, through the Louvre Museum, was a by-product of my fascination for steamers. Almost every Thursday and Sunday, I would rush

---

[3] I have no doubt but my sustained interest in the long projected Paris Ship Canal (Paris-Port-de-Mer) was due to my early love for these little cargo boats. The scheme is sound; it was proposed by great engineers, Belgrand before 1870, Bouquet de la Grye some twenty years later. The only obstacles —but apparently they are insuperable—are the selfish opposition of Rouen and the indifference of the Parisians. I have written many articles about it, which were found cogent by competent judges. But at the core there was the dream of a Paris gamin.

to the Louvre, and hurry through its magnificent galleries
in order to reach the collection of naval models on the third
floor, a toy shop for the children of the gods. I knew every
piece intimately, stately three-deckers with their hulls of
ebony and ivory, modern ironclads, venomous monsters of
the deep, worthy of their spiteful names—*Vindictive, Formidable, Devastation*—and best of all a marvelous miniature
of a cargo liner, *Paraguay*, with one side removed so as to
reveal her whole intricate anatomy. The artistic spoils of
centuries simply cluttered the anteroom to my paradise. I
could not help noticing a picture or a statue as I rushed by.
Ultimately, I came to know them all, and some remained
lifelong friends. I never had much use for the antiques: their
blank eyes met the same indifference in mine. Even the
"Venus of Milo" inspired in me neither awe nor love. Serenity
can be carried too far. I had, on the contrary, a genuine admiration for the "Victory of Samothrace," symbol of all victories,
winged and poised to fly away, and above all headless. But
perhaps it was because she stood on the prow of a vessel,
lashed by the salt breeze, as I longed to do in those far-off
years, as I am still yearning to do now that I am old, and that
"the sky and the sea are as dark as ink."

So I grew intimate with masterpieces in the oddest fashion
—unhistorical, untechnical, unaesthetic. I was impressed, but
not charmed, by bigness. The "Wedding Feast at Cana," the
"Coronation of Napoleon I," the "Battle of Eylau," the "Triumphs of Alexander," the swelling mountains of soft flesh and
heavy brocade in the Rubens series on Marie de Médicis:
these glorious enormities received the cool recognition due
to record-breakers. I loved, of course, melodrama: "Divine
Justice Pursuing Crime," by Prud'hon, and "The Raft of the
Medusa," by Géricault, half blotted out by bitumen, always
demanded a stop. I was intrigued by difficult feats, reminis-

cent of the circus: a family of acrobats by Girodet-Trioson, attempting to climb out of the Deluge; St. Paul carried to the seventh heaven, a capital puzzle picture, in which I tried to disentangle the legs of the apostle from those of the sustaining angels. I had picked out for myself a mysterious St. John, by Leonardo da Vinci; but the pearl of great price, "La Gioconda," had to be pointed out to me. I did not arrive of my own accord at the profound interpretation offered by Clifford Bax: "the smile of a rapacious landlady at the seaside." My deepest predilections, Rembrandt and Watteau, grew unawares.

The Louvre was my stately pleasure dome. Before I had in mind even the clumsiest definition of art, I relished, not only the teeming painted scenes and their myriads of actors, but the halls themselves: the Grande Galerie losing itself at dusk into a distant haze, the Galerie d'Apollon with the gilt-framed Delacroix ceilings, a fit casket for the crown jewels, the grand staircases in their cold stateliness, the unfinished *Escalier Daru,* an architectural nightmare with a Piranesi effect. And, in this world of gorgeous ancient dreams, an open window here and there affording a glimpse of modern life: my beloved Seine, the Tuileries Gardens, with, miles away, the great Arch of Triumph, a gateway to a golden Walhalla.

Well, this is a "true confession." I must admit that, in my mind, the Louvre has gone the way of the Port Saint Nicolas. Not that it has vanished, or grown absurdly small; it is richer than ever, and more intelligently planned. Yet my last visits were a heavy disappointment: the glory has departed. The wholesale accumulation of "Old Masters," most of them third rate, is depressing. A museum is a necropolis. I thank the Lord that I am emeritus, so that I may brazenly proclaim that I do not like galleries which do not know when to stop. I have become John Doe, the average American husband, whom Mrs. J. D. drags ruthlessly through miles of dingy masterpieces—and the dingier the more masterly. I began life like Walter Pater, and I am ending like Mr. Jiggs.

Paris never was, like Los Angeles, a hundred suburbs in search of a city. The features of the capital are strong and harmonious; foreign visitors are impressed by this organic unity; and the Parisians themselves are aware of it, and proud. Yet in my days Paris contained a hundred villages. The métro —the first line was opened in 1900—has rubbed down some of these local differences. People dive into the subway—one station is very much like another, with the same smell of creosote—and pop out again three miles away. In the days of horse-drawn vehicles, people lived within a narrower circle. Ten minutes' walk marked the radius of their daily experience. Doctors and lawyers had their offices in their own apartments. Everyone went home for lunch, and took his time to it: no grabbing of sandwich and pie, against the haggard crowd, the harassed operators, and inexorable Time.

So the familiar unit was not the mighty Paris as a whole, or the pious and learned Left Bank, or the twenty purely administrative *arrondissements,* or even the official *quartiers,* fourscore of them. It was the quarter in a less formal sense, the intimate neighborhood, a few blocks with its own shops, and its parish church around the corner. Our "commercial street" was the humble rue de Verneuil. To me, the name evokes the pungent exotic fragrance of roasting coffee; for our local groceryman was kind enough to perform this delightful operation on his doorstep. Some of these quarters had actually been villages within my parents' memory; and in my youth, Ménilmontant, Montmartre, Charonne, Passy, Auteuil, for instance, still showed traces of their former independent status. The famous Place du Tertre, near the

Sacré Coeur, now the haunt of sight-seers from Patagonia
and Keokuk, was then what it still looks before nightfall:
the public square of a very modest country town. The little
theater at the foot of the Butte Montmartre, with its miniature plaza, might have graced Montfort-l'Amaury or No-
gent-le-Rotrou. St. Médard and St. Germain de Charonne
are unpretentious village churches. In the rue des Canettes,
there is a memorial tablet to the poet Franconi, who died in
the First World War "to defend his house, his street, and the
Place St. Sulpice." This is concentrated patriotism, "the soil
and the dead," *Blut und Boden,* even though the "soil" be
asphalt or paving stone. I wonder if this intense love of the
neighborhood unit has its equivalent in New York. There are
innumerable quarters within the five boroughs. But some are
simply segregated areas—Harlem, Chinatown, Little Italy,
Little Czechoslovakia, a squalid slice of Puerto Rico. Greenwich Village is as synthetic as modern Montparnasse. (Synthetic does not mean unreal. Chelsea is not a memory, but a
revival. Perhaps Yorkville with its beery Teutonic flavor?
Would a man die as did Franconi to defend Eighty-second
Street or Third Avenue?

I am a Parisian patriot, citizen of no mean city. But I have
little sentimental yearning for the Paris of the 1880's, although it lies so far away and so long ago. There was no
soft idyllic glow about my childhood. My own life was shel-
tered and comfortable, but I saw a great deal of hard work
around me, and not a little distress. A cab with a heavy trunk
strapped on top; a man running after it. Why? In the hope
of earning a few sous by lugging the box up four flights of
stairs. At six o'clock, a line of beggars would form along the
wall of the Municipal Guard barracks across the street. They
carried wooden bowls or tin cans; and what was left over of
the soldiers' coarse fare was ladled out to them. On every
face was imprinted: "Leave all hope behind." Among the

ragged crew, there was an old gentleman, flotsam of the
Second Empire so recently wrecked: short jaunty overcoat,
gray top hat, white whiskers, a Morny of the gutter. To pick
up cigarette butts was almost a recognized profession. To
forage among the garbage cans before they were collected
at dawn was a coveted privilege. These scenes were part of
my education, no less than the harmonious line of the quays,
the magnificent Louvre, and the noble residences of the
Faubourg St. Germain. There are lovely days in Paris, in
every season. But if their perfection has such a poignant
charm, it is because of the sober, and even somber background. I have tenacious unpoetical memories of trudging
through the slush of melting snow, colder than ice, dirtier
than mud; with an accompaniment of earaches, toothaches,
cold feet, chilblains, stuffed nose, and all the ills and discomforts gamin flesh is heir to, in the city of sweetness and light.

So I have few illusions about the Paris of President Jules
Grévy. I am far from deprecating the métro, the taxi, the
autobus, heralds of undeniable progress. Yet it is patent that
giant cities—London and New York even more than Paris—
have acquired within the last hundred years a Dantesque
quality unknown to our forebears, and which no engineering
remedy can cure. Paris was already suffering from congestion
in the days of Boileau, who translated his wrath into pedes-
trian but vigorous and colorful verse. But Boileau could walk
away from the crowded districts in ten minutes, and into the
open country in half an hour. Perhaps Paris as I first knew it
was at its best from the point of view of circulation. The ruthless surgery of Haussmann had given definite relief. He had
provided generously for the kind of traffic he could foresee;
and his bold planning remained adequate until the advent of
the automobile. My chum Fock and I used to chase a ball from
our high school, Chaptal, on the Boulevard des Batignolles, to
the left bank of the Seine, past St. Lazare Station and the

Madeleine, across the boulevards and the Place de la Concorde: I have seen no Manhattan guttersnipe attempt the
same feat on Broadway, Fifth Avenue or Forty-second Street.
I am not voicing an idle regret: a memory may also be a goal.
If a trend proves unfavorable, it should be reversed.

The streets of Paris were a playground for great and small.
A song of Aristide Bruant put it pithily: *"T'es dans la rue, va!
t'es chez toi."* "You're in the street? Well, you're at home."
After the busiest streets in Paris ceased to be my football
field, they remained my favorite reading room. There were
plenty of seats on the tree-lined quays or boulevards. For
the thirsty who could not afford a bock, Sir Richard Wallace
had provided his slender, graceful and unsanitary fountains:
bronze caryatids supporting a rococo cupola. For the hungry
boy with one cent to spare, there were in little niches the
vendors of roasted chestnuts, the "winter swallows" who
descended from the mountains of Auvergne with the first
nip of frost. And all the year round, there were the fried
potato stalls: a poke of heavy, porous brown paper, a few
crisp and tender golden slivers, a sprinkling of rock salt, and
the Paris air in your nostrils: a feast for the gods, not to be
matched at the Waldorf. Especially if, like a true gourmet,
you got your pennyworth from rue Coquillière, near the
Halles. For a wise child knew the right places, and would go
a long way to buy a brioche rue de la Lune, near the Porte
St. Denis. No need to dwell on the terraces of cafés, and the
sidewalk tables of the restaurants, with a decorative screen of
potted box trees: they are as familiar as the Eiffel Tower or
Napoleon's tomb.

Half a century ago, itinerant tradespeople went about cry-
ing their wares or their skills, just as they did in the Middle
Ages. The glazier, his assortment of panes on his back, blew
a lively tune on his shrill little trumpet; it had been taken up
as a marching song by the Light Infantry, the swift-paced

Chasseurs. A woman chanted: "Pimpernel for your little birds!" And the water-cress man, long before the era of vitamins: "Straight from the fountain! The health of your body!" In the quiet of the street, you could hear a block away the merchant who bought old clothes, or empty barrels, or rabbitskins, and get your stuff ready. The mender of crockery sat down in the entry to ply his deft and patient trade: no glue for him, but invisible holes and tiny wire fasteners. He could have repaired Sully Prudhomme's *Broken Vase* and (more doubtfully) Greuze's "Broken Pitcher." Once in a while, a woman passed hawking *oublies,* not *oblivion,* for that is beyond purchase, but thin, brittle, waferlike biscuits; and her melancholy little song said:

> *Voilà l'plaisir, Mesdames, voilà l'plaisir!*
> *N'en mangez pas, Mesdames: ça fait mourir.*

"Here is pleasure, ladies, here is pleasure. Don't taste of it, ladies, for it brings death." The interplay of death and pleasure is a commonplace of Renaissance poetry: how did it ever become a street vendor's cry?

A shepherd's pipe was heard, a pure Virgilian note in the dingy street; and around the corner there came the shepherd, complete with his blue smock and his wooden clogs, his dog and his flock of goats. He had steady customers: children for whom goat's milk had been prescribed. The goatherd was still going his immemorial rounds in the first decade of this century; after 1910, I never saw him again.

Ubiquitously, there were the fruit and vegetable dealers with their little pushcarts, "merchants of the four seasons." Their chaffing and chaffering, their mocking, resigned, realistic philosophy, their hardships, their constant bickerings with the law—are they not written in Anatole France's *Crainquebille?* Those shopkeepers on wheels were an intermediate species: half respectable, quasi legal, frowned upon

but tolerated as long as they kept moving, on terms of un-
friendly, precarious neutrality with the cops. Woe to the
dealer who did not even own or rent a barrow, but displayed
his stuff in an upturned umbrella! As in New York, he was
usually eloquent, with a glibness racy of the sidewalks; as
in New York also, he was fair game for the force. He did business with his weather eye constantly alert. Strange life, that
of the street hawker, honest to a large extent, yet an outlaw;
irreproachably animated by the profit motive, free enterprise
and the spirit of competition—a miniature capitalist, a sturdy
if ragged individualist—yet his existence as startled and fitful
as that of the smaller animals in the jungle. He was called a
camelot, and his shoddy stuff was known as *camelote.* I still
remember my amusement when I found the familiar term
"Camelot" in a highly romantic poem of Tennyson's. (To
make matters worse, *The Lady of Shalott* evoked the taste of
shallot, which, as Webster's Dictionary avers, is closely akin
to garlic.)

Apropos of *camelots,* a semantic digression: those "pious
hooligans" (so they were called by the venerable Vicar of
Ste Clotilde, Monsignor Gardey), whom we decorously referred to as "the King's Henchmen" had chosen the name
Camelots du Roy. They too were voluble and picturesque;
they too had incessant trouble with the police; they too
gathered little knots of suckers, including a few Americans.
But Paris would have none of their *camelote.*

It is an easy transition from *les Camelots du Roy* to the
heroes of a Punch-and-Judy show. Both groups were traditionalists, and both loved to beat up the police. Guignol—not
le Grand Guignol, a Little Theater specializing in a con-
trasted fare of uproarious farces and horror stories, but the
good old-fashioned puppet show—at one time held for me a
fascination rivaling that of steamboats. Very young children
were seated inside the roped-in enclosure; but older children,

poorer children, and not a few grownups stood outside, and enjoyed a free show. I was among the deadheads. The hero was little Guillaume, a gamin with blue overalls and a red cap, as impertinent as Charlie McCarthy, but a trifle more sophisticated. Comic relief was provided by his father Cassandre, whose name and costume perpetuated the eighteenth century: cocked hat, queue, and the red waistcoat which long remained the badge of cab drivers. The fun was as rough and elementary as in *The Doctor in Spite of Himself* or *The Merry Wives of Windsor*. The Big Stick (Henry IV coined the phrase long before Theodore Roosevelt) settled all legal, social or financial problems in the most satisfactory fashion: there are still a few of us who believe in that philosophy, and call it "realism" or "power politics." In 1913, I took my three-year-old daughter to the Guignol in the Champs Elysées, hoping to recapture the delights of my childhood through her mind, still dewy with the dawn. But the child had been properly brought up, in that wholesome atmosphere of the American home which it was the business of Puliter prize novels to depict.[4] The brutality and cynicism of the Paris puppets revolted her, and she fled screaming: "I don't like this kind of church!"

For six years (1893–1899) I walked to my high school, Collège Chaptal; [5] the métro did not exist; there was no convenient bus line, and cabs were not within my reach. A five-minute detour would enable me to go by way of the Champs Elysées, or to take in the Opéra and the Place Vendôme. I was thus intimate, at the formative age, with some of the noblest examples of urban architecture.

[4] Such were still the terms of the Pulitzer prize when Pearl Buck won it for *The Good Earth: lucus a non lucendo.*

[5] A French lycée or collège is the equivalent of high school and junior college, with a six- or seven-year course.

I knew other parts too, through long *flâneries. Flâner!* an old-world term for an old-world art: to stroll, to saunter, to wander with apparent aimlessness, yet with mind constantly alert; sketching mentally a landmark, a scene, a silhouette; noting the rhythmic wail of the newsboy: *"Résultat complet des courses!"* the distant siren of a tugboat, the sudden laughter of a *midinette.* The dictionary taught me that *flâner* was "to loiter," and when I first saw the harsh Anglo-Saxon sign: LOITERERS WILL BE PROSECUTED, I realized that there were still salt, unplumb'd, estranging seas between civilizations.

But if I came to explore every district in Paris, even the remotest and the most commonplace, it was through a strange conjunction of influences: a great deal of Victor Hugo, with a dash of religion.

We had few books in our home, and not all of them good. A curse on the salesman who managed to clutter our cramped quarters with the seven big volumes of Anquetil's French History, a monument of vapidity! We had some reference works, not so bad: Bescherelle's Dictionary, Jules Verne's Geography of France, two volumes of popular medicine by Dr. Rengade: the crudely colored anatomical and pathological plates had a morbid appeal. But, best of all, there were two tattered, unbound (perhaps *disbound*) illustrated books which were turned over to me before I knew my A B C. They were *Five Weeks in a Balloon* together with *Voyage to the Center of the Earth,* and Hugo's *Notre-Dame.* In these, I actually learnt my letters. I was familiar with every character and with every scene—Otto Lidenbrok belched forth by the volcano Stromboli, or Quasimodo defending the cathedral singlehanded—long before I could make out a single word. These were my Mother Goose Rhymes, my Grimm's Fairy Tales, my Alice, my Oz Books, my Superman. The books were my very own; but although I handled them with reverence, their decay was irremediable. My parents promised me

new and well-bound copies as soon as I could read; they
kept their word, and these two volumes, which I practically
memorized, were the nucleus of my library and the first basis
of my education.

I cannot tell how much I understood at any particular age.
I am today discovering new depths in the tortured soul of
Dom Claude Frollo. "Intelligence" is a complex, uneven,
capricious thing: it cannot be reduced to a numerical symbol.
When a child meets a genius, how deeply do they commune?
There is, of course, a popular, a primitive, and even a juvenile
aspect to some of the greatest masterpieces. In 1921, when
the whole scholarly world was feverishly preparing lectures
for the sixth centennial of Dante's death, I brought home a
Divine Comedy with Gustave Doré's spirited illustrations.
My children were delighted: they wanted to learn Italian at
once, in their eagerness to know more about Geryon and
other fantastic characters. I do not know whether our birth
is but a sleep and a forgetting. But I am persuaded that
children—aye, and animals perhaps—feel obscurely those
eternal verities which adults strive in vain to formulate. At
the age of six, I did enjoy Hugo's *Notre-Dame*. The fact that
I also relished the most elementary kind of juvenile fiction
does not embarrass me in the least. In a child's brains, as in a
man's, there are many mansions. Threescore years later, I
have room in my Pantheon for Kafka, Paul Valéry, Yvor
Winters, Moon Mullins or Andy Gump. There is no single
mental age, any more than a single intelligence quotient. In
December, 1928, I was crossing on the *Olympic;* there was
on board a prodigy, a seven-year-old Polish violinist. He was
a beautiful child, and when he played, he had the rapt expression of the true artist. But the concert over, there was a noisy
party; the young virtuoso sat on the floor, like the other children, blowing a penny trumpet with manifest delight. A dog's
eyes may be luminous abysses, with the unseeing-allseeing

depths of a yogi's; the next moment, he is blissfully gnawing
a bone.

I am attempting to explain to myself a fact which is both
incredible and undeniable. I was no prodigy; yet, between six
and nine, I read with rapture; I knew, almost by heart, those
very passages in Hugo's romance which American students
find such a stumbling block: the descriptive Book III (*Notre
Dame* and *A Bird's-eye View of Paris*), and the philosophical
chapter "This Will Kill That." Of course, I did not catch every
allusion: who ever does? Current literature is full of references to baseball, business and politics which to me are as
cryptic as Etruscan. I shall never know why the people from
Missouri "have to be shown." I love to chant to myself Mallarmé's great sonnet on *The Tomb of Edgar Poe;* but I have
not yet discovered what "angel" and what "hydra" he was
talking about. So, when Hugo wrote: "Rétif de la Bretonne
brings his hodful of broken plaster," I was nonplused, yet
the phrase satisfied me. I have a pedantically clear mind:
yet I revel in the deepening twilight.

I knew for certain that Hugo's orchestral prose was not just
sonorous nonsense, incidental music to his melodrama. His
magic was true, for his Sesame did open the secret door. For,
before I was nine, I already went on repeated pilgrimages to
Notre Dame. I sought, not the wraiths of la Esmeralda and
Quasimodo, but the cell of the archdeacon, with the tragic
word, ANANKE. And I conversed, not with the bland virgins
and bearded saints on the portals, but with the chimeras
(wrongly called gargoyles) on the parapets. I sought particularly the "Stryge" so admirably drawn by Méryon: beast,
angel and man, his head heavy in his hands, looking down
upon Paris with a mysterious blend of cynicism and despairing pity.

It cost, I believe, six cents to go up the North Tower. Six
cents! A fortune, but well invested. The gloom in the narrow

winding stairs was alive with dark romance: this sudden little door might lead to the chamber of Claude Frollo. The rare slits in the thick wall revealed entrancing vistas of Paris, wider and more magical as you climbed. Then, there was the marvelous interlude when you reached the gallery on top of the slender colonnade: that is where the fantastic monsters stand guard at every corner. Finally, the broad platform, Paris at your feet, the soft sheen of the Seine, the Eiffel Tower just rising in the West, still unfamiliar and hostile. I have long preserved my love for climbing to the top of monuments, and preferably of churches; elevators have no appeal. It was not in Paris, but at Chartres and at Santiago de Compostela that I had at last the perfect experience so well described by Hugo: to feel the mighty edifice trembling under you, as though the booming of the bells were the clangor of titanic hoofs. The most exciting experience was reaching the dizzy top of the Strasbourg spire, with my two young children. My farewell performance was getting into the ball above the dome and lantern of St. Paul's, under the cross. That was in 1937; I nearly got stuck in the narrow well that contains the ultimate ladder, and I had to acknowledge that my climbing days were over.

But it was not merely the enchanted forest of Notre Dame that Hugo revealed to me: it was old Paris, Gothic art and the soul of architecture. I have just read over those archae-ological digressions, so easy to skip: they are truly great. Victor Hugo provided a unique album of etchings; but there is more to his book than picturesqueness. When most writers were raving (as many still do) about the mystery, the mysti-cism, the otherworldliness, the haunted gloom of the Gothic, Hugo understood that the cathedral is a hymn of life and joy, not of death and despair; that it embodies civic pride as well as religious faith; that the House of God, in those lusty, tur-bulent days, was also the House of the People. Once the churches were gleaming white, and their jeweled windows were pure of grime.

Hugo understood also that carved stone and stained glass were not mere ornament, like the saints gesticulating in a baroque church. They were the Bible and the encyclopedia of the people, the "mirror of the world," *speculum mundi.* Viollet-le-Duc, Ruskin, Henry Adams and, above all, Emile Mâle did but follow where Hugo first trod. And there is power in his thought: "This will kill that." Architecture no longer is the sovereign among the arts. The printed word now carries the main stream of human culture. And, who knows? It may be superseded by the spoken word and the immediate vision, more evanescent, but more ubiquitous still. The great book may soon have the fossil majesty of the great church. Who cares for the letter, if the spirit finds swifter wings?

So Victor Hugo sent the Paris gamin, well under ten, not to Notre Dame alone, but to all the other medieval churches that survive in Paris, and there is a good dozen of them. I discovered St. Julien-le-Pauvre, then hidden in what seemed to be a farmyard, back of the leprous walls of the old Hôtel-Dieu. I knew, of course, the glory of that incomparable shrine, the Sainte-Chapelle; the robust austere elegance of St. Germain-des-Prés; and jewels gayer and more delicate, reached through a labyrinth of ancient twisted lanes, like St. Séverin.

Through Hugo, I came to love the past even in its decay, but never because of its decay. I had to wrestle, many years later, with the perversions and the diseases of the historical spirit; but even when I was, unwittingly, a deep-dyed little Tory, meanness and stupidity never seemed venerable to me. I never could see anything hoary about the sacrilegious blunders of dead architects. If they have defaced a masterpiece, let us remove the stain. I know it spells "restoration," a word which is anathema to the exquisite. I am glad Notre

Dame and the Sainte-Chapelle were delicately, tenderly restored. I should like to see St. Germain-des-Prés with its three
towers, and St. Denis with its splendid spire. I admit the line
is hard to trace. Viollet-le-Duc may have been ruthless in
some of his restorations. The absurd, the incongruous may
have a charm which the banal never possesses. I remember
St. Nicolas-du-Chardonnet when its main front was a blank
wall. Against it there had grown like a fungus a narrow
five-story house, parlous and verminous, leaning on crutches.
It had a perverse appeal, and I dreaded the time when it
would finally crumble into utter decrepitude. The new Jesuit
or baroque façade which has taken its place is good of its
kind. Yet, when I first saw it, I had to repress a morbid regret.

So, with the pages of Hugo in my memory, and the drawings of Méryon, Viollet-le-Duc, Hoffbauer, I wandered in
quest of vanished time. I evoked the feudal Louvre, a fortress
with the grace of a palace; and across the Seine, the Tour de
Nesle. I had already memorized Villon's ballad: "In like manner, where is the Queen— Who commanded that Buridan—
Be thrown, sewn in a sack, into the Seine? But where are the
snows of yesteryear?" Who was that Buridan, a fit hero for
Alexandre Dumas? The one Buridan known to history was not
a man-at-arms and not a lover, but a scholastic philosopher.
Buridan's idiotic donkey starved and parched to death between a bundle of hay and a pail of water, in order to maintain his "freedom of indifference." But he was an ass to start
with.

In one respect, Hugo taught me better than he knew. I
agreed that architecture, with the decline of the Middle Ages,
had lost its pre-eminence, and much of its vitality. Still, I
could not spurn, as Hugo did, all later works. The Renaissance and the Classical period may be silver ages: but good
silver is a thing of beauty. There are few pure Gothic churches
that enchant me like those miraculous hybrids, St. Etienne-

du-Mont and St. Eustache. If a dome be a hump, as Hugo will have it, then there is for me a perverse fascination in those glorious hunchbacks, the Invalides, a gilded spiked helmet, and the Pantheon, antique majesty with a Louis XV smile. The towers of St. Sulpice may be two huge clarinets; but the main front shows that there could be simplicity and grandeur in the century of Voltaire.

I have mentioned almost exclusively churches, as though Paris were first of all an ecclesiastical city. Rare are the secular buildings that have survived through the classical centuries: the Conciergerie wing of the Palace of Justice, a few aristocratic residences—Hôtel de Cluny, Hôtel de Sens—a tower or a turret here and there. God, His Mother and His saints followed architectural fashions more slowly than the fine lords and ladies of this world. But the chief reason is that I loved, and still love, Catholic churches just as churches. I was pious then, without mystic visions or agonies of fear. When I pushed the red leather-padded, iron-studded inner door, I was seeking neither sanctuary nor adventure. The hush, the subdued light, the blended odor of burning wax and incense, the coolness in summer, the gentle warmth in winter brought to me the peace and comfort of a well-ordered home.

So I decided, when I was about twelve, to visit every Catholic church in Paris, and, at that time, there were about a hundred. It was an architectural, and historical, but also a devout pilgrimage. Piety at times would blur my taste. In the Christmas season, when I explored the little booths on the boulevards, bright with the latest toys and the ingenious novelties of the Paris trade, I never failed to kneel before the Nativity scenes in the churches that were on my way. These scenes were, I am sure, in that conventional style known as *bondieuserie St. Sulpice*, saccharine and devout. As I grew, they turned into toys, familiar, elaborate and naïve; but they had still a sweetness which I can never hope to recapture.

That pilgrimage, often interrupted, extended over three years. I saw the Roman basilicas built at the end of the eighteenth century or early in the nineteenth, like St. Philippe-du-Roule and Notre-Dame-de-Lorette, the exterior barnlike and forbidding, the interior heavily decorated, but hardly ecclesiastical. La Madeleine was an old acquaintance, but not a favorite: pagan without and mundane within. I saw the many Romanesque or Gothic pastiches, some of them, like St. Pierre-de-Montrouge, rather successful. I saw the churches of the Second Empire, set in well-proportioned plazas, and not devoid of elegance: St. Augustin, Florentine, Byzantine and industrial, La Trinité with its graceful Renaissance tower copied from a Norman model,[6] and, in a proletarian district, St. Ambroise. I knew the Sacré-Cœur when it was but a crypt; I watched the nave rise course after course, and the cluster of cupolas, and the campanile in the rear. Even during my last visit, a couple of years before the Second World War, I felt a little tremor of joy when, unexpectedly, from some place on the Left Bank, the white-robed Sacré-Cœur would appear, soaring, remote, unreal; massive withal, and watching over Paris like a citadel of prayer.

[6] Avranches, I believe.

CHAPTER TWO

My Paris:
Servitude de Beauté

─────────────────────

MY TEACHERS were cities rather than individual men or books. No influence could compare with that of Paris. In this, I must admit, I was highly fortunate: Paris is an incomparable museum, but not a necropolis. In close touch with the past, it is constantly straining toward the future. But it would be a breach of taste for a Parisian to praise his birthplace. Victor Hugo had the right to be dithyrambic about the City of Light: he was born in Besançon.

I love Paris tenderly, and, as Montaigne put it, even in its warts. I am not blind to the warts, and not averse to a minor surgical operation. I have seen much ugliness, much squalor and not a little stupidity in Paris. Not every *bistro* or *bougnat* [1] is the paradise of epicures; it may well be a *gargotte* worse than a Greek restaurant at Gopher Prairie. Not every grisette is Mimi Pinson or Louise; not every gamin is Gavroche or Anatole France.

---

[1] *Bougnat,* for *charbougnat,* alleged Auvergnat form of *charbonnier:* the little Auvergnat coal dealer who also runs a small and cheap restaurant.

45

As a matter of fact, although my love for Paris is both instinctive and reasoned, I have for London a feeling which, while totally different, is no less deep. I knew at one time every street corner in Paris; London, because I never could explore its full immensity, has remained stranger and more romantic. Novels with a London background appeal to me more than stories of Parisian life. As far as the setting is concerned, I find Dickens more fascinating than Balzac. I spent only two consecutive years in London; but they were years of complete freedom, intense study and sudden conscious growth. Paris was a delightful immemorial habit, London was a revelation and a challenge. In New York, I never was more than a country cousin, an entranced visitor, until I was well over sixty. Then I had a full, long, potent draught of New York life. But it was very late in the day; and the center of my activities, the French Section of the Office of War Information, was a transplanted bit of cosmopolitan Paris. Still, I feel profoundly the chaotic and feverish charm of the giant city. I have my favorite quarter, where I am as much at home as on the banks of the Seine; and I have at least one family of perennial friends, upon whom I never fail to call, the sea lions in the Central Park Zoo.

I shall repeatedly discuss, in these farewell pages, the mystery of nationalism. It is the central spiritual enigma of our civilization, as atomic energy is the crucial physical problem. Both are fraught with disaster, yet, if we master them, they may be no less potent for good. Two hints will suffice at this stage. Instinctive patriotism, the kind that is experienced, not taught, is intensely local. The only love that needs no prompting is that of our own, our native land in the most literal sense of the term: the earth our feet have trod, the contours and shades familiar to our gaze. No child born in Maine grows up with an intuitive love of New Mexico. The national state is a construction of the mind. To realize the bonds between the various localities, to love that historical and political entity, the United States, is a triumph of education, not of instinct. I am too good an American not to "love" Chicago; but I must confess that it is an acquired taste.

Then, if we quietly, deeply, cherish what is familiar, we are also strangely moved by the exotic. We do not love Rome, Rio, or Peiping quite in the same way as we may love Kansas City: but there are no scales on which such imponderables can be measured. I am conscious of being, first of all, a child of Paris, not of France. Yet there are chords in my being which vibrate more purely in London or in New York.

Every *Parigot* obscurely loves his *patelin*—his street, his quarter, the whole splendid, ardent, and cruel capital. But my interest in Paris reached consciousness at an amazingly early age. This I owed to Victor Hugo and his *Notre-Dame,* but also to humbler guides, my father and my uncle Charles Collot. Both of them had a proprietary interest in the city. No building could be torn down or erected, no street repaved, no public work undertaken, but they must inspect the scene at once. This required no small effort, for they were not gentlemen of leisure. Once in a while, I trotted by their side; and always I heard their reports at the family table. My mother was more interested in people than in steel and stone. So her usual response was: "You two ought to get jobs as inspectors of street pavements." David Starr Jordan defined success as "doing the thing you like, and getting paid for it." My father and my uncle never achieved that kind of success. Their concern with the growth of Paris was strictly art for art's sake.

So I acquired from them, by the time I was ten, the sense that a city was not a mere backdrop, and something to be taken for granted. A city is the incessant work of man; it can be marred and it can be improved. One expression recurred like a refrain in my father's talk: "*Il faudrait faire ceci ou cela,*" this or that ought to be done. Among very modest

working people, I thus breathed an atmosphere of city
planning. There was nothing exceptional about this: the
common folk of Paris are keenly aware of their heritage. This
may be the reason why, in spite of politicians and profiteers,
of ruthless engineers and dogmatic architects, Paris has managed to preserve its beauty; not unspoilt by any means, but
still vigorously alive.

I had an incontrovertible example of city planning a quarter of a mile from our home: the Tuileries Gardens. An English park looks like a bit of nature; nature touched up no
doubt, and even faked; but its meadowlike swards, its clumps
of trees, its glades and glens, seek to create the impression
that they just happened. No such delusion is possible about
the Tuileries, and, beyond them, the Place de la Concorde,
the Champs Elysées. Such things were not evolved by chance.
They are the monuments of intelligence and will power; and
they are not ashamed of it. Thus I was taught the wisdom of
planning, not from day to day, not even for a decade, but
for hundreds of years ahead. If Paris is enjoying gardens of
unique magnificence in the very heart of the city, it is because the kings had willed it as early as the sixteenth century.

Another lesson was impressed upon me a little later, when
I was about fifteen: the discovery of Haussmann. My parents
were good orthodox anti-Bonapartists; they never had a good
word for "Badinguet"—their name for Napoleon III—or for
any of his minions. But the presence of Haussmann was still
felt. The plans of the great prefect were still being followed;
even today, three-quarters of a century after his fall, they
have not yet been fully carried out. In my youth, the Boulevard Raspail, the Boulevard Haussman, the rue Réaumur
were still uncompleted. I saw buildings pulled down, and new
vistas opened, in accordance with a long-range, all-embracing
scheme. People had planned before, generously or crudely,
from Major L'Enfant to the forerunners of George F. Babbitt;

but it was in the open fields. Haussmann demonstrated the possibility of replanning, of making over, an ancient city, an enormous city, with a heavy and glorious heritage. It was human reason substituted for the random cowpath; it was radicalism against the wisdom of prejudice.

I know that Haussmann hacked and hammered with a clumsy hand. There is much monotony, false symmetry, banal elegance, about a great deal of his work. His wide and straight thoroughfares, meant for the cavalry charge or the raking artillery fire, destroyed not a few charming intimate nooks which might easily have been preserved. Still, with many blemishes and a few egregious blunders, the transformation of Paris under the Second Empire was a magnificent enterprise. It was showy, like the Opera, its prize jewel; but it was also solid. Haussmann was seconded by admirable technicians: Alphand for the gardens, Belgrand for sanitary engineering. Markets, railway stations, were marvels for their time. And if the architects of the period are not outstanding, they formed a very competent team: Hittorf, Duc, Lefuel, Visconti, Ballu, Baltard, Garnier.

That great achievement was radical, but not revolutionary. Haussmann did not impose an abstract, brand-new formula: he rationalized the practice of the classical centuries. Haussmannism is found in the districts planned under Louis XIV and Louis XV, Champs Elysées, Invalides, Ecole Militaire. It is the style that prevailed at Versailles, Nancy, Bordeaux; it inspired the Washington of L'Enfant and the Regency London of John Nash. It is the conception of Le Nôtre, the great landscape architect: a city is treated like a park, with vast avenues, circles and stars. It is not the only conceivable style; it does not automatically solve all our modern problems; and especially, it has been imitated *ad nauseam* and vulgarized. But in Paris, it is not a conventional beaux-arts mask. It is rooted in tradition. One passes without a shock

from the best eighteenth-century planning such as the Place
de la Concorde and the rue Royale to a Haussmann thoroughfare such as the Boulevard Malesherbes; or from the aristocratic restraint of the Place Vendôme to the appropriate
gaiety of the Opera. The devastating prefect, the new
Scourge of God, as he was called, worked truly in the grand
manner.

. Haussmann was but a rough and efficient tool: the guiding
thought belonged to Napoleon III, the socialist emperor, "St.
Simon on horseback." Grievous as the sins of the Second
Empire may be, the regime turned resolutely away from that
laissez faire which too often means *laisser aller:* let everything drift as it pleases. Planning, that is to say foresight, is
generosity. Yes, the creaking old machine would probably
last our lifetime. It is not impossible to make ourselves fairly
comfortable in it. What will happen when it breaks down is
one of those "iffy" questions that wise men shrug away. The
other attitude is one of responsibility toward the past and toward the future. We have received the Champs Elysées from
our ancestors. We should transmit our heritage undiminished
and, if possible, increased, improved, to our descendants.
This lesson is a little harder to learn in a new country. The
pioneer is self-made: let his sons create their own world.
When the land is exhausted, and the "templed hills" have
been eroded to the rock, move on. We have turned our backs
on the past, and what has posterity done for us? There is
something vital and primitive about that grand indifference.
But it is not the whole truth. The problem is to blend the
pioneering and the historical into a spirit of dynamic reverence.

Tracing grand vistas in the open fields, as did the architects
of the Bourbon kings, is a noble but simple task. But to mod-
ernize and improve an ancient city, without destroying the
unique savor of its past, is a problem beyond the reach of the

mere Functionalist. No need to be a genius like Le Corbusier
to suggest that the whole center of Paris be razed to the
ground, and large cruciform towers erected on the site. This
brutal solution simply ignores one essential term of the equation: to keep alive the delicate flower of a civilization. Health
and convenience must never be sacrificed. But the first *func-
tion* of Paris is to be a thing of beauty. Even though an elevated had been practical along the Champs Elysées, it was
inconceivable. There is a word which Alfred de Vigny rightly
associates with Grandeur: it is Servitude. Here it means not
enslavement, but moral obligation, *noblesse oblige*. As a legal
term, *une servitude* means a building restriction. Paris is
burdened with a heavy *servitude de beauté*.

My interest in city development was first of all of an aesthetic nature. This has not evaporated: I still consider planning as the most complex of arts, and Marshal Lyautey as a
great virtuoso. But quite early, the romance of the practical
demanded its share of attention. I have already noted how I
loved the Seine and its utilitarian steamboats. I should not
have been a normal boy if I had not fallen also under the spell
of railways. When the paleotechnic period defined by Lewis
Mumford passes away, when the few remaining trains are
streamlined, glittering and silent, some primitive magic will
have departed from the world. There was something dragon-
like about the dark, puffing, clangorous monsters, hot and
greasy, belching forth steam and smoke. My grandchildren,
poor little things, waste a nickel taking a few turns on a miniature railway: I had the Belt Line for my toy, and Paris for
my amusement park. For twenty centimes, you took a ticket
to the next station; but you stayed on and went first around
the whole loop, a little over twenty miles. You saw the con-
nections with the various main lines; you went through more

tunnels than there are between Leningrad and Moscow; you crossed the Seine on high viaducts; you had a glimpse of industrial Paris near La Villette; Auteuil was still a placid bourgeois suburb, and Vaugirard was rural, with carefully tended market-gardens. To watch the trains at St. Lazare, on the way to Chaptal, was a delight that the years could not dull.

So I loved railroads, and particularly underground railroads, before there were any in Paris. I was entranced by a book on *Metropolitans,* by that indefatigable popularizer Louis Figuier. When I went to London in 1896, the chief attraction was not Buckingham Palace, Westminster, St. Paul's or the National Gallery; next to the Thames' shipping, it was the sooty and acrid Metropolitan and District Railways. Every child loves the subterranean world: Freud must have an interpretation for that appeal of the chthonic depths. *The Voyage to the Center of the Earth* was much more fascinating to me than *Five Weeks in a Balloon;* just as even today, I feel much more at home in Dante's *Inferno* than in *Purgatorio.* I had a much cooler interest in surface transportation. Yet in the late nineties, Paris had become a delightful exposition of streetcar oddities: a cable line in Belleville, plain steam, compressed steam, instantaneous steam without boilers, compressed air, and every form of electric traction: storage batteries, contact plots, slots, anything except the standard overhead trolley, kept out of the center for aesthetic reasons. Old guide books still referred to tramways as *chemins de fer américains.* In that transitional period, horse-drawn cars would alternate with engines, at least on short stretches. In a surprisingly short time, horses got used to those noisy fellow travelers; it took poets three generations to discover that locomotives would not destroy religion, love and the Muse.

A taste for historical beauty, a love for transportation: to-

gether they form a pretty good equipment for a budding
urbaniste. By the time I was twenty, I was, although self-
taught, a fairly competent student of city planning. Much as
I loved railroads, I was indignant when vandals cut down
trees and dug brutal holes in the majestic Esplanade des
Invalides. And, although no engineer, I was right in one case
at least against the technicians. I prophesied that the new
and very expensive line, Courcelles-Champ de Mars, would
never be of any use. It lost money from 1900 to 1914, and has,
I believe, been abandoned ever since.

My active interest in city planning had to be left in abeyance. I had to work hard for competitive examinations; then
I left Paris for England, for a year of military service, finally
for America. For a while "urbanism" had to remain a hobby
and an unfulfilled desire. But in teaching French Civilization,
I came to realize what an excellent center my knowledge of
Paris provided; and later, in studying political problems, I
saw that the "urbanistic" method was valid in larger fields.
Combine aesthetics with engineering; do not willfully destroy
the past, do not deplore the present. Remember that the
life of a city, and of a nation, is not instantaneous; that Time
is the fourth and greatest of dimensions; that the future is
real in so far as we realize it. I understood that my eager wan-
derings in the streets of Paris, my pilgrimages to Notre Dame,
my exploration of the proposed sites of the seaport at Clichy
or Gennevilliers, my circular tours on the Belt Line, were
not childish pastimes merely, but a most valuable part of my
education. And when in 1910 and 1913 I visited Paris again,
I went over the same rounds, not to recapture the ghost of
my boyhood, but to bring my planning information up to
date.

These thoughts came to fruition in 1918. I was then, as I
shall relate, a liaison officer in the A.E.F. General Pershing
had unaccountably overlooked my talent for leading a divi-

sion into battle; so with the modest rank of lieutenant, I was a casual officer, an odds-and-ends man with long periods of abysmal idleness. To fill these dismal hours, I wrote a series of city planning articles, published in *La Revue de Paris* (then edited by Ernest Lavisse) and in other magazines.

Nearly ten years later, a very dear friend of the war days, Paul Bouju, had become prefect of the Seine. He made it easy for me to meet his chief lieutenants, Bienvenüe, Malherbe, Jayot, Drogue and others. So I expanded and organized my scattered essays into a book, *L'Avenir de Paris*. It did not take the capital by storm; for the antiquarians, it was too cheerfully modernistic; too pragmatic for the doctrinaires, too aesthetic for the engineers, too starry-eyed for the ward politicians; but it was appreciated by a few kindred spirits. It remains an honest study in integrated planning within extremely definite limits. Urbanism is the meeting ground of the historian, the artist, the sociologist, the engineer, the businessman. And, in a city like Paris, the historian has a right to be heard, provided he realizes that history did not stop abruptly the moment he dropped his pen. Paris is "a lady with a past"; but as a Senator wisely remarked about aviation, "most of her future lies ahead."

Thanks to my book, I became acquainted with a number of fellow workers in the field: high officials like Henri Giraud and Fontaine, architects like Jean Royer and Tony Socard, historians like Marcel Poëte and André Ménabréa, engineers like Humery, men in active politics like Senator André Morizet, Mayor of Boulogne Billancourt. Simply because I loved Paris, these gentlemen welcomed me—a free lance, a mere visitor—as one of themselves. I was, informally and for a brief season, a member of the team. It was a new and a delightful experience. In my various activities, I had so far worked in isolation. My association with the Paris *urbanistes* in 1937 made me feel more deeply, in retrospect, the great loneliness from which I had suffered, and which I had accepted without question. I had twice again the privilege of working with a group, for a cause in which I heartily believed: in the Office of War Information and on the Committee to Draft a World Constitution. It may be true that man is never so strong as when he stands alone; but he is never so happy as when he works with comrades.

In all three cases, this teamwork among men of good will implied no totalitarian uniformity. We labored together for a definite purpose, and we enjoyed it. We knew full well that beyond our chosen meeting ground, we differed, on vital points, and radically. André Ménabréa was a Catholic, William Oualid an Algerian Jew; many of my temporary associates were conservative bourgeois, André Morizet was a Communist. Everyone has had some experience of this kind; yet we refuse to recognize that it is the very negation of the party spirit. There is no Republican music totally different from Democratic music; there is no Republican chemistry at odds with Democratic chemistry; there is no specific Republican justice, medicine, engineering, which it is the duty of Democrats to deny *in toto* and oppose tooth and nail.

These few weeks in Paris, in 1937, had a unique charm, as of a tardy spring with the poignancy of Indian summer. There was anguish in the air: the insolence of Nazis and Fascists, the rebellion in Spain, the sorry farce of neutrality, the craven cunning of the British Tories, the obstinate blindness of America formed an angry, and indeed a tragic background. We forget that there was also a surge of hope. The people of Paris were alive to the gathering perils; but it seemed as though Soviet Russia and the Western democracies could work together at last; and the victory of the Popular Front was thought to herald a decisive revolution without bloodshed. As in 1788, there were violent contrasts of light and shade. This chaotic situation was well symbolized by the Exposition of Arts and Crafts. It was woefully and ludicrously behind time, through incompetence, squabbling, sabotage; but it was also full of admirable and delicate things, the promise of a less brutal world.

My city planning activities came to a delightful climax with a luncheon at the Pavillon d'Armenonville, in the Bois de Boulogne, on June 30, 1937. With M. Boutteville as host, we gathered to discuss my proposal for a new kind of exposition. Every eleven or twelve years, since 1855, the very heart of Paris had been desecrated by world fairs. Flimsy buildings of aggressively bizarre architecture were piled up on the banks of the Seine, in the Champs Elysées, on the Esplanade des Invalides. It took three years on the average to get the thing ready, and at least six months to clear up the debris. The festival turned into a fever. Hectic prosperity was invariably followed by a depression. I do not deny that the spectacle was impressive, brilliant at times, and even memorable: like Sir Patrick Geddes, I am fond of expositions. But the center of an artistic city is not their proper place; and a modicum of foresight may avert a *Katzenjammer*.

One, the Colonial Exposition of 1931, was held at Vincennes. It was Marshal Lyautey's last victory: it was ready on time, and left no deficit. But, as a rule, hotelkeepers, retailers, and their agents the ward politicians, insisted on keeping the expositions to their traditional site. They argued that the temporary galleries were but a pretext anyway: what the throngs from all over the world wanted to see was Paris itself, and not Vincennes, St. Germain or Gennevilliers.

There was some truth in their plea; and I thought that once at least, we might attempt to draw the logical consequences of their contention. Let us have an exposition without emergency buildings; let the whole of Paris be the world fair. First of all, Paris must be cleaned as it had not been for a genera-

tion; for a great deal of slackness had been tolerated after the
First World War. Let every museum organize special ex-
hibits; and especially, let every quarter, every street, every
store display its best wares. Why have a special pavilion for
jewelry or dressmaking, when Paris has the rue de la Paix?
The shops of the Palais Royal, so admirably located, might
be revitalized for the occasion. This Exposition of Paris at
Work and Play would be truly a world fair, for Parisian life
is cosmopolitan. It would be prepared, classified, advertised,
engineered, in the traditional fashion. But instead of being
a heaping-up of bric-a-brac, it would show the achievements
of our civilization organically. Instead of being housed in
pretentious lath-and-plaster monstrosities, it would have for
its setting permanent Paris, normal Paris, brought to a fugitive
point of perfection.[2]

It would, we believed, have been good business, and at the
same time a great historical, artistic and technical demonstration. We had selected the year 1948: to preserve the normal
periodicity of Paris world fairs, and to celebrate the centennial of 1848, the actual beginning of our modern world.
Alas! 1948 is with us. Paris is still struggling with scarcity
in every essential; and a free, joyous, peaceful gathering of
reconciled nations seems the wildest of Utopian dreams. I
left Paris on July 21, 1937; and I doubt whether I shall ever
see it again.

I offer no apologies for dwelling at such length on the problems of my native city. Paris belongs to the world: the Parisians are only its custodians. It particularly belongs to

[2] Something of that kind had been realized in 1937. Instead of having an
artificial Exhibition of Dramatic Arts in the fairgrounds, four theaters had
been placed at the disposal of the great directors, Copeau, Jouvet, Baty, Dul-
lin; and each gave a most instructive "season."

America. The ancient jest still has its grain of truth: "Good Americans, when they die, go to Paris. Americans not so good do not wait quite so long."

I shall not list my many suggestions for the development of Paris; they would need technical explanations and illustrations which are not within the scope of the present book. The few reflections I want to submit apply to other cities beside Paris, and to other disciplines beside city planning. They are a confession of faith. Above all, they are part of my personal equation. Men fulfill themselves in many ways—sport, work, gambling, art. Napoleon was first of all a virtuoso who used an army as a violin. City planning is my instrument. I have seldom played it in public, but I cherish it all the more.

First of all, I am averse to megalomania. Macropolis, the enormous city, is a morbid growth, the price we have to pay for the absence of national planning. There are advantages in great size; but there is also a law of diminishing returns. Practically everything we prize in Paris is found within its eighteenth-century limits. If Levallois-Perret and its likes were to fade away, I should feel no regret. And this might well apply to the Bronx and Brooklyn.

But the idea of *Greater Paris* is no puerile megalomania, no desire to jump statistically ahead of Berlin, Moscow or Chicago.[3] It means integrating the whole region; in other terms, daring to face a palpable fact. For lack of such an organization, the growth of the Paris suburbs has been chaotic, unsanitary, hideous. Because Paris has not been provided with a Green Belt of health and beauty, there has grown a menacing Red Belt of sullen resentment. It is meanness that breeds revolt. The Rights of Man include "resistance to oppression"; and it is no mere playing upon words to affirm

[3] The population of the department of the Seine, which has almost exactly the same area as the city of Chicago, is about five million; that of the Paris Region is well over six million.

that the atmosphere of the industrial suburbs is oppressive.

The one pressing need is not merely to check, but drastically to reduce the human density of congested area. Theoretically, this could be achieved by means of skyscrapers, if properly spaced, as well as by means of bungalows. But the skyscraper, even in New York, is no longer considered a magic formula. It never favored a healthy, city-wide development; and now it has ceased to be profitable even to its owners. The United Nations Center on the East River may be the last of the clumsy and wasteful Titans. But Paris has no choice in the matter. The skyscraper solution is ruled out, at any rate within the historic districts. There is a Parisian module of proportion. It is determined by the scale of the ancient monuments, of the Seine, of the trees. Tall buildings are not condemned as such: the cathedrals were skyscrapers, and it took America several decades to rival the Strasbourg Cathedral. But they should stand in isolation, like the custom house in Boston, or the city hall in Los Angeles. Paris, I repeat, is under a *servitude de beauté:* the world could not afford to have even a thirty-story building by the side of Notre Dame.

It is easy enough to translate this *servitude* into a restriction of building heights—let us say seventy feet. The problem of style is far more complex. Paris has too varied a heritage, and is too eager in the vanguard, for a single architectural idiom to be rigorously imposed. Least of all could that idiom be Gothic. Paris has long ceased to be the city of serrated gables, bristling with spires, so glowingly described by Hugo. No sentimental love of the picturesque should serve as an excuse for the squalid. Streets that reek with disease and decrepitude are not "medieval": in those days, the churches were white, and the people bathed more than they did in the classical age—the nadir of personal cleanliness. Let the Street of the Fishing Cat join the rue de Venise in richly deserved oblivion: there is no virtue in meanness.

America may carry too far the worship of the deodorant: it
is not true that heaven and earth will be yours, if only you do
not smell. But the odor of slums, the halitosis of cities, is a
symptom of civic failure. The rue de la Huchette, I am glad
to say, is doomed—even though it should break the romantic
heart of Elliot Paul.

There are a few points upon which all lovers of Paris are
in accord, except perhaps a handful of rabid functionalist
doctrinaires. Certain aspects of Paris should be religiously
preserved because of their intrinsic beauty combined with
historical appeal. No doubt the Place Royale [4] and the Place
Vendôme are "antiquated," as antiquated as Descartes or
Racine; but we love them, and would resent any alteration.

I have often considered city problems in terms of dollars
and cents. Frankly, an adequate civic programme is not good
business, as chewing gum and slot machines are. If strict
individualism and the profit motive are to be our only guides,
we cannot afford to live decently. Even by combining farsighted capitalism with enlightened municipal assistance, as
in the case of Stuyvesant Town, the result is far from adequate; when this was pointed out to Commissioner Moses,
he could only sneer at the "perfectionists." So far, we have
proclaimed: Let the system have its way, for it is holy; men
must learn to adjust themselves to it. Many, in Europe and
in America, not revolutionists by any means, believe that
the terms should be reversed: Let us make a determined
effort to provide adequate living and working conditions,
and let the system adjust itself to human needs. *If it can.* If
it cannot, let us devise another system. For an economic
regime is but an instrument, and men are men. As Henry
Churchill rightly reminded us, "The City is the People."
Human values are more realistic than real estate.

[4] Officially Place des Vosges.

CHAPTER THREE

My Paris:
The People

===========

Sixty years ago, the quarter, in Paris, was still to a large extent a self-contained community. It did not offer that radical separation between business and home which, in my opinion, leads to a kind of moral schizophrenia. The aristocratic Faubourg St. Germain, where, through an odd twist of chance, we were to live for some twenty years, was far from solidly aristocratic. It had its ancient princely residences: late in the seventeenth century the nobility had started moving from the *Marais* to the less crowded Left Bank. But it also had bourgeois apartment houses, and whole blocks so dingy that to call them humble was a conscious euphemism. This close proximity of all ranks and fortunes existed, not merely in the quarter as a whole, but in individual buildings. Our house was a social microcosm. The rue de Lille had a good name; so the front apartments were occupied by members of the lesser nobility and upper *bourgeoisie*. The floor that was graced with a stone balcony, and which the French would call *first*, the English *second*, the Americans *third,* the Germans *bel-étage* and the Italians *piano nobile,* was the winter home of titled families who, in the early summer, returned to their provincial *châteaux.* A flat, to be sure, was but a poor substitute for a private residence of one's own, between a court of honor and a formal garden, such as the richer nobility were able to maintain. But those were evil days for the descendants of the Crusaders (a courtesy title, by the way, for very few families can trace their lineage to the Middle Ages). That awful bourgeois Republic had come to stay, much as the Right People tried to ignore the intruder. Soon His Holiness himself was to advise the faithful that they had better resign themselves to the scandalous fact. "This," said the Pontiff, clasping a crucifix to his breast, "is the only corpse to which the Church should cling." So families with authentic armorial bearings had to put up with a ten-room apartment in a decent middle-class house, provided it was untainted by trade—shops or commercial signs of any kind. One other condition was hardly less essential: there must be a porte cochere, i.e. one that would admit a carriage and pair. Ours was never used; but the principle was maintained. One has to draw the line somewhere. The French have often been called the Chinese of the West; this applied at any rate to old France and old China, now one with Nineveh and Tyre. Both peoples were addicted to ripe scholarship and intricate bureaucracy (what the French call *chinoiserie* is probably *françaiserie* in Chinese); both can boast of excellent cooks and dexterous laundrymen; both cultivate elaborate politeness, a strong family feeling, and a common-sense philosophy. Like the Chinese, the French nobility were meticulous about saving face.

The entresol or mezzanine, traditionally less desirable, was at one time given over to a very select *Pension de Famille.* No sign or advertisement revealed its existence; it was an open secret, hushed by tacit agreement. As you ascended, the social standing decreased, for there were no elevators in that ultraconservative neighborhood. So above the *belétage* were found a wine merchant from Bordeaux, a member of that Peerage of the Cask and Bottle so mercilessly described by François Mauriac; a great architect, Emile Raulin; on the top floor, a venerable senator, Jean Macé, founder of the National Education League; at seventy-five, he climbed alertly his five flights of stairs.

Those front apartments were our Mayfair or Park Avenue; our Bayswater, our Upper Broadway, stood immediately behind, between two inner courts. This second building was divided into three- or four-room flats. The more eligible were occupied by well-to-do bachelors: a member of the Council of State, a high official in the Colonial Service, a deputy who kept his main establishment in his constituency. The balance were rented to very unpretentious people: minor government employees, clerks in department stores, retired elderly couples. No Bohemianism: there was a gifted young musician, *but* he was a gentleman. He dined out in the best circles, never forgetting to bring his violin. Thus he was well fed, once in a while; however, it did not pay his rent, and barely met his cab fare. He gave a few lessons, and, every year, one grand benefit concert at Erard's or Pleyel's.

In the garrets—slanting walls, small casement windows, no heat, a single toilet and cold water faucet for the whole floor—there lived our proletariat, if the term will fit such un-class-conscious and unorganized people: the lower servants, a few workingmen, and a very decent old couple, M. and Mme Chapart. They had an official and respected situation: "Mendicants at Ste Clotilde's." Beggars are an essential part of the conservative scheme. Without them, the lovely virtue of Charity would fade away, revealing the forbidding face of Justice. Since, according to the Gospel, the poor are always to be with us, we might as well have them as quiet, respectful and innocuous as possible. It is a sort of social homeopathy.

During the two world wars, the air raids forced everybody, pell-mell, into the same cellars; I had an experience of that kind during my brief stay at Chaumont. It was idyllic as well as tragic: for a while, rank was obliterated. It took a world catastrophe to turn Christianity and democracy, for a fleeting moment, into realities. The world in which I grew up was a normal one, and everyone knew his place. The situation was neither a recognized feudal hierarchy, as in the last act of *The Admirable Crichton*, nor a Marxian sense of implacable conflict. As a rule, we did not like the *larbins* or flunkies, who gave themselves airs, and had to wear a mask: as Thackeray noted, they are the very essence of snobbishness. But we did not resent the nobility, who did not in any way lord it over us. When we caught a glimpse of them in the common entrance, they struck us as rather ordinary. Dowdiness, of course, is the privilege and the badge of the bluest blood; chic was found across the Seine, among actresses, *nouveaux riches* and South Americans. But, the nobility, in our eyes, were *provincial*, the most damning term in our vocabulary.

The dividing line between the various elements was drawn by the school. Those who depended on the nobility, or genuinely shared their opinions, sent their children to the Brothers of the Christian Doctrine; the others, although good Catholics, to the municipal, or Communal, schools. There we were taught that the ancient regime had come to an end in 1789. Those benighted aristocrats, with titles and coronets, were simply ill-informed provincials, who had never heard of the Bastille, and of the scrapping of feudal privileges. It was about that time, in 1892, that François de Curel, one of their class, called them "Fossils," not without a touch of gloomy pride.

The Church was a neutral ground rather than a common home. Who knows? I may have seen Oriane de Guermantes kneel gracefully at Ste Clotilde's; though she may have attended St. François-Xavier's, which is even more aristocratic. We met the scions of the nobility in catechism class. We did not hate them, and we did not envy them. They were no bigger than we, no better dressed, no less pimply, and not so quick of tongue. No friendships were formed at the foot of the altars; but there was mutual courtesy.

A full quarter of a century later, as I shall relate in its place, I met the provincial aristocracy in its natural habitat. It was during the First World War. I had shed most of my Parisian prejudices. I was ready to admit that a man might have been born three hundred miles from the rue du Bac, and yet not be a "M. de Pourceaugnac." [1] I was then a gentleman by act of Congress, and the bronze eagle on my cap was as good as any crested helmet. So I met the nobles of Anjou with unjaundiced eyes, and I found them delightful. Some were a trifle dim and dusty; but this happens also in college faculties, and even in chambers of commerce. As I chatted pleasantly with them, it was amusing to evoke, from half-forgotten depths, the little plebeian of the early nineties. I wonder if Palamède de la Grandière, as handsome as his name, ever remembered that we had taken our First Communion together at Ste Clotilde's?

I had no doubt, in those early days, that we the people of Paris were the vanguard of progress, with the nobles limping a hundred years behind. I don't know how far we have progressed, they and I. Our paths may have been spirals, or more erratic involutions. At any rate, they crossed in 1918; and if the meeting was a miracle, I am none the less thankful.

[1] A ridiculous country squire from Limoges, in Molière's farce by the same name.

So in the rue de Lille we tacitly agreed to keep our distances. They, in their ancestral pride, stood immeasurably above us; we, in our own conceit, were ages ahead of them. In our eyes, they were an anachronism which might at any moment turn into an obstacle, like a steep and narrow bridge marked for demolition. Our snobbishness in reverse, which amuses me in retrospect, saved us at any rate from the sin of envy, which is the most degrading of all.

Our natural associates comprised the whole range of Parisian life, from the lesser *bourgeoisie* to the humblest working people. We had, in our family connection and our rather narrow circle of friends, at one end *rentiers* living on a modest income, minor officials, well-to-do shopkeepers, a contractor with a meteoric career; at the other end, mechanics, janitors, a dressmaker in a small way, the owner of a suburban restaurant, a stone mason and a porter at the Central Market, mysteriously nicknamed *La Cacouère*. These porters were officially known as "strong men"—*les forts de la Halle*—and they proudly wore soft hats with two-foot brims.

On the whole, they were mostly *petites gens*, little people. I was conscious of that "littleness," which, frankly accepted, is not demeaning, any more than the lifelong poverty of priest, soldier or educator. But when circumstances are too narrow, they cramp the soul, and I felt it among some of our acquaintances. The honest, hard-working, thrifty, unsuccessful poor may be more materialistic than the millionaire. I'd rather chase dollars than pinch pennies. But I do not think I'd be good at either. Fortunately, I have been saved from both extremes.

There is an expression I remember with a mixture of genuine pity and irritation: *"Nos pauv' 'tits quat' sous,"* our poor little four cents, i.e. our savings. The French workman's four cents, like the peasant's woolen stocking, went into Panama bonds, Russian funds, and the bottomless pit of war expenditures. History has tried its hardest to cure the French of their thrift. Perhaps they are incorrigible.

If there was no waste, there was no want. The *petite bourgeoisie* and the common people lived well in those days. There was wine in abundance: we had our own cellar, a dank, unlit, sepulchral vault which greatly appealed to the romantic gamin. If we made a meal of lentils once in a while, it was because we liked lentils; but I remember also golden-crusted white bread, chops, steaks, roasts and fowls, snails too (I never had frogs' legs until I reached Houston, Texas, where they were served at a grand banquet for Maurice Maeterlinck); on gala occasions, an elaborate cake from the pastry cook's—Mocha, Savarin or St. Honoré. Of course, we had no car, rarely took long trips, and clothes, for women as well as for men, were made to last many years; but the party dinners in very modest homes were such, in abundance and refinement, as I have seldom seen equaled in America. *Cuisine* was part of the family ritual. This is the one aspect of the bourgeois regime that its most determined opponents do not challenge. I have seen restaurants—one called *Au Rendez-Vous des Prolétaires*, another *Au Rendez-Vous des Artistes*— with the boast and the promise: *Cuisine Bourgeoise*. For us, *cordon bleu* did not evoke the Royal Order of the Holy Ghost, but the apron strings of a capable cook. After a particularly good meal, we would sigh with gratitude: *"Encore un que les Prussiens n'auront pas!"*: another one that the Prussians will not get! I wish America would ponder the significance of that popular tradition.

My early experience made me immune to the crudely abstract scheme of Marxism, the sharply defined class struggle. Life never was like that in my Paris or in my London; it is not like that in my America. The Marxians confuse *classes,*

that is to say social levels, with economic interests. We were
well aware of class differences, which we accepted as a fact
of natural history, just as we were conscious of racial types:
a blond is not a brunet, and a Chinaman is not a Negro. It
would be nonsensical to deny obvious facts; it is a monstrous
fallacy to maintain that they create ineradicable antagonisms.
Our conception of classes was much more elaborate, and
much more scientific, than the rudimentary Capitalist-Pro-
letarian dichotomy. Each of the three "estates," upper class,
bourgeoisie, common people, had many kinds and degrees.
The Guermantes, the Prince of Borodino, Charles Swann,
and the provincial Cambremers were all *"de la haute,"* they
belonged to Society; but there were sharp distinctions between them. We were plain working people, and did not call
ourselves "bourgeois." Yet my parents kept a *bonne,* usually a
young peasant girl from Brittany, paid three dollars a month;
and my mother would not go shopping in the next street
without a hat. Wealth was not the sole criterion. An impover-
ished noble still belonged to a class which was not of easy
access to parvenus, although there were Lavals even under
Louis XIV. An official outranked a shopkeeper with a much
larger income; a clerk felt himself superior to a mechanic.
"Capitalism" was not the test: as I noted before, a street
hawker is a capitalist in miniature, yet a pariah; the director
of a great public service lives on a salary. We do not seriously
believe that a justice on the Supreme Bench is one of the
downtrodden; or that the village blacksmith, who "owes not
any man," is one of the oppressors.

For us, classes were undeniable, but they were many,
delicately shaded, and to a large extent fluid. Our realistic
and classical sense warned us that it was difficult to jump
several hurdles at one time. We accepted implicitly the doctrine formulated later by Paul Bourget in *L'Etape:* the necessity, as a rule, of intermediate steps. With one exception,

however. There was an immemorial tradition that the service
of the spirit and the service of the State obliterated the accident of birth. The clergy under the ancient regime was the
first Order, above the nobility of the sword; and it was possible for a swineherd to become pope. Poets and artists con-
sorted with kings. Louis XIV, with an exquisite and almost
fanatical sense for social distinctions, yet treated Boileau with
greater deference than he did Lauzun. An officer was a gentleman, even though he had no handle to his name, and not an
écu in his purse. The students who graduated with the highest honors from Polytechnique, the great engineering school,
chose government service as a matter of course, for it carried
greater prestige. I did well in my studies and it was taken for
granted that I would rise in a profession as yet undefined. So
I thought of myself, in all simplicity, not as bourgeois or
proletarian, but as a future engineer, architect or writer.

After so many years, the use of the term "bourgeois" to denote the capitalistic system still annoys me like a barbarism.
The mind of Marx was formed at a time when the *bourgeoisie*
had sharply defeated the old aristocracy, both in England
and in France. Democracy still appeared, as bolshevism does
today, in the sinister glare of the Terror. The reign of Louis
Philippe was thus the apotheosis of the middle class. For a
brief season, plutocracy reigned and governed, precariously
but insolently. Marx mistook that fleeting and uneasy dictatorship of the moneybags for the very nature of the modern
world. Because he borrowed from the critics of Louis Philippe the word "bourgeois" as a term of opprobrium, he burdened us with an ambiguity which has become inextricable.
The virtues and the faults of the typical capitalist,—the pro-
moter, the captain of industry, the empire-builder, the robber
baron—are exactly the reverse of those we discern in the
perfect bourgeois: staid, cautious, somewhat dull and sluggish. The true capitalist is a gentleman-adventurer, as in the

days of Queen Elizabeth; there is something of the conquis-
tador about him. Balzac, because he was a romanticist, could
give a prophetic portrait of the capitalist, who did not reach
full stature until the Second Empire. The two types, bourgeois and capitalist, are antithetical—which does not mean
that they may not be allied. In the economic field, I prefer the
capitalist, for his dash and brilliancy. But the bourgeois offers
a more favorable ground for a rich, slowly matured culture.

It is absurd to call a duke a bourgeois, even though he
should be on the board of financial companies; or to stamp
a successful artist as bourgeois, even though, like Sargent,
he should paint the portraits of millionaires. The use of the
word "bourgeois" has become as hopelessly confused as the
Santa Claus story, in which a shadowy Bishop of Myra, the
Christ child and a jolly Nordic gnome who looks like Andrew
Carnegie are bewilderingly tangled. I like fairy tales in their
place, and my children were not denied their Santa Claus;
but political economy is no place for myths.[2]

No doubt there was still in my youth a sentiment that the
service of God, of country, and of the human spirit was nobler
than the quest for gain. It would be easy to interpret this feeling as a survival of the feudal, and as an anticipation of the
socialistic, both transcending the profit motive. This sounds
very lofty, and it is not untrue. But I must confess that reality
had also more sordid shades to offer. The quiet acceptance of
class as a fact often changed into class assertion, most bitter,
naturally, on the boundary line. Class consists in the right to
be rude: white against colored, Big Five against small fry,
blue blood against commoner, millionaire against pauper,

[2] To make confusion almost absolute, the Romanticists used "bourgeois"
for "philistine"; *épater le bourgeois* was one of the chief tenets of their creed.
That tendency was manifest even in Baudelaire. The cream of the jest was
that most writers, and their public, were bourgeois themselves. Fortunately
the term, in that sense, has become antiquated.

self-anointed artist against Philistine. I have seen members
of the very small Parisian *bourgeoisie* treat their underpaid
servants with an arrogance born of secret fear.

It is well not to make a fetish of gain; but what many a
French bourgeois despised was not gain, it was manual labor.
The white-collar man, however insignificant or parasitic, was
a *monsieur;* the man with calloused and grimy hands was
relegated to the abyss. *That is* the petty bourgeois spirit which
I saw at close range, and against which my soul rebelled
even when I was a child; that was the Carthage I prayed to
see destroyed; that, and not a complicated economic formula
about which experts cannot agree.

I have been told that the French bourgeois spirit perished in the war; if it be so, men have not died wholly in vain.
But I am skeptical. That spirit is fully seven hundred years old;
and when I last came across it, there were no signs of decrepitude on its plain and robust countenance. (Somehow,
and unjustly, I clothe that unlovely myth in the semblance of
Raymond Poincaré.) I wish it were dead, for then I could
sing a palinode. For there were very fine traits about the *petit
bourgeois.* Whatever we called ourselves in those days, we
sought to practice the bourgeois virtues, and I trust they will
not disappear from the world. The first of them was steady,
conscientious work, with a definite element of pleasure and
pride. Here we must note a contradiction. The bourgeois
hoped to retire and set up as a gentleman. The earlier the
better: an uncle of mine was greatly envied because he had
"made his pile" and given up his business by the time he was
forty. But until repose had been earned, diligence was a duty.
We had a strong sense of working-class solidarity; but we
included the owner-manager among the workers. Even today, I believe that the laborer has genuine respect for the boss
who is on the job. It is the absentee landlord, the gambler and

the profiteer that are intolerable. We bunched together in our contempt *"les oisifs et les fainéants,"* idlers and loafers, whatever their social rank.

Another distinction cut across the formal division of classes: *"les honnêtes gens et les autres,"* honest people and the rest. The rest included pilferers, pickpockets, and other pitiful delinquents; but it comprised also grafters and swindlers on the grandest scale. Finally, we drew a very sharp line between *"les gens qui savent se tenir et les autres,"* people who know how to behave, and those who do not. It was not a question of good manners merely, although the common people of Paris could be very punctilious on that score; it was a matter of discipline. *Laisser aller,* or laxity, was a sin. Drunkards, gluttons, debauchees, bad debtors, spendthrifts, came under the same condemnation, whether they belonged to the dregs or to the alleged elite.

I was brought up to be "punctual, abstemious, chaste and thrifty," like the small groceryman of Montrouge in the poem of François Coppée. These qualities are those of the Puritan; and there was a strong tinge of Puritanism among the Parisian people I knew. Max Weber believed in a pre-established harmony between the Protestant ethic and the spirit of capitalism. The spirit and even the techniques of capitalism were brought to perfection in Catholic Florence, an economic community if ever there was one, in which the guilds ruled the commonwealth, and a successful banker assumed princely power. On the other hand, the manifest Puritanism of my Parisian acquaintances was tinged with a cold distaste for Protestantism, which, very inaccurately, was considered as un-French.

This conception of the true Parisian as puritanical is, I freely admit, a paradox. Foreign visitors prefer to believe the evidence of their own eyes; but they may easily be deceived by superficial differences in manners. Paris liked to have a good time on Sunday, in the period when a London, Midland or Scottish Sabbath was palpable Stygian gloom. (The difference is far less striking today.) Free thought was common even among nominal Catholics, and Bible reading was practically unknown. But we should distinguish between sectarian habits and a moral code. The Stoic philosophers were Puritans without the benefit of Calvin and Knox.

I repeat that I am speaking of the Parisian born and bred. It is not an extinct species, but even in my days, it was a minority; and in the last fifty years, the population of the Paris region has more than doubled. Paris is a submerged province. For the immigrant and the visitor, Paris is not simply a place for unceasing and modestly rewarded labor, it is, as Paul Valéry put it, the great gambling resort. People flock thither to win, by a sudden stroke of luck, wealth, power, fame or love. This conception is admirably symbolized in Balzac's hero, Rastignac. The young provincial has just buried, with his old friend Goriot, the scruples and delusions of his youth. He contemplates Paris from the heights of Père Lachaise, and hurls to the giant city the famous challenge: *"A nous deux, maintenant!"*: now let us fight it out, you and I! Rastignac forced his way into the narrow, strenuous, frantically advertised circle known as *Tout Paris;* but he never was a Parisian at heart. He was a buccaneer, and Paris was his field of operations.

There is the glory of Paris, and there is the glamour, and between the two, the unwary fail to discriminate. *"La vie parisienne"* means a round of pleasure, with the proper condiment of scandalized and delighted sinfulness. This Paris is a bizarre and sumptuous flower of evil. It lies in that fabulous region East of Suez, where the Ten Commandments are in abeyance. It shines with a peculiar phosphorescence in the moments of dissolution: the twilight of the ancient regime. the last few years of the Second Empire, the very eve of the two world wars. It is to be noted that in all these cases, alleged "Parisian Life" was extremely cosmopolitan. The man who best rendered the sultry atmosphere of 1867 was Offenbach, who came from Cologne. The queen of that pleasure-crazy world was an Austrian, Princess Pauline Metternich.

The attitude of the true Parisian toward that fevered hunt for amusement is one of realistic but contemptuous tolerance. In his eyes, the habitués of promiscuous dance halls are purely and simply suckers, as they were so aptly called by Miss Texas Guinan. As a child, I knew vaguely of La Goulue, Grille-d'Egout, and other high priestesses of the cancan. As I grew up, they and their successors never aroused in me the slightest curiosity. I never entered the Moulin Rouge or the Folies-Bergère; even after I became an American, there was still enough of the Parisian in me to preclude any interest. This was by no means virtue in the self-righteous and defensive sense: there was no temptation to resist. I took it for granted that these alleged pleasures were intended for provincials and *rastacouères;* [3] they did not appeal to me any more than flashy scarfpins.

Do not forget that I am evoking the memories of fifty years ago. The contrast between French and American life was then glaring, at any rate on the surface. I have seen a radical change come into the tone, if not into the substance, of the American mores. Paris now reads American books for their daring. Today, New York is far more "phosphorescent" than Paris; probably because New York is going through a period of dissolution, and Paris through the pangs of a new birth. But prejudices take an unconscionable time dying. Somehow, Paris still has an aroma of fascinating, sophisticated wickedness. When Gopher Prairie wants to give its most risqué night club the proper (i.e. improper) allure,

[3] A word denoting all-too-vivid foreign visitors, particularly from South America.

it picks the name *"Chez Paree."* All this would be distressing enough, if it were not such an old story.

We often fail to bear in mind the unrealism of literature and the press. "The humble truth" has very little chance in fiction, or in newspapers; once in a long while, it may appear with the piquancy of the unexpected. "The slice of life" is selected, cut and flavored so as to tickle our palate. Our journals tell us nothing about the millions who were not murdered or who did not divorce. We read so as to escape the oppressive dailiness of life. This is not unhealthy, so long as we make the proper adjustments. It would be disastrous, on the contrary, if we thought that the atmosphere of a Parisian home is that of a Palais-Royal bedroom farce.

Many French writers, including some of the greatest, have given us despairingly somber pictures of Parisian life: Balzac, Zola, and, in our own days, Duhamel, Romains, Carco, Céline, Aragon, Sartre. Most of them, except perhaps Zola, would disclaim any moralistic intent. Yet their works, even those of the most extreme among them, Céline, are denunciations; they imply a norm, against which their darkness stands out. (If they did not, their pictures could not be distinguished from that simple and profound masterpiece: *Fight between Negroes in an unlit cave at midnight.*)

This tacit moralizing is acceptable, were it only because it is inevitable. The same excuse cannot be offered for what might be called "differential moralizing." Some writers pick out vice and squalor in Paris, depict them as the norm, and contrast them (by implication) with the wholesome atmosphere of Minneapolis or Cleveland. This does little good to the cause of morality, and a great deal of harm to that of international understanding.

But there is a still lower level. The writer professes his great love for France and for Paris. Then he picks out a particularly nauseous spot in the hard-working, clear-thinking cap-

ital—let us say The Flower Basket, a cheap bawdyhouse in
a decaying slum. He grows sentimental over it; he proceeds
to idealize it as the very symbol of ancient and indomitable
France. This is a marvelous recipe for popular success. It
has pornography for the prurient, a challenge to the conven-
tions for the emancipated, tributes to the Paris spirit for the
Francophile. At the same time, the author knows that most
of his readers will render thanks unto the Lord—that they
are not like those sordid and degenerate Parisians. So you
cast your net over the righteous and the unrighteous, and
draw in a miraculous haul. There are few more damaging
epithets in French than *équivoque* and *louche* ("squinting"):
this kind of literature deserves both. I am glad to say that
when I denounced this "love that France spurns," I secured
the vigorous endorsement of many unknown friends.

The Parisians of my day had another trait in common with
the Puritans: an unquestioning and insufferable faith in their
own superiority. Perhaps this is the price that has to be paid
for every kind of Puritanism. You would not impose upon
yourself a rigorous discipline if you were not conscious of
being counted among the chosen few. This is true of the
Huguenot and the Covenanter; but it is no less true of the
monk, the soldier, and, in many cases, of the revolutionist—
Robespierre, Saint-Just or Lenin. In long retrospect, I feel
detached enough to appraise this attitude which I had
adopted without a thought. It was, in certain lights, stiff and
unlovely; in other lights, naïve and ludicrous; yet it had its
merits. An aristocratic code does confer a certain degree
of nobility. The elite is to be despised only when it seeks
privileges and exemptions, the refuge of the cowardly; when
alleged superiority is an excuse instead of a discipline. There
is an excellent point about collective pride: when you do

overcome it, you are liberated at the same time from the worship of other artificial superiorities. I smile at my conceit as a child of Paris; but I regard with the same irony the glory we find in race, nation, caste, church or wealth: vanity of vanities. One shibboleth is as futile as another. Pride is a feeling that it is well to have transcended, just as Latin is a language it is well to have known. You will best attain the full stature of the "common man" if at one time you have thought yourself uncommon.

I have a suspicion, which I cannot put down as a historical truth, that Parisian conceit was more intense in those days than it is now. Any caste feeling is exacerbated when it is menaced; and the long unchallenged supremacy of Paris was then slipping away. Within the last fifty years, the population of France apart from the Parisian region has barely increased at all, while that of the metropolis and its suburbs has doubled. Yet the dictatorship of the capital, once absolute, is now as dead as the Bourbons.

Old France was the slow achievement of many agencies; first among them the monarchy, the Church, and Paris. The Capetians began as counts of Paris. The language of Paris, the University of Paris, the Parliament of Paris gradually imposed their authority through their unrivaled prestige. They were the king's, but the king was theirs. Not seldom, king and capital were at odds, and the king emerged victorious. Louis XIV dreaded Paris, and established the seat of his power at Versailles; the Paris rabble felt this hostility, and came to carouse on the line of the king's funeral procession. But even in the full splendor of Versailles, Paris remained a financial, social and spiritual force. French culture was for a time bifocal: *"Etudiez la cour et connaissez la ville,"* study the court and know the city. With the failure and death of the Grand Monarch, Paris came into its own. Versailles under Louis XV was but a wasteful parasitic show. It was toward

Paris, its salons, its cafés, that the eyes of Europe were turned. There dwelt the rulers of fashion, in dress and in ideas. This unofficial leadership of the capital became patent in 1789. While the king fumbled and the Assembly palavered, Paris acted. The fall of the Bastille was decisive. On the fifth and sixth of October, the mob marched on Versailles, and forcibly brought back the royal family. Thus was brutally confirmed a situation which, veiled in twilight haze, had existed for at least seventy years.

For another half century, Paris reigned and governed, whoever the occupant of the Tuileries might be. France accepted with docility the dictates of the capital. Sometimes it was the mob that appeared as the protagonist, as in 1792, 1830, February, 1848; sometimes a change of regime was engineered by a small group, as in 1799, 1814, 1815 and 1830,[4] but always with Paris as the point of origin. At the very height of the Napoleonic Legend, Louis Napoleon found that it was impossible to launch a movement from Strasbourg or Boulogne.

In February, 1848, the rural masses accepted the latest change with resignation, but without enthusiasm. In June came the showdown. Paris rose again, to recapture the leadership of the Revolution. Instead of capitulating, the rest of France reacted fiercely. Had the outbreak been successful, it would have been great and glorious; it failed, and was branded as a criminal insurrection. The repression was ferocious; the victor, Cavaignac, won the title: the butcher of June.

The advent of Louis Napoleon was the victory of the rural

[4] There was in July, 1830, both a popular uprising and a liberal-bourgeois intrigue. The bourgeois won out, tricked the people out of their victory, and enthroned their candidate, Louis Philippe. Lafayette, who might have led the masses, effaced himself out of timidity, fatigue and chivalry. He gave the new sovereign his ambiguous blessing: "Take him: he will be the best of Republics."

masses; the new regime received its baptism of Parisian blood
on December 4, 1851. For nearly twenty years, Paris voted
steadily against the sovereign who was pouring upon it new
wealth and splendor. The Second Empire was killed at Sedan;
Paris had only to register its death. But Paris was not allowed to succeed Napoleon III as it had succeeded Louis XVI.
Thiers challenged the divine right of the capital. The result
was civil war: Versailles vs. the Commune, the provinces
against Paris. Such was the clear-cut issue.

This time, the defeat of Paris was crushing. France was to
be ruled from Paris, but no longer by Paris. The Third Republic, even after it had moved back from Versailles to Paris,
was steadily, and at times overtly, anti-Parisian.

In my childhood, the memories of the Commune were still
very vivid. The ruins of the Cour des Comptes were a grim
reminder of the civil war. The exiles were just returning from
abroad, or from the convict settlement of New Caledonia.
My parents were not Communards: my mother was a young
girl in 1871, and my father a twenty-year-old volunteer in
Algeria. With the proletarian and socialistic aspects of the
Commune they had but little sympathy. (It should never
be forgotten that the Commune was democratic and patriotic
at first, and not communistic.) Yet the Commune, for them
as for many other Parisians, was the Lost Cause. Thiers,
the leader of the victorious Provincials, was hated even worse
than Badinguet (Napoleon III). Even though, in his latter
years, he was to ally himself with Gambetta against the
Royalists, he could never wash away the stain of the Bloody
Week. In the teeming open-air Pantheon of Paris streets and
gardens, there was no room for his statue. You might as well
have attempted to erect a Sherman monument in Georgia.

We felt ourselves defeated, and unjustly defeated. For
did not Paris stand for progress and light, *"la Ville-Lumière,"*
and the provinces for darkest reaction? Of this faith in Paris,

Victor Hugo was the last and greatest exponent. He had not been a Communard; but he had, nobly, jeopardized his popularity by pleading for mercy. For him, Paris was not merely the capital, but the incarnation, of democracy and free thought. In him, this Paris worship was not sheer rhetoric or politics. With his primitive capacity for creating myths and believing in them, he had evoked a tremendous figure, the Spirit of the City, as a latter-day Messiah. Paris was to him what "Israel" or "Jerusalem" was to the prophets of old: not a collection of individuals, but an entity more ardently alive than any mortal man.

So a revolution springing from Paris was holy, a victory against Paris was a sacrilege. Napoleon III had not been endorsed by Paris; so his conquest of power was a crime. The man who is with God laughs at majorities; the democrat who has Paris on his side spurns plebiscites. What if Napoleon III received over seven million votes? They were provincial votes.[5]

The funeral of Victor Hugo is my first memory. I was well under five. My recollection is at the same time luminous and blurred: a vision of teeming masses on the Faubourg St.-Germain, a great hush, and something like a stifled sob. Who knows but I had then, in instinctive, quasi-animal fashion, a revelation of the collective soul? I cannot remember that feeling being instilled into me at a later date; it has remained with me; and there is a tremor of awe in the depths of my being as I write these lines. It was my First Communion. If the common people of Paris turned the elaborate official ceremony into an apotheosis, it was not to the poet, to the romancer or to the Republican that they were doing homage, but to their champion, to the man who believed in

---

[5] This apocalyptic conception is expressed in Hugo's little book *Paris*: his preface to *Paris-Guide 1867*, and sundry pieces in the same vein. The same doctrine may be found in more moderate form in Alfred de Vigny's poem, *Paris*.

the spirit of Paris, and who had uttered words of compassion on the dishonored grave of the Commune.

This was the dirge of a dying faith. Paris is not merely an enormous city; it has remained an incomparable center. But its unique spirit, which for two centuries had been a pillar of fire, is now the memory of a dream. I have seen great popular demonstrations in Paris, during the Dreyfus Case and the First World War; and there were notable "days" in the streets of the capital, until the sinister sixth of February, 1934. But all these explosions of anger or pride were *in* Paris, not *of* Paris. Only the liberation of the great city by its own people, in 1944, which my son was privileged to witness, showed a revival of the old passionate unanimity. Still, it was merely a brilliant episode, not a world symbol like the defense of Stalingrad. Paris the city is bursting with material and intellectual vigor; but Paris the incarnation of struggling humanity has been wrapped, to borrow Renan's phrase, "in the purple shroud in which dead gods repose."

I am a student of history, and so I must find a tremendous historical background for my petty prejudices. In my scheme of the universe, the Parisians were the elect, the provincials were the lost. There was some hope for the foreigners. Their differences from us were accepted as picturesque oddities, not as badges of irremediable inferiority. We detected their accent with amusement, but with sympathy; whereas the speech of the countryside aroused derision and contempt. To go abroad might have the charm of an adventure; to be exiled into Champagne and Poitou could be nothing but a harsh punishment. The Paris workers rebelled in June, 1848, because it was suggested that they might find employment draining the marshes of Sologne. Of course, if I had remained in France, I should never have been resigned to provincial gloom. It was much easier for me to go to Williamstown than, say, to Romorantin. I did not discover the provinces—and the provincial nobility, as I noted before—until 1938. I hope the Parisians of today are free from my old prejudices. They may have discovered that within thirty miles of Tours were born Rabelais, Ronsard, Descartes and Balzac; not a bad showing for a placid countryside.

I do not want France to be governed by Paris; indeed I believe it would be better if France were not governed from Paris. Paris has played its part in the unification of France, which, in not a few cases, has been ruthless. I have become a thorough believer in regionalism, within the World Republic and within the national states. Centralization of the Richelieu-Jacobin-Napoleonic type is a process which may easily be carried to an absurd extreme. France would be better off if she had twenty local capitals. She might be better off too (this, for a Parisian of my generation, would have been a particularly outrageous blasphemy) if the federal capital were no longer Paris. It is not wise for the Assembly to meet within a stone's throw of the square so ironically called "Place de la Concorde." America is right: as a rule it is advisable that the political capital should not be located in the largest urban center; and it was an egregious blunder to establish the headquarters of the United Nations on the East River. As I have no special fondness for politicians and bureaucrats, I should like to pack them all off to Bourges, the geographical center of the country. Paris would not be the loser if Deputy Tartempion had to orate on the banks of the bucolic Yèvre.

CHAPTER FOUR

Collège Chaptal:
The Four Winds of the Spirit

I ATTENDED Collège Chaptal for six years, exactly in
my teens. I have remained a loyal and grateful alumnus of
that excellent school. But I am not tempted to turn it, in the
golden haze of memory, into an academic Utopia. It suffered
—or rather we suffered—from the two great deficiencies in
French secular education: our physical development was
neglected, and we had no social life whatever. A third accusation against secular schools, that they fail to provide
a moral and spiritual armature, seems to me undeserved. We
were formally taught ethics and civics, and Chaptal, without
doctrinal stiffness, was committed to a Kantian sense of duty.

But if our souls received a plain substantial fare, our bodies
were loftily ignored. There was no medical checkup at any
time. A gymnasium was provided, and some of us proved to
be good little acrobats; the others gaped. Organized sports
were not within the purview of our Kant-like instructors.
We managed to have our games during recess; but the conditions were incredibly unfavorable. We played a rudimentary
kind of soccer, with a tennis-size, three-cent ball. Half a

dozen teams were using at the same time the same narrow courtyard, with endless confusions and collisions: a pluralistic pandemonium. We hardly ever kicked the ball without a spray of loose pebbles. We played in our heavy street clothes, and sweated profusely; no showers were available.

The amenities of life were reduced to a Spartan minimum. I was at school from eight-thirty in the morning till eight at night. Hundreds of meals in the bleak basement refectory have left no unpleasant memories, only a neutral blur in which pallid veal and navy beans are the dominant notes. We were served *abondance*, which is water barely tinted with red acidulous wine: not a bad drink at that.

No dances, no theatricals, no competitive sports, no clubs, no newspapers, no student government: in a word, none of those "activities" which turn the American "high" into a delightful microcosm and a training school. Naturally, coeducation was one of those absurd revolutionary dreams that sensible people shrug away.

I do not want to create an impression of gloom, or even of excessive austerity. My Chaptal years were happy. I enjoyed our hit-or-miss, rough-and-tumble, lawless brand of football fully as much as if I had been taught scientific tactics by Pop Warner himself. I traversed the center of Paris twice a day, and I had my home life, narrow and warm. Those who were to be pitied were the full boarders or *internes*. Fortunately, they were very few: boys without a home in Paris, or whose home was no fit place for them. With the callousness of adolescence, we gave no thought to their loneliness and secret tragedies. They were derelicts, "interned," incarcerated, and we took it for granted that they had deserved their fate. In return, they protected themselves with an armor of surliness. In six years, I do not believe I exchanged one friendly word with an *interne*.

It is true that at Chaptal no "activities" interfered with the strict business of study. It is true that the curriculum, definitely prescribed, was full and well balanced. It is true that we had in our teens teachers like Paul Wiriath and Georges Dumas, who would have been a credit to the staff of any university. It is true that some of us at least got the equivalent of a good college education by the time we were eighteen. But our bare and frigid temple was not free from absurdities. I have learnt many things so mechanically that, although worth remembering, they have vanished without a trace. On the other hand, my memory is still cluttered up with useless stuff. Why should I remember that Robert the Pious reigned from 996 to 1031? Why should I still be able to recite the three or four hundred French subprefectures?

At present, there is, I admit, a nostalgic charm to that futile knowledge, which is barely fading away. It means youth, and it means France. I like to chant:

Barcelonnette, Sisteron, Castellane, Forcalquier, or: *Parthenay, Bressuire, Melle,*

in preference to any canto ever penned by Ezra Pound. Did not Abbé Bremond find the essence of pure poetry in:

Orléans, Beaugency,
Notre-Dame de Coucy,
Vendôme, Vendôme?

I have lost track of my schoolmates, I repeat; but there are quite a few whom I remember to this day with great affection. They were not eccentric in any way; they had honorable but unsensational careers; and they did not perceptibly influence me. So they have no place in this inquiry. The merest *Salve atque Vale* will suffice. But two, for very different reasons, were part of my life and must be mentioned here: André Bénier and Albert Thierry.

I knew Bénier for a few months only, when we were about sixteen. We never saw each other except at school: he lived at Puteaux, a western suburb. We had no dominant taste and no intellectual interests in common. This strange, immediate, ardent friendship was a pure mystery. As Montaigne said of La Boétie: "I loved him because he was he, and I was I."

I know that Freudians, Proustians and Gidians have an explanation in readiness; and I admit that the obvious interpretation must have contained a modicum of truth. There was something soft and gentle about Bénier. He was slender, with a delicate almost nacreous complexion, and a quiet merry smile. He was by no means effeminate; he took part in our rough games, and excelled in them because of his swift suppleness. I had no brother or sister, and not even a dog. It was natural that my cabin'd tenderness should seek an object; natural also that there should appear in it a faint premonitory gleam of the change which, at sixteen, was stealing upon us. There is nothing unusual about such an experience; and I believe that as a rule, such friendships are unsullied by impure thoughts. With Anatole France, I may claim that I am a good grammarian: I never got my genders mixed. I have to accept a great deal of modern literature on trust, as children swallow fairy tales.

We knew that our friendship had a strange delicacy, and we treated it with curious reserve. There was no gushing: our understanding was unexpressed. It did not need the mask of boyish roughness. When I look back upon that *amitié amoureuse,* there is in my wistfulness not the slightest tinge of shame. Our affection was abnormal only because of its exquisite purity. We both felt that it could live in its perfection only "the space of a morning," and in fifty years we have not inquired about each other. But my favorite poet Alfred de Vigny taught me to love above all things "that which will never be seen again":

Aimez ce que jamais on ne verra deux fois.

I have had two other attachments of the same kind, equally free from the practical, the intellectual or the sexual. One was for a young pecan tree that grew under my study windows in Houston; the other, for the fox terrier who has been my companion for fifteen years. I have no race prejudice, and particularly no prejudice in favor of the human race. That tree and that dog are more profoundly dear to me than the vast majority of mankind.

My friendship with Albert Thierry was characterized by the same ardor and reserve, but it was of a different nature. There was nothing attractive about Thierry's appearance. He was sturdy, but short, and devoid of elegance. His head was too large and of uncertain shape, as though packed hard and carelessly. His forehead bulged with obstinacy, his brows were knitted with determination. As long as I knew him, he was afflicted with pimples. He spoke in a quick eager whisper. He wrote a miraculously small and neat hand. His smile, rare and shy, was unbelievably sweet.

My sentiment for Thierry was based entirely upon admiration. I was not free from schoolboy conceit; I was a good student, and won prizes as a matter of course. When Thierry joined our class, his superiority was at once so manifest that it precluded envy. He was only sixteen, but he already possessed a unique style, with the fevered glow of Michelet's. Although he was a year younger than I, I immediately ranked him among my masters; a master more respected than some of the classics we had to read, and than most of the teachers who expounded them. We remained in close touch until his death, some eighteen years later; my faith in him never faltered.

Was that faith a generous adolescent delusion, a "crush" on a different plane? Thierry, when he was killed in the First World War, had reached years of full development. Yet he

was still, to the general public, unknown; to his friends, a
promise. There is searching power in his short stories (*The
Wounded Smile*), and in the romanced account of his teaching (*A Prey to Children*). There is courage in the notes he
jotted down in the trenches (*Conditions of Peace*). But there
was no revelation. The very first essay of his that I read when
he was sixteen offered the same maturity of thought as the
last, with a poetic tremor of deeper appeal.

But I was not alone in my faith. There was from the first,
and without the slightest effort on his part, a Thierry chapel.
It never grew large, whereas the followers of his elder friend
Charles Péguy now need a cathedral. But young men born
after his death still seek in his few volumes, and in every
page that he chanced to write, something far beyond the
letter: the key to a personality which might have been our
guide. The quest is not vain, even though Thierry himself,
had he lived, might never have fulfilled our hopes. If Thierry
be a myth, his value to me will not be decreased.

With his innate courtesy, he never treated me as a disciple,
but as an equal. It was well that we took different roads: I
English studies, and he German; thus we could enrich each
other without duplication or imitation. It was through him I
acquired a taste for German literature that my teachers had
never been able to impart; and I treasure my handsome
Luther's Bible as a memento of our friendship.

He taught me to respect intellectual anarchism, that of
the Reclus brothers and of Jean Grave. This at the time
when "anarchists" denoted either the bomb throwers, or
their shallow aesthetic apologists, like Laurent Tailhade, the
decadent poet who minted the counterfeit phrase: "*Le geste
est beau.*" Intellectual anarchists used to call themselves "lib-
ertarians"; and a libertarian I have remained, against state,
party or clique. I remember with what a rueful quizzical
smile Thierry told me, in 1900, that at a Congress of Anarch-

ists, some were ruled out for not submitting to the discipline of the group.

Thierry's anarchism, or self-reliance, was the key to a favorite principle of his, *"le refus de parvenir."* The phrase is hard to translate. A student of mine, in my course on Art for Art's Sake, proudly announced his determination "to set up as a failure"; whereupon a colleague remarked: "I hope he will make a success of it." Thierry did not admit the prospect of failure. There was no renunciation in him, and no humility. He meant to forge ahead. He did not desire to succeed at the expense of others; but he knew that competition exists under every regime, and particularly in the state of nature. There is no liberty without equality of status; but the effect of liberty is to make inequalities manifest.

Parvenir did not mean to him "getting out of his class." His parents were working people. But as soon as he had been destined to become a teacher and writer, he knew that he had joined a class that ignored class distinctions. He would not plume himself on being a proletarian.

Parvenir, according to his conception, was to entrench yourself in vested interests, to reach such a situation that you no longer needed to exert yourself. Honors, an official position, solid wealth, confer upon you security, authority, prestige. You are one with the comfortable virtues; *you have arrived.* Your sole duty is to preserve the standards which protect you; and, if you are nobly philanthropic, to teach the young how they may reach the same secure eminence. You are assured, self-assured, reassuring. Any man with a system is a parvenu. He lives on his investments and needs no further efforts. Thierry, I know, would never have given up the quest.

In this Thierry resembled André Gide, whom he probably met, for both were associated with Paul Desjardins and his Union for Truth. Gide ever was the reverse of reassuring. A bourgeois, he hated the privileges of his class; a Protestant, he sought to break down the walls of orthodoxy; for every citadel turns into a prison. He refused to belong to a school, or to found a school; if there were a coterie of Gidians, he would consider it his punishment. He was with the Soviets (and it took courage) when communism meant liberation; and he withdrew his support, when he had to face the fact of brutally enforced conformity.

I surmise that Thierry would have followed the same course, erratic only for those who see the crosscurrents, but not the remote star. Yet this is only a surmise. How little I knew of him, whom perhaps I knew best! I shared his hope, but never his secret anguish. As he was not histrionic, he never boasted about his inner flaws.

Chaptal, in those days, put the emphasis on a scientific course. In that line, it was one of the best schools in Paris. When I entered it, I firmly planned to become an engineer. An untoward incident deflected me. I had a certain gift of lucid expression; I happened to win an interscholastic Essay prize, and my fate was sealed. My teachers groomed me for an academic and literary career, coached me privately in Greek and Latin. My life has been happy, and I have no right to complain. What little science I ever knew has evaporated long since. When it comes to Einstein, atomic energy, or filterable viruses, I am in sooth John Doe worse confounded. But from my very early training, I still retain a belief in the primacy of science. I am still at heart an engineer *manqué*, and I respond to great public works as I do to very few poetic masterpieces.

Our language and literature courses, even for scientific students, were very good. We were thoroughly drilled in parsing and "logical analysis," in synonyms and families of words, and in that elusive study that Michel Bréal had not yet christened "semantics." We had excellent editions of the classics, ancient and modern, French and foreign, with introductions and notes that we read with actual pleasure. My memory is still well stocked with fine classical verse, including Malherbe's inevitable *Consolation to Du Périer.* Yet I remember all this intelligent teaching with polite indifference. Like Malherbe's *Consolation,* it has in retrospect the quality of marble: colorless, opaque and cold. My literary initiation came from other sources.

Our curriculum was, deliberately, a full half century behind the times. Chênedollé and Soumet were still above the horizon. Of the great Romanticists, only a few innocuous poems were admitted into our anthologies. Realists, Parnassians, Naturalists, Symbolists, were not mentioned. Perhaps there was sound method in that extreme conservatism. It takes nearly a hundred years for a writer to be safely embalmed as a classic; and living literature should be enjoyed, not taught. I am not sure that it is wise to "teach" Faulkner or Dos Passos: it may create a prejudice. My unformed taste was very fallible: would college teaching have proved a safer guide? I thought François Coppée and Jean Richepin were poets: but so did the French Academy. Outside of his esoteric circle, Mallarmé was known—and that to very few— as an elaborate mystifier. Oh, the blunders of the wise, and the heresies of the orthodox! Goethe admired Béranger; Walter Pater took Octave Feuillet seriously; and a Yale professor closed a capital little text book by linking together, *ex aequo,* Gustave Droz and Guy de Maupassant. Perhaps it is as vain, and as wrong, to teach contemporary literature as to teach contemporary politics. Normalcy and the New Deal have no place in the curriculum until they have receded into the vasty halls of death.

Students at Louis-le-Grand, Saint-Louis, Henri Quatre, Sainte-Barbe, schools which lie in the heart of the Latin Quarter, may have been in closer touch with the latest fad or vogue. Yet Stéphane Mallarmé lived in the vicinity of Chaptal, rue de Rome; but we were unaware of the Presence. We were among the uninitiated who do not blush to be seen in a car of last year's model. In the nineties, Hugo had disappeared into a somewhat dubious empyrean. Leconte de Lisle, who died in 1894, was our demigod, worshiped with the frigidity that he taught and practiced. There is a despairing magnificence about his *Qain:* a massive temple of black marble, defiant against an angry sky. His *Antique, Barbaric,* and *Tragic* poems were a briefer *Legend of the Centuries,* dense and without a gleam of pity. Then came José Maria de Heredia, who reduced the same epic survey of world history to a jeweled miniature, without a glimmer of thought. We should have expected next a poet who could engrave on a cherry pit a condensed version of the mighty *Legend;* but literature took a different turn. We could all write Parnassian verse in those days, harder than corundum, studded with lovely semiprecious words like "chrysoprase," and crowned with rhymes rich beyond the dreams of avarice. Of my Heredia days, nothing remains but a smiling fondness for monosyllabic sonnets, the acme of concentration, *Trophies* reduced to one-twelfth. Two random quatrains happen to flit across my mind:

I
Eat
Meat
Pie,

which is sound, down-to-earth realism (you cannot stick "chrysoprase" into a monosyllabic sonnet), and the gloomy reflection of a modern Ecclesiastes:

Steel
Rusts;
Trusts
Steal,

which at any rate is an excellent tongue twister. *Desipere in loco,* as Quintus Horatius Flaccus used to say.

It is a truism that adolescence is the formative age. The masters of my youth, Hugo, Renan, Taine, Vigny, have remained with me to this day. They are "the Four Winds of my Spirit." It does not mean that I rank them highest—if ranking, a professor's trick, has any validity in literature. Even in those days, I was aware that there were other, and mightier, gods. I never had for them the jealous, fanatical worship found in very small chapels, and particularly in crypts and catacombs: there was nothing esoteric about my masters. But they opened avenues of experience; they were my initiators. In a circuitous and fortuitous manner, it was through Renan that I came to Anatole France, Voltaire, Montaigne, Jonah; through Taine that I reached Auguste Comte, De Maistre and Burke; through Vigny, Pascal, Aeschylus, Job and Unamuno; through Hugo, Goethe, Shakespeare and Dante. This is purely a personal confession, and not the syllabus of a course in world literature.

My Hugo-worship requires no explanation: I was born and brought up in the faith. During my Chaptal years, Hugo's fame was suffering a partial eclipse. Literary Paris made him pay for years of absurd idolatry. His funeral had been a great popular demonstration—all too popular, and with a flagrant political tinge. No wonder the reactionaries sought to discredit the champion of democracy and free thought: Edmond Biré brought out his painstaking and wholly partisan studies, and it could not be denied that the giant had warts. The Pococuranti found it humiliating to kneel at the same shrine as the rabble; in the literary heaven, there must be special

sections reserved for scholars and gentlemen. For the De-
cadents, Hugo's robust fighting faith was a reproach. The
ruling masters of the day, Renan and Taine, were anti-Hugo-
lian. For opposite reasons, Taine imagined himself to be a
scientific realist, a positivist (while he was above all a frightened bourgeois conservative); Renan, in his closing years,
was all elusive shades and subtle ironies. For both, Hugo
was Demos, that is to say Caliban.

Hugo could not be expunged from French literature; but
he was accepted with a deprecatory smile, like a rich uncle
whose manners are none too good. André Gide, whose mind
was shaped, more than he cares to admit, in the Yellow
Nineties, was to give perfect expression to that weary and
apologetic tolerance: "Who is our greatest poet? Victor Hugo,
alas!" That *alas!* was the password of the Happy Few.

So Victor Hugo was voted bombastic and shallow, a formidable word-monger, an apocalyptic Philistine, the idol of
the semiliterate. To the world's loss, admirable works of his
were published during that depression, and to the present
day they remain half in shadow. *The Full Lyre, The End of
Satan, God:* if Hugo had written nothing else, he would still
have few peers; but his glibbest and haughtiest critics in
modern America barely know the titles, and have not opened
the books.

Oddly enough, I was conscious of this disparaging trend;
and instead of feeling wounded, I smiled with impish glee.
The Paris gamin likes to take liberties with the mighty;
he is the sparrow perching, incongruous and saucy, on the
shoulder of the bronze statesman or general. Roman triumphs
had an accompaniment of riotous jibes. Apparent irreverence
seasons, but does not destroy, profound convictions. There
were caricatural carvings of monks and nuns in Gothic
churches, and the rollicking festivals that took place in the
cathedrals would seem sacrilegious to our more squeamish

faith. Hugo was a household god: we could count on his indulgence. I might have been tempted to pull his snowy beard, but only because, with all the children of Paris, I felt myself his grandson.

Victor Hugo poured forth spates of magniloquent nonsense. Yet I doubt whether the proportion of the mediocre in him is as great as in Baudelaire, or greater than in Shakespeare. The work that is good is enormous; but the part which is of surpassing beauty is hidden under a double veil. The most impenetrable of all veils is obviousness. Victor Hugo expressed great ideas, and he was a master of form: for the true connoisseur, these are sins against the Holy Ghost.

His great themes are eternal: love, pity, nature, liberty, justice, religious awe; eternal and therefore commonplace. The Devil's advocate might say that Hugo believed ardently in his ideals, and expressed them superbly; but stern judges brush aside mere extenuating circumstances. Gustave Lanson, swimming with the tide, wrote in 1894 that Hugo was not very intelligent. Granted: his intelligence was no match for that of Emile Faguet, the Admirable Crichton of the lecture room, or for that of Remy de Gourmont, the arbiter of mental elegances. He would have been infinitely more intelligent if he had proclaimed himself, like Mr. T. S. Eliot, a Classicist, a Royalist and a Catholic; he might with advantage have made himself the apostle of Blood and Iron, like Bismarck, or of Blood and Soil, like Hitler. He might have reflected that Machiavelli's *Prince* is infinitely more clever than the Gospel—witness the magnificent success of Machiavelli's most brilliant disciple, Benito Mussolini. It happened that Victor Hugo's creed, in 1849, was scrupulously the same as that of our most advanced liberals a century later, only a great deal more definite. As the Bourbons (we have it on their own authority) have a monopoly of Intelligence, Hugo and his fellow fighters are *ipso facto* branded with imbecility.

As for his technique, it suffered from being incredibly rich and under masterly control, like that of a great symphonic orchestra. In many of his early pieces—most of the *Ballads* and *Orientals,* for instance—Hugo was the virtuoso rather than the poet. And to the end of his career, he could juggle with words, images and rhymes in bewildering fashion; the haggard dreamer must have his sport. Although the sacrifice would not be light, I wish that Hugo, the laureate of justice and fraternity, were profoundly forgotten, and that all his verse before *The Contemplations* could be lost to the world. For the Hugos we understand too well, the humanitarian and the prodigious word-artist, obscure for us the greater Hugo, the "weird Titan, cloud-weaver of phantasmal hopes and fears."

If poets have to be labeled (critics and professors must live), Hugo is a Romanticist. It is common to equate Romanticism with Rousseauism, and Rousseauism with a naïve faith in the essential goodness of human nature. But although the thesis was defended by Irving Babbitt, it is as shallow as it is common: learning and profundity may be placed at the service of egregious fallacies. Romanticism and Rousseauism are almost as Protean as "religion" and "democracy." Their various connotations blend and clash with a lawlessness which is a scandal to the precise theorist. Victor Hugo is accused of being a believer in progress and the ultimate victory of the good. To this "cheap" optimism is opposed the tragic sense of life in Christianity; the haunting, implacable conviction of original sin. But the opposition is wholly artificial. There is an optimistic side to Christian theology, Catholic or Protestant. After all, it is difficult to conceive of God as otherwise than good and omnipotent. If you accept these two simple premises, Leibniz, Fénelon and Robert Browning are irrefutably right: so long as God is in His Heaven, all must be for the best in the best possible world.

On the other hand, there is no doctrine, whatever its label may be, that can avert its eyes from the somber enigma of evil. Call evil a delusion, an error, a lie: still, the delusion causes sufferings which brook no denial. For Rousseau himself, evil is there, in the shape of tyrannical institutions; but these embody pride and greed, which are rooted in the human heart. There was, according to Rousseau, a man who first enclosed a field, and said: "This field is mine." It was the origin of servitude and war. Thus is the Fall translated into economic terms; Property appears as the original snare set by Satan. Hugo was no blind optimist. He knew the three Fates that grind the face of man under their iron feet: "the *Ananke* of dogmas, the *Ananke* of laws, the *Ananke* of Nature." For, turning away from the facile quietism of Wordsworth, of Lamartine and of his own younger days, he saw in Nature the blind forces from which man must expect no mercy. No one had a more shuddering sense of the "chthonic powers" so dear to German—or Danish—obscurantists. Only, like Pascal and Vigny, he refuses to bow before that which is crushing him.

Evil was no less real to the second Hugo than to his contemporaries, Baudelaire, Lautréamont or Rimbaud. He had suffered more deeply than they in his private life, for he had had glimpses of joys they never knew. And the brutality of history struck him harder, for he had been no mere spectator. The mighty hope of 1848, a fraternal world in which Christianity, democracy and social justice were to be reconciled, had been dispelled by the "realists" with the irrefutable logic of a Nazi bomb destroying a cathedral. Hugo had lost faith in his last idol, Demos. *Vox populi,* "the collective incarnation of the divine," had eagerly endorsed Napoleon III. Hugo was driven back from all parties and creeds to the impregnable rock of his own conscience: "If only one be left to resist, I shall be that one."

From the same data, Vigny, whose greatness is so strangely ignored in America, extracted a philosophy as dense and as luminous as a diamond. Such an achievement was beyond the reach of Victor Hugo. Fortunately: Vigny said what had to be said, and Hugo had a different domain. He felt intensely, in his very flesh, the tragedy of mankind; and he was obscurely, compellingly aware that this tragedy was a mystery. He was no logician and no scientist. His very limitations saved him: he knew that the problem was beyond logic and science. A defiant survivor of Romanticism, he spurned the latest key: realism, positivism, the materialistic interpretation of history, all that hard mechanistic determinism now gathering dust in the museums of the mind. So he the man of words wrestled in the night with the unutterable, and won a blessing. Greater than his boasted skill, he ventured into the realms where articulated thought is but a clumsy tool. His was the gift to see, to feel, to know, in a single living immediate process. So he expressed himself spontaneously in myths. As Charles Renouvier the philosopher was to make it clear, Hugo was of the breed of the ancient prophets, an Ezekiel in the age of Herbert Spencer and Ernst Haeckel. Of course, his free thought, his republicanism, his virtuosity, clung to him. They burdened, but they steadied his flight. Without his Philistine ballast, he would have been lost in the twilight between the worlds; without it, he could not have expressed the horror and the glory. He was so equipped —to use an odd but telling phrase of Stephen Leacock's— that he could venture "behind the beyond" with a return ticket. Because the Seer was also an artist, he could play, consciously, in those dim ultimate regions where reality, dream and madness join hands.

All the forerunners and masters of modern poetry recognized that eerie power, under the stodgy, exasperating garb of the Freethinker and the humanitarian. Baudelaire knew it, and Rimbaud: they had the vision to salute in him the Seer. André Gide strove to exorcize him from his own mind, and failed: Hugo followed Gide as the Eye followed Cain.

Now at last, poets have torn away the gaudy garments of the obvious. Surrealists have published an anthology of Hugo's verse, in order to claim him as one of their company: the first, the greatest, the least understood. They borrowed the title from the philosophical poem in *The Contemplations:* "The Mouth of Darkness." Some passages have Miltonic grandeur. Others, vying with Blake and the Apocalypse, seem to rend the shimmering veil of the palpable world. Others gambol riotously in illimitable nonsense. Hugo may take us, in deep earnestness, to the sphere where "a hideous dark sun is ir-radiating night"; but there is no Romanticism without irony. The mysterious is also the absurd: Hugo explored its depths, within and without. The failure of the world to conform to a neat symmetrical plan—Bossuet's, Locke's or Karl Marx's— verges less on the grotesque, in which the ludicrous is tinged with horror. Victor Hugo, who can be witty in the eighteenth-century tradition, can also indulge in epic buffoonery. The ascent of Nimrod in his eagle-drawn machine (*The End of Satan*) is one of those defiant flights. Of course, good taste will shake its smooth vacuous head; good taste that once pro-claimed that Shakespeare wrote like a drunken savage.

It was at home also that I came under the spell of Renan. We had a well-worn copy of his *Life of Jesus,* which was a great favorite of my mother's. It came into my hands when I was about twelve, and very pious. I read it as I believe it was written: in a spirit of reverence. If my faith, a few years after-wards, swerved away from Church discipline, Renan was not to blame: his book, to my uncritical mind, was a fifth Gospel, with all the beauty and tenderness of the others. If, on the contrary, I have *preserved* my faith, all the stronger for being free, it was thanks to Renan's guidance. His intense concern with religious matters, his scorn of all pretense, his contempt for shallow scoffers, his monastic dedication to the service of the spirit were for many years my steady if unattainable models.

For me, as a very youthful reader, his book had the fascination of a story. It is not romanced biography, except in so far as all biography must needs be romance. The most scrupulous scholar, if he be more than a card index, inevitably disposes ascertained facts in such an order and in such a light that they will appear credible. This, and not dashes of melodrama or splashes of color, is the true gift of life. Renan possessed it, and his quiet even voice was more convincing than the vociferations of Carlyle or Michelet.

The Life of Jesus does read like a novel. Mérimée, wishing to rail at Renan's popular success, reported that a young lady could not drop the book, so eager was she to find out "how it would end." The jest is obvious; but there are at least two depths of truth beneath its mocking surface. When we read a classical tragedy, we know in advance the fate of the characters. What interests us is *how*, through what psychological paths, the inexorable end will be reached. In the case of Renan's *Jesus*, the phrase "how it would end" has another meaning. Would the narrative take us up to Golgotha and close on the despairing cry: *Eli, Eli, lama sabachthani?* Or would there be the happy ending that we crave in our hearts, the triumph over the grave?

It was not until much later that I discovered the full significance of Renan's *Jesus*. The work was a crucial experiment, admirably performed, and decisive because it failed. Renan elected to treat Jesus as he would treat Luther or Loyola: as an individual historical character. In spite of his learning, his sympathy, his art, he could not make such a Jesus credible.

Between his young village prophet and the tremendous fact of Christianity, there is an abyss, which human history cannot bridge. The man Jesus does not suffice; the God alone offers the key, the God, whom Renan had ruled out *ex hypothesi*. That a man Jesus actually lived, that there actually was in those days a city called Nazareth, is not established beyond reasonable doubt. But the material facts are immaterial. For the true believer, the essential element is the Word, Who was with God in the beginning, and Who was God. The "mythicists," Kalthoff, Robertson, B. Smith, Drews, Brandes, Couchoud, who see in Jesus only the God and deny the man, are much closer to the orthodox than is Renan. The great characters of history are not of flesh and blood. The taut efficient Napoleon of material fact is puny compared with the Napoleon of legend, the Revolution with crown and sword, the Prometheus of democracy.

I read much later all the historical works of Renan, and found his *Antichrist*, for instance, far more absorbing than *Quo Vadis?* As an artist, Renan was revealed to me by my professor of Philosophy Georges Dumas. Dumas was a psychophysiologist at a time when official philosophy was still committed to the three solemn abstractions, the Faculties of the Mind.[1] Psychophysiology is a perfect instrument for desiccating the soul. But Dumas had too rich a nature to be dried up by any scientific process. Trained in medicine and pure philosophy, he took great interest in sociology and in literature. He wrote, quite early, a good little book on Tolstoy; and he was a lifelong student of "the Positivist Messiahs," Saint-

---

[1] We had a most edifying display of the clash between philosophical generations. An inspector general—M. Evelin, I believe—dropped in one day: a venerable defender of the Eternal Verities, and among them, of the Soul and the Mind as entities sublimely aloof from material conditions. Dumas was telling us that our emotions were but the consciousness of physiological states: we feel angry because we are red in the face. Evelin quaveringly made Dumas repeat this outrageous paradox; then he raised his hands to heaven, and silently tottered out of the room.

Simon and Auguste Comte—as Messiahs rather than as Positivists. His prestige was immense with us. He had the athletic build, the strongly marked features, the marble pallor, the abundant low-growing hair of a young Roman god; and when he looked at us fixedly with his enormous heavily lidded eyes of abysmal darkness, we Parisian gamins felt that he belonged to a different race. But the god was barely thirty, and had a boyish laugh. He read to us, as a relief from metaphysics, passages that he loved; and in particular, the *Flax Crusher,* from Renan's *Souvenirs.* After the dust of Kant or Hegel, it was a vision of delicate beauty. *The Prayer on the Acropolis,* although more obvious and too complacently ornate, still remains in my ears as an incomparable sonata.

Renan and Thierry together gave me a deep respect for German thought. I never had any superstitious awe of German philosophy and scholarship, such as I found in American universities; but I too felt, as soon as I could read German with ease, "as though I were entering a temple." This intellectual love for Germany was by no means exceptional in France: Hugo, Quinet, Michelet, felt it and expressed it long before Romain Rolland or André Gide. It has never left me, even at the height of the two world wars. I still believe that I am a better German at heart than Bismarck or Hitler, just as I am a better American than Decatur or Hearst. The final victory for world peace will have to be won in the German soul; and it cannot be won, unless we the victors abjure the German sin, faith in brutal power.

To the Pharisees of all faiths—Christian, democratic, or even scientific—Renan's attitude in his old age was a scandal. He was a dilettante, a skeptic, an anarchist, a hedonist. "He concocted candies with a flavor of the infinite." (The phrase applies far better to Maeterlinck than to Renan.) He did not deny the reality of pleasure, the one thing as certain as death; and he acknowledged the supremacy of beauty, as the sign and promise of pleasure. In the tepid flood of his universal and contemptuous indulgence, all moral values were dissolved. Thus ran the indictment; and much of it was true.

Yes, to the frivolous, Renan was frivolous. Not so to those who had followed the triumphant tragedy of his spiritual life. His irony was a weapon, no doubt: why thunder, when a smile will do the work? "Jonah, saith the Lord, Doest thou well to be angry?" But it was also a reward. He had fought, without faltering, while so many of the tough-minded capitulated, sneaked back into the safe, comfortable holes of systems, parties, institutions. He had the right to enjoy the evening hour. He had erected for himself an Ivory Tower? So be it: as a fortress, not against responsibility, but against compromise. For the true meaning of the Ivory Tower is the strength that is in purity. He could be indulgent, because he was austere. He would have blushed to praise the stern virtues which were the essence of his nature. He was skeptical out of stoic pride. He had led a good life, and claimed no remuneration. For others, the performance of duty posited a rewarding and avenging Power: else goodness would be a delusion. Renan was not afraid of being a dupe: he obeyed his conscience, and refused to exact payment.

Renan was not unconscious of the Renan legend. In his lighter moments, he played the part for which he had been cast, exactly as Franklin and Hugo did. It was a pleasant society game. But, at the end of his career, he took care to dispel all ambiguities. He had devoted his whole life, not to the amusement of the sophisticated, but to the fearless quest of truth; and he published at last his very early book, massive, confused, teeming and generous, *The Future of Science*. The work was truly defined: "Thoughts of 1848," and 1848 is the last peak in our culture; in a hundred years, we have not regained its height. In a different key, the Renan of 1848 had the same ardor, the same dawn-lit eagerness, the same intolerance of slothful conformity, the same purposive energy as the other prophets of that age, Karl Marx or Michelet. The kinship had long been concealed. Renan spurned eloquence and hated rigidity; he had kept aloof from the humanitarians, be they Romantics or doctrinaires. Yet, in 1848 and in 1890, at his own post, he was one with them. In the great adventure of mankind, he was not among the galley slaves, and not among the profiteers. He believed in conscious striving, however distant the goal.

My relations with Taine were intimate and acrimonious. I learned much from him, mostly through the process of fighting him. I might call myself a follower of Taine in the same way as Irving Babbitt was a follower of Jean Jacques Rousseau.

First in my experience came Taine's method of presentation. It was taught me by Paul Wiriath, my professor of history, and the best loved of my teachers. Wiriath's lectures were marvelously constructed after Taine's pattern, and we youngsters listened spellbound. The discipline was rigorous and profitable. Taine precludes indifference: if you have anything to say, you must be convinced it deeply matters. His seriousness is never passive, like that of the Dryasdusts. He feels intensely: not a page of his, even on the most abstruse subject, is without a tremor of intellectual excitement. But he scorns irresponsible passion: sentiment is no argument. He expresses himself in logical form. Every paragraph develops a single idea, stated in the opening sentence, redefined and enriched in the last. The paragraphs are linked with the same inevitability as the triple rhymes in Dante. But Taine is not satisfied with the abstract frigidity of Euclid or Spinoza. His logic is constantly supported by vivid, realistic instances. The blend of restrained passion, cool masterly argument and telling, picturesque illustrations is extremely impressive.

Of course, the method had to be resisted, for it was purely and simply rhetoric, the approach of the retained advocate— criminal lawyer, propagandist, journalist. There was no dishonesty on Taine's part. I have called him *"un esprit faux,"* an intellectual instrument both powerful and delicate, but *untrue*. Untrue, not insincere. The style was the man. Taine had never measured his personal equation, and his most virulent prejudices seemed to him the objective truth. He despised the Romantics for their appeal to the heart, and condemned the French classical spirit for its excessive rationalism; but he did so quivering with righteous indignation and with an orgy of logical arguments.

He was saved, in his own eyes, by his abundant use of definite, concrete facts. If he could support his passionate assumptions with incontrovertible instances, his conscience was at peace; he was a scientist, a realist, a positivist, in constant touch with material facts. He was unaware that he never allowed the facts to speak for themselves. He summoned them, in limited numbers, and cross-examined them as witnesses for the prosecution. Of the millions of facts about the French Revolution, he called to the bar ten thousand, which were "significant," because they meant what he wanted to prove. At times he passed unconsciously from fact to metaphor. He described the Jacobin as a crocodile, with the same symbolic imagination as Melville evoking the White Whale or Hugo the octopus. But he called himself a "naturalist."

In this he was in full harmony with his younger contemporary Zola. Zola too belonged to the era of Darwin, Spencer and Claude Bernard, and was scientifically minded. When he described a case of human autocombustion, or arranged the family tree of his Rougon-Macquart so as to "demonstrate" the effects of heredity, he believed he had "performed an experiment." When he made up his mind to write a novel about railways, he went on the cab of a locomotive from Paris-Ste-Lazare to Mantes, fully thirty-seven miles. In the same way, Taine would repair to the National Library, and dig out of the dust the facts he needed to support his thesis. All the while, he would pour contempt on amateurs, sentimentalists, Romantics, logicians, in the name of his austere implacable goddess, Scientific Truth. I have found the same haughty infallibility among Marxians. Scientific Truth, if there be such a goddess, must smile wearily at many of her priests.[2]

On one point, Taine helped me greatly, without the necessity of a fight. He strengthened, although he did not create, my interest in English life. I read his *Notes on England* with delight, and his *English Literature* was not a bad initiation. He was at times misinformed, and he had his delusions, but this caused no irreparable harm. A wounded patriot, he constantly deplored that the French were not English. "How happy they are, and how unhappy we!" It was a disciple of his, Desmolins, who was to seek "The Causes of Anglo-Saxon Superiority." Logically, they, like my professor Camille Guy, should have regretted Joan of Arc's mission: without the Maid, the two countries would have remained united. Taine's ideal was the intelligent English conservative, i.e. the old-fashioned liberal. The breed did not then exist in France: the conservatives were reactionaries who wanted to abolish the Revolution and the Enlightenment. Taine did his best to acclimatize British conservatism in France, by helping in the creation of the *Ecole Libre des Sciences Politiques;* and the

[2] Taine could be arresting and impressive: he never was lovable, for there was no love in him. My mother, when she caught me echoing the harsh doctrinaire tones of the Master, hummed to a French hunting tune:

Je n'aime pas ton ton, je n'aime pas ton Taine,
Tontaine, tonton. . . .

discipline which molded such *grands bourgeois* as André Siegfried is not to be despised.

On two other points, I have been wrestling with Taine all my life, and my resolute hostility is not incompatible with respect and with gratitude.

The first is his materialistic deterministic interpretation of literature, in terms of race, environment and time.[3] Materialistic and deterministic: the words are familiar. Taine was the contemporary of Karl Marx, and they wore the same garb. In literary criticism, this rigorous scheme simply has no standing. Taine's method, carried to its perfection, would explain everything about literature, except literature itself. It takes us only to the threshold. Under Louis XIV, there was a third-rate dramatist Pradon, whom a cabal pitted against Racine. For a few nights, Pradon's *Phaedra* was extolled, and Racine's was damned. Race, environment and time, as well as subject matter and form, were the same in both cases. What Taine cannot explain is why Racine is not Pradon. Nor can he account for the fact that, in scorn of race, environment and time, I enjoy Ecclesiastes and Jonah today far more than the latest American best seller.

There is a negative validity to Taine's method. We need to study the Elizabethan in Shakespeare, in order to discount the historical deformation and get at the essential Shakespeare. But above all I learned this from Taine: all threads of history are woven into the same tapestry. Philosophy, religion, science, politics, economics, social life, art, constantly react upon one another.[4] Taine made the relations too rigid, too simple, too one-sided; but he stood above the cramped compartments of the *Fachmänner*. There are trends in history which manifest themselves in every field of endeavor. No discipline is autonomous. Writers are not affected purely

---

[3] Time: French *moment*, more accurately momentum, acquired velocity.
[4] Cf. his "law of mutual dependence."

by writers, economists by economists, politicians by politicians. The *Zeitgeist,* the spirit of the age, is no abstraction, but a confused and potent reality. Taine and Marx were contemporaries. So were, a generation later, Theodore Roosevelt and Rudyard Kipling. They did not influence one another; the undeniable family likeness is due to the fact that the same *period* light falls upon them. What we call history of civilization is the study of these dissolving lights.

The second point is the problem of the French Revolution, and of revolution in general. I was brought up in the belief —which unworldly Kant had in remote Königsberg—that the storming of the Bastille was one of the glorious summits in the destiny of mankind. I read Hugo's *Ninety-Three* soon after his *Notre-Dame;* I was soon to read at least the most glowing pages of Michelet's great dithyramb. I remember very distinctly the celebration of the centennial, in 1889, the ceremonies at school, the flood of speeches, the spate of books, a few of which are still on my shelves. Taine, as a *petit bourgeois,* had first considered himself a son of 1789. In his essay on Carlyle, there is a vehement defense of the Jacobins against the anathema of the Scot obscurantist. The Commune literally frightened Taine and Renan out of their wits. Renan, with his feline suppleness, recovered his balance. Taine, far more dogmatic, spent the last twenty years of his life demonstrating, in his *Origins of Contemporary France,* that the Revolution—the Enlightenment with a guillotine—had been a curse, a grotesque and bloody nightmare. The damaging histories by Louis Madelin and Pierre Gaxotte were but popular versions of Taine's somber masterpiece.

My prejudices were all on the other side. But I was impressed. Neither Aulard nor Mathiez could bring me back to revolutionary orthodoxy. Later Anatole France (*The Gods Are Athirst*) and Goldwin Smith deepened my doubts. I reached the conclusion that bloodshed never is idyllic: revolutions, like wars, are catastrophes. Whatever good they achieve would have come without them, if human reason had not collapsed. They inevitably bring brutal elements to the fore. They retard progress by frightening the intelligent moderates, and most of all by arresting the growth of the Revolutionists themselves. It is not in America alone that the Sons and Daughters of the Revolution are reactionary influences. The French bourgeois Radical of the Edouard Herriot type lives still in 1789, which makes it difficult for him to understand 1948. And I surmise there are not a few Russian Communists incapable of moving beyond the fossilized 1917 pattern.

This dread of revolution as a virulent disease is not an attitude of a weary old man; I am not weary, and these ideas were clearly formed in my mind some thirty years ago. But this is not the place to discuss them at length. On the main issue, Taine and I remain on opposite sides of the barricade. He stands for vested interests; I am against privileges. Revolutions are evils; but the perpetuation of injustice would be worse. Who must bear the responsibility for violent upheavals and their disastrous consequences? The Bourbons, the die-hards. It takes a General Dyer, the hero of Amritsar, to lose India, a Sir Edward Carson to drive Ireland out of the British Commonwealth. Progress had been dammed too long in eighteenth-century France; yet, even as late as 1789, the change, however swift, might not have been destructive, but for the unyielding pride of Marie Antoinette. The Danube basin would not have been Balkanized, if Francis Joseph, and especially the Magyar aristocracy, had shown in time a spark of intelligence and generosity.

I have become thoroughly imbued with the historical spirit, which is the consciousness of change. Not all changes are for the good of mankind: I am the reverse of a fatalist, and I believe in selective evolution. But upon those men whose sole thought is to arrest the course of history lies the guilt of disaster. I hate war and I hate revolution. But when hostilities have broken out, I want the side that stands for justice to win, on its own merits, whether it calls itself conservative or radical. I favor gradualness. An atomic bomb would be a wasteful method of slum clearance. But if, through some natural or man-made cataclysm, a city has been wiped out, I would not rebuild it with all its traditional absurdities, in the hope of improving it through some slow and cautious process. Preserve monarchy, if you will, wherever it does little harm: I am not suggesting that the British should behead George VI, or even send him to a pleasanter clime. But do not forcibly restore a king who, through his alliance with a dictator, has forfeited his rights. Evolution is clogged and sluggish as it is; man's mind is moving swiftly in this epoch, and institutions find it hard to keep up the pace. If a disaster should straighten the channel, let us regret the cost; but it would be stupid painfully to rebuild the obstruction.

Alfred de Vigny was the fourth of my masters, and the most revered. I came to him last—in 1897, to be exact. It was not an unaided personal discovery. I was carried by a general current, and guided by a particular and somewhat incongruous hand.

In the nineties, Vigny was dimly remembered by the general public as a very honorable minor poet, somewhere between Théophile Gautier and Victor de Laprade. The "Romantic Triad" meant Lamartine, Hugo, Musset. In the drama, in the novel, in the lyric, Vigny had preceded Hugo; but he had faded like a pale star in the glow of the Romantic day. It was for him that Sainte-Beuve borrowed from the Litanies of the Virgin the lovely phrase *Turris Eburnea:* "Vigny, more secretive, before noon withdrew into his Ivory Tower." His great philosophical poems, *Destinies,* were published posthumously; and Sainte-Beuve himself, greatest and most fallible of critics, was blind to their somber and delicate beauty. The only poem of his I knew was *The Frigate "La Sérieuse,"* which is the acme of mediocrity. At fifteen, I knew I could do fully as well.

Of course Vigny still lived in a few kindred spirits, including, unexpectedly, Anatole France. But the common reader and his appointed guides, the professors, the critics "in the know," stuck by the traditional values. The discovery of Vigny came with the celebration of his centennial in 1897. Ceremonies of this kind as a rule are sheer waste, except for the organizers, who manage to scrounge a bit of red ribbon for themselves. In this case, the result was immediate and profound: thirty-five thousand copies of Vigny's poems were sold in a short time. From that date, fifty years ago, his rank in French poetry has not been challenged. Baudelaire, of course, is immensely more popular, and Mallarmé has more fanatical disciples. But for his devotees, Vigny's quiet fame is second to none.

My professor of literature in those years, Emile Hinzelin, took active part in the festivities. He inspired in us a proprietary interest in the risen master. He delivered a lecture on Vigny at the Odeon Theater, for which he presented us with free tickets—worth no less than fifty centimes, a dime. I liked Hinzelin, and his burly presence is inseparable in my mind from Vigny's aristocratic mien; it hovers on the wall of my memory like a grotesque shadow. So the austerity of my Vigny cult is tempered with a smile. For Hinzelin was as eccentric as a character in Dickens.

He was our Professional Poet, and took sedulous care to look the part: leonine mane (somewhat oily), vertiginous brow (he was getting bald), Vandyke beard, and the sure badge of the artist: a billowy black silk lavallière tie. His garb was unique: a top hat of dull finish with flat brim; and, in all weathers, a loose overcoat known as a *macfarlane,* with large flaps instead of sleeves. When he shuffled along, leaning forward and beating his flippers, he looked for all the world like an enormous penguin. His heavy none-too-solid flesh was well concealed by his ample garments; but it was pitilessly revealed in his mottled and bloated face. He doused himself with perfumes. His smile was enigmatic, perhaps because, like Mona Lisa and Josephine, he had bad teeth. At times his lower lip would protrude, giving him the expression of a sly and benevolent prioress. Thirty years later, I saw in Proust an admirable description of that smile.

Hinzelin's career was pathetic. He had talent, in verse and prose, but not quite enough to find a niche even in the most hospitable anthologies. Ill at ease in Paris, he strove to be a power in Nancy; but his "regionalism" was interpreted as provincialism. Above all, there was a Musset, a Count d'Orsay, a Beau Brummell, imprisoned in that huge sagging mass. On that level, the incongruous becomes tragic. So it was in the cases of Balzac and of Madame de Staël. But their genius conquered the handicap of their bodies. Hinzelin remained an *almost.*

Yet he was a true poet, even in his own verse; enough of a poet to feel poetry intensely. In his high, affected voice, he could convey the sacred awe better than Sarah Bernhardt herself; for he made us oblivious of the fleshly performer.

He was absurd, and equivocal, as I vaguely surmised. But I liked him, and I am truly grateful to him. I was glad when I met him again at Chaumont in 1918. He had not perceptibly aged, and his uniform as a military interpreter was more becoming than his old *macfarlane.* He had lost none of his tricks, and he could still give a good lecture. Still? He probably was not much over fifty; but to me he seemed like a ghost from a deeply buried past. As we chatted about Chaptal days, I half expected him to grow misty and melt away. But to the last, there was nothing misty about Hinzelin. He ate and drank lustily, and we parted, as we had met, excellent friends.

Vigny wrote little. His poems form a slim volume—a little larger than Mallarmé's, a little smaller than Baudelaire's. Obviously, bulk is not of the essence: else Strada the epic monger would outrank Dante, Milton and Hugo. Vigny is more unequal even than Baudelaire. Some of his early poems, like *Dolorida*, are not merely poor, they are bad. Even in the magnificent *Destinies* some passages are indifferently versified prose. Yet he rises to incomparable heights. In the first stanzas of *The Shepherd's Hut*, for instance, or in the last, there is a music that is low, grave, intense, absolutely pure, and above all, mysterious. It is elusive; you cannot miss the beauty of *Correspondences, Evening Harmony*, and a dozen other pieces in *The Flowers of Evil*, but you might well read the overture to *The Shepherd's Hut*, and pronounce it "very nice indeed."

The one point in Vigny's philosophy upon which I want to dwell is the manliness with which he faced his own despair. It takes no genius to be a pessimist: Christians and pagans, the learned and the simple, the wise and the foolish, meet in the conviction that this is an evil world. Some whine; some shriek; some strike a stiff defiant attitude; some indulge in bitter Mephistophelean laughter. Some settle comfortably in the utmost depths of their pessimism as in a cozy spiritual haven. Schopenhauer evidently found infinite pleasure in taking all joy out of this life, and denying the life to come. The "Lost Generation" shook their heads angrily when you told them that the highroad was just a few steps away: they were lost, and enjoyed being lost. Like the Scottish lady who was "brought up on total depravity," they would not be deprived of their most cherished spiritual possession.

Not so Vigny. The thoroughgoing denial of all fallacious consolations was but his starting point. In this he reminds us

of Pascal. There is no higher praise: for Pascal is the summit
where all schools of thought and art meet, the wit, the scientist, the believer, the Classicist who was also the perfect example of Romantic agony. But if the *Thoughts* are an immensely richer and more tragic document than the *Destinies*,
Vigny has his points of advantage. For—no use mincing words
with a giant of the spirit—Pascal cheats. He introduces a
factor which is not in the original terms; he pulls a *deus ex
machina*. He deliberately gives up thinking, out of weariness.
He takes a short cut, not to the solution, but to the dismissal
of the problem: the throw of dice, the wager. Vigny was too
proud to gamble away his responsibility. And there is in Pascal the terrible, the damnable admission: "Follow the practices of your Church; tell your beads; it will stupefy you."
For Vigny, religion was a stimulant, not an opiate.

He explored his despair without faltering, even to the inevitable and fearful end, antitheism. Like Dante, he escaped
from Hell not by retracing his steps, but through the lowest
depths. He did not destroy despair: he transcended it, just
as Descartes used doubt as the arduous and inevitable path
toward certitude, just as those Existentialists who are worth
their salt use absurdity and chaos as stepping stones. Vigny
was free from the major heresies: he did not foolishly deny
darkness; he did not love darkness; and above all, he was not
afraid.

"Here endeth the lesson": at nineteen, when I left Chaptal,
my schooling was over. I was to have at least seven more years
of formal studies; I was to learn much from books, and men,
and life. But I never stood again in the position of a pupil
or disciple. I was *emancipated*. A proud thought. But, in
these fifty years, another thought has grown, and will not be
denied; the two are still struggling within me. "What paltry
use I have made of my boasted freedom!"

CHAPTER FIVE

The Dreyfus Crisis

I NOW COME to the greatest spiritual crisis in my life, the Dreyfus Affair. My coming to America, the First World War, the Russian Revolution, the Second World War, the revelation of atomic power, shook the very depths of my being. Yet they did nothing but sharpen ideas which were already well established in my mind. It was between 1897 and 1900 that these ideas were formed.

The change that took place within me, in those crucial years, was not exclusively my own. I was carried by a mighty stream. But it would be idle to speak of my "generation." The Dreyfus test, which was a very searching one, absolutely ignored age differences. Age is a fallacy. Among Dreyfusists, there were old men who had been Republicans under the Empire, like Ranc and Clemenceau. There were also, oddly enough, survivors of the maligned Imperial regime, the Empress herself, Princess Mathilde, Emile Ollivier, Paul de Cassagnac, General de Galliffet. On the other hand, among my schoolfellows, many were fanatically against Dreyfus.

You cannot foretell a man's opinions by his age; you cannot even foretell his temper. Many are cooler and more sedate

115

at twenty than Clemenceau was at eighty. There is a radicalism of the right and a radicalism of the left; but radicalism is
not a youthful rash. Does anyone believe that all men are
born red, and turn white with age? Not a few pass, in later
life, from the conservative to the progressive position; so it
was with Gladstone and Victor Hugo. Youth is handicapped
by insufficient knowledge, age by physical infirmities: there
are few adolescents like Joan of Arc, and few octogenarians
like Clemenceau. But experience is not invariably Tory. Experience may teach us that it pays at times to be drastic, to advance boldly and swiftly. There is no church, no party, no
school of thought, that does not contain both young and old.
The old are not invariably the wiser, nor the young the more
generous.

By 1896, my literary taste was beginning to take shape. My
religion was in an uneasy twilight, outwardly undisturbed.
My political and social ideas were unformed. My father died
early in 1890, a victim of the great influenza epidemic, before
he could guide me. He was, as a matter of course, a good
Republican. But I remember his telling us that he would vote
for Denys Cochin, the Royalist candidate, an upright man,
against Terrail-Mermeix, a somewhat equivocal Boulangist.
Years later, I heard Dr. David Starr Jordan express, with
a smile, the same political philosophy: "I always vote a
straight ticket, by weeding out all the crooks." My mother, at
that time, was very reticent in political affairs.

The atmosphere in which I grew, at home and at school,
might be defined as *petit bourgeois* radicalism. (The terms,
of course, are contradictory; but not more so than *orthodox
Protestant,* or *Catholic Nationalist.*) We were attached to the
traditions of the French Revolution and the immortal principles of 1789; but we deplored the excesses of the Terror,
and were averse to any new upheaval. We had great faith in
public education: Danton had said: "After bread, it is the

first need of a people." This suited me very well; for I was successful in my schoolwork, and Jean Macé, the venerable founder of the Education League, had patted me on the head. We thought that priests were all right in their place, which was the Church, but that clericalism in politics should be resisted. We looked forward, without impatience, to the separation of Church and State. The government should see to it that working people got their rights; but there was no substitute for the *petit bourgeois* virtues, hard work, honesty, thrift, legitimate ambition, and independence. We were at the same time patriotic and peace-loving. We liked parades and reviews, but we hated military service. We cherished the Army as the symbol of national integrity and pride; we considered the treaty of Frankfort not merely as a humiliation, but as an injustice; but we had no desire to reconquer the Lost Provinces by force of arms. We recited the artless, folk-like *Soldier's Songs* of Paul Déroulède. I still remember a few; a bugle is a rudimentary but pleasing instrument. But we did not take Déroulède's quixotic clamor for *Revanche* very seriously. Indeed, we calmly reversed Gambetta's famous dictum: "Think of it all the time, never speak of it." We spoke of it abundantly, comfortably, as we were quite determined not to think about it at all.

As I sum up this faith of the French *petit bourgeois*—an enormous section of the French people—I am struck by its American character. The creed of the average Parisian about 1890 might be that of the Middletown citizen between the Revolution and the New Deal. When I came to America in 1906, I found fully realized on this side all the things I had been taught to hope for and work for. This was not to me "the promise of American life": it was too obvious. Our *petit bourgeois* radicalism was the mildest of fighting creeds; still, it had some dynamism. The same ideas in America, unchallenged for generations, had become respectable, complacent, static. I felt, not the joy of fulfillment, but the drowsiness of satiety. Sensible compromises were taken for granted, in which I did not feel the slightest interest; and issues were ignored, which had become vital to me.

Such was the tepid but not unhealthy atmosphere in which I lived, just before the storm. I do not remember when I first became aware of the Dreyfus Case.[1] All I know is that I must have caught my Dreyfusism from my mother: Chaptal was divided, and the teachers, at first, strictly neutral. She and her brother Charles Collot had a morbid horror of injustice; unconsciously, they were in the Voltairian tradition. I parroted them when I was in the elementary school. I would rise, an indignant little citizen in short pants and black pinafore, and shout: *"C'est pas juste!"* with a fierceness that seemed to presage a career on the soapbox. The usual result of my quixotic outbursts was to be kept after school.

Note that this protestant temper of ours might have inclined us either way. I suppose that when I first heard of the captain's condemnation in 1894, I resented the leniency with which he was treated. *"C'est pas juste!"* A common soldier who, in anger, raises his hand against a superior could be shot; a rich and educated man who might have brought disaster to the whole country escaped with his life. And his friends would get him out, never fear! For quite a number of honest anti-Dreyfusists, the captain's defenders were the hirelings of a wealthy, unscrupulous crew attempting to defeat justice.

At any rate, we were ardent Dreyfusists at a very early stage of the agitation. Oddly enough, our faith first found sustenance in conservative papers which neighbors used to lend us: *Le Figaro, Le Soleil, Le Siècle; Le Temps,* for which

---

[1] The Dreyfus Case has turned into a legend, at the same time lurid and misty. A brief chronological summary may not be superfluous. The reader will find it at the end of this chapter.

we felt a kind of superstitious awe, was pontifically Yea-and-Nay. We read *L'Aurore* from its first number. Zola's great letter—*J'accuse!*—was for us not a revelation, but a glorious confirmation, and a call to arms. When I left Chaptal at eight o'clock in the evening, I rushed to public meetings, shouted myself hoarse, and returned home broken with emotion. Then it was that I learned the vanity of formal divisions: all ages, all classes, all faiths and parties were mingled in those tumultuous gatherings; out of the dust, and the reek, and the din, there seemed to rise a common soul, fierce and pure.

My mother felt even more intensely than I did, and I knew it. At the climax, it was of her I thought first. We were spending the summer at Chatelaillon, a small resort on the Atlantic coast. I had gone with my bicycle to La Rochelle, ten or twelve miles away. There I saw the headlines: COL. HENRY CONFESSES FORGERY, COMMITS SUICIDE. Henry was the chief instrument of the anti-Dreyfus machinations. The truth had been made manifest. I pedaled back to my mother with wings on my heels, for I was bringing her tidings of great joy; and we sobbed happily in each other's arms.

I am not going to tell again the story of "*The* Affair." It is a well-made drama, so well made that modern playwrights would scorn it, complete with villains, mysteries, sudden revelations and reversals, relapses into despair, noble champions of the truth, and, in a grand final tableau, Virtue vindicated and triumphant. In the midst of the sophisticated nineties, it was a piece of primitive folklore. Its one weakness was in the central character. Dreyfus was an upright man, an ardent patriot, a diligent officer; but he lacked the flamboyancy we expect in romantic heroes. He was inert. This was partly a matter of physique: he looked and sounded wooden. Dreyfus felt intensely, as we can see in his letters to his wife; but in public, he was paralyzed. When he cried with his whole soul, at Rennes: "I am innocent!" there was not a tremor in the audience. "Ah!" said Labori, his junior counsel, "if *I* could have said that for him, the very walls would have trembled."

The hero was disappointing for a deeper reason. Very soon, from the time of Zola's intervention, the case had become a spiritual fight. The Dreyfus movement placed righteousness above established authorities and vested interests; it was profoundly revolutionary. On that different plane, Dreyfus was not a Dreyfusist. He was a conservative, a capitalist, and above all an army man. His brother Matthieu and his counsel Demange shared the same views. If they had had their way, the Affair would have remained a purely individual case, to be settled on its own merits and by strictly legal means. Even at Rennes, they still tried to placate the military jury. Their way was sane; but they could not have their way. It was blocked by the stupid obstinacy of a few officers, and by the passion of journalists like Drumont and Rochefort. So the higher and more arduous Dreyfusism remained the only path: "Let justice prevail, though the heavens should fall."

The issue was that of irresponsible and mysterious author-ity: "Theirs not to reason why." Dreyfus had been con-demned in the dark. On the strength of the documents com-municated to the defense, no conviction was conceivable. There is a foolish notion among American journalists that in a French court, a man is presumed to be guilty until he can prove his innocence. This is contrary, not merely to the formal Declaration of the Rights of Man, but above all to the temper of the people. If the military were allowed to judge in secrecy, the Bastille was restored, and the old *lettres de cachet*,[2] and that *raison d'état* so hateful to human reason. The Third Republic would have been delivered, bound hand and foot, to the General Staff. Freedom could not breathe in such an atmosphere. As Zola put it, if you stifle, and they won't let you

---

[2] Arbitrary orders of imprisonment, issued in the King's name at the re-quest of some powerful individual.

open the window, smash it. Such was his purpose when he wrote *J'accuse!* They had to prosecute him, and when he appeared in court, he asked searching questions. The judge consistently ruled them out; but that negative attitude was an admission. There *was* a mystery, and therefore a breach of the law. His monotonous refrain: *"La question ne sera pas posée"* sounded like an alarm bell calling all free men to the fight. No evasion could be tolerated.

"Do not lay hands on the Ark of the Covenant! Do not peer into the Holy of Holies!" It is too easy for men in power to wrap themselves in sacrosanct mystery, and denounce all inquiry as a sacrilege. The French have ancient traditions; one of them is that of Abélard, Rabelais, Montaigne, Pascal, Molière, Voltaire, and above all, Descartes. "Never accept a thing as true, unless it appears to you clearly and evidently to be such." And *évidence,* in the French sense of obviousness, results from *evidence* in the sense of proof. Prove, i.e. try and test, all things. Anything that claims to be above proof may well be a hoax.

Although the Dreyfus case became political to a large degree, originally it was intellectual. The Dreyfusists' leaders were branded by their opponents as *"les Intellectuels."* As long as Dreyfus was kept on Devil's Island, human thought was denied freedom. There was volcanic passion on both sides; but the essential appeal of the Dreyfusists was to reason, and the method they urged was scientific criticism. To me, the crucial contribution to the cause was not Zola's admirable *J'accuse!*—an impassioned and heroic question mark. It was the series of articles by Jean Jaurès, entitled *The Proofs,* published in *La Petite République.* In these he examined the scanty documents which had been adduced by War Secretary Cavaignac as decisive. He analyzed them with the rigor of a trained logician, historian and lawyer, and from internal evidence, he exposed them as forgeries. It was a triumph similar to that of Leverrier locating, by calculation only, the unknown planet Neptune. The series was barely completed, when Captain Cuignet "discovered" at last Colonel Henry's falsifications. Seldom had pure reason won so swift and so signal a victory.

We all profess: "The truth is great, and shall prevail." But we are inclined to add *in petto:* "Let it not prevail too soon, if it be likely to disturb our comfort." We hear a steady chorus from England: "Let us not be logical!" with a mighty echo from America: "Let us be realistic!" To these equivocations, the Dreyfusists opposed their faith: "Truth is Truth, even if it should destroy us. There is no pious paltering with the truth. God has no need of our lies."

A secondary lesson that was impressed upon me was the complete divorce between talent and intellectual integrity. Many Dreyfusists were common folks, and uncouth. The leaders on the other side, and most of the rank and file, were by no means stupid. Witness the case of Charles Maurras, the most persistent, the most subtle, the most resourceful of all anti-Dreyfusists. He is so very clever that I find it hard to believe that he can delude himself. All his life, he has built impressive and intricate structures of thought; and he has said to himself, with secret pride: "And it is all my own invention! If I chose to blow, the whole thing would collapse!" It is incredible how clever men can force themselves to think the unthinkable when their prejudices demand it. Because the guilt of Dreyfus was with the Nationalists an article of faith, Esterházy must be innocent; not merely innocent, but the pure and noble victim of international traitors. Now Major Esterházy was, as William James called him, a fantastic scoundrel. His one excuse for selling the secrets of national defense was that, under the French uniform, he was no Frenchman. He was virulently, insanely anti-French, and dreamed of entering Paris at the head of a Uhlan regiment. Yet this incredible villain, a gambler, a swindler, an investor in bawdyhouses, was turned into a hero. A Prince of the House of France, the explorer Henri d'Orléans, embraced him publicly. Triumphantly acquitted, Esterházy was escorted by raving crowds shouting: "The Army for ever!"

There were other instances of perverse distortion. The essential document, the *bordereau* or invoice of pieces to be delivered, was in a handwriting resembling that of Dreyfus, but not identical with it. So Bertillon must needs rig up an infinitely complicated scheme to demonstrate that Dreyfus had attempted, by mechanical means, to imitate his own handwriting. Because Henry had admitted cooking up a proof to reassure the waverers, Charles Maurras invented the magnificent theory of "the patriotic forgery." For reasons of national security, the authentic documents could not be shown. Henry manufactured their moral equivalent. He drew on the bank of truth. A check is not a swindle, if there be sufficient funds to cover it.

So the ultimate proof, not shown to the accused, could not be shown to anyone else either. It had to be accepted on faith. It was darkly hinted that it consisted in a copy of the *bordereau* annotated by William II himself in his own imperial hand. Had the fact been revealed, it would have brought immediate war. Why, and how, no one ever knew. "Hush! It is a matter of life and death for our beloved France!" My country, right or wrong! Of "my country," the flag is the symbol; it is the Army that holds the flag; it is the General Staff that guides the Army. Therefore the General Staff in its corporate capacity can do no wrong. Else the Army would fall to pieces, the flag would be dragged in the mire, the country would lose pride and independence. The very existence of France and the infallibility of Colonel Henry stand and fall together. Dreyfus is guilty; but he must remain condemned, even if he were innocent. "If he were innocent," said an anti-Dreyfusist with faultless logic, "it would be his worst crime."

I was eighteen, and the lesson was branded in my soul. From that moment, I have examined many hypotheses, with eagerness. I know that plain reason does not suffice for the discovery of truth. There must be imagination, and a leap in the dark. But no poetic intuition can be considered as actually true, until it has been submitted to the utmost rigor of a critical examination. Don Quixote made for himself a pasteboard helmet, tested it with his sword, and smashed it; then he made a second helmet, likewise of pasteboard, but refrained from giving it the same trial. In that sense at any rate, I refuse to be quixotic. Whenever an orthodoxy of any kind, religious, political, social, artistic, scientific, claims infallibility, attempts to raise itself above criticism, my old Dreyfusist blood boils as it did in 1898. I am a Fundamentalist, and anti-dogmatism is my fundamental dogma. I reserve the right to challenge the Constitution, Joseph Smith, Madame Blavatsky, Karl Marx, T. S. Eliot, Sigmund Freud and Jean-Paul Sartre. I want to find out whether their helmets are made of steel, or pasteboard. I must know whether their glitter is tinsel or gold. It is only through honest doubt, which seeks to assay and not merely to destroy, that we can reach honest belief.

The anti-Dreyfusists chose to be known as Nationalists; and nationalism was indeed the major issue. Anti-Semitism was purely incidental. Probably Colonel du Paty de Clam would not have been so prompt to suspect Dreyfus, had Dreyfus been, like himself, a practicing Catholic. But the situation would not have been different, had Dreyfus been a Protestant, a Freemason, or (an impossibility at the time), a Socialist. The anti-Semitic journalist Edouard Drumont,

who had a smoldering, fuliginous talent, with sudden magnificent flames, gave the Affair from the first something of his
own intensity and bitterness. But Drumont was a fanatic
whom people read for his style, not for his opinions. The
Jews, few in France at the time, and thoroughly assimilated,
were not hated as Jews. They were distrusted as international-
ists: Dreyfus, to some extent, was made to suffer because the
Rothschild family had branches in several capitals. One of
the prominent anti-Dreyfusists was Arthur Meyer, editor of
the Royalist and fashionable paper *Le Gaulois;* Arthur Meyer
was a Jew, and was not baptized until, a few years later, he
married into the highest Catholic aristocracy. At the worst
moment of the Affair, there was in the Chamber an anti-Dreyfus majority, but only a handful of professed anti-Semites.
If I remember correctly, not one of them was returned by
Continental France; they had to seek election in Algeria,
where the situation was totally different.

Among Dreyfusists, the sole effect of Drumont's campaign
was to create sympathy for the Jews. I had never given them
a thought before, although some of my comrades, and the
principal of Chaptal, were Jews.[3] When the fierce light of the
Affair was turned upon them, I realized what an admirable
people they had been through the centuries. This was the
origin of a philo-Semitism which has grown with the years.
As usual with me, it assumes today an unpopular and paradoxical form. But of that later.

Nor was Catholicism the battlefield. Many devout Catholics
were on our side, among them Abbé de Bréon, one of the
priests who had instructed me at Ste Clotilde's. Certain religious orders, and a rather unscrupulous press, threw them-

---

[3] Many Jews at the time were unconscious of being set apart. Eugène
Manuel, a minor poet and a high official in public education, wrote at the
height of the crisis: "I had forgotten I was a Jew; they are persecuted; I
claim my place among them." Cf. also *I Remember*, by the Jew Emile Herzog
(André Maurois): no sign whatever of his feeling branded, or even different.

selves into the fray, and on the wrong side. A few years later, they had to pay the price. Of course, the Church is by nature authoritarian. There are admirable Catholic philosophers; there cannot be any Catholic Freethinkers. *"Les Bien-Pen-sants"* (right-thinkers, i.e. docile believers) and *les Libres-Penseurs* are poles asunder. All problems, ethical or social, lead to an ultimate choice which, of its very nature, is religious. Here, the choice was between a religion of the spirit, respecting the full dignity of the individual soul, and a Church imposing conformity on the strength of traditional authority. Long before the Affair was over, I had made my choice, and I have never repented. But most people do not care to draw the line so sharply. They think they believe, they believe they think, and so they are at peace. Clear thinkers among Catholics (and I do not mean *bien-pensants*) saw the danger of engaging the battle between authority and liberty on a purely individual issue, in which no point of Catholic dogma or Church discipline was at stake. Thanks to them, if clericalism suffered a sharp defeat as the result of the Affair, Catholicism did not. Some of the most ardent Dreyfusists, like Charles Péguy, returned to the Church; and there was after the Separation a magnificent flowering of Catholic thought and art.

Nationalism was the one essential tenet of the anti-Dreyfus coalition: Barrès and Maurras, the theorists of the movement, made this perfectly plain. Royalism and Catholicism were but corollaries. The monarchy was to be restored, according to Maurras, because it was "integral nationalism"; it had created the nation, and was the core of national unity throughout the centuries. Catholicism was to be preserved and revitalized, because it was part of the *French* tradition. Maurras called himself a Catholic but not a Christian. He did not attempt to revive Gallicanism, i.e. the full autonomy of the French church; he knew it was a lost cause. But he was

true enough to the Gallican tradition to oppose the Holy See
in political matters: his paper *L'Action Française* was for
years under a Papal ban.

Nationalism as a doctrine was an impressive pile of paradoxes cemented with sophistry. The Nationalist cohorts were
made up of Catholics, Royalists, aristocrats, army men and
capitalists. Now Catholicism, by definition, transcends national boundaries. The aristocracy is far more cosmopolitan
than the proletariat; and most of all the very highest aristocracy, that family which claims to be identical with "France,"
the Bourbons, in whom there is hardly a drop of French
blood. Army officers, as late at any rate as the First World
War, formed a curious Freemasonry that ignored frontiers.
Münster, the former German ambassador in Paris, wrote to
Schwartzkoppen, who had been military attaché at the time
of the first Dreyfus trial: "The liberty and the future of an
officer are at stake; an officer whom, whether he be a Frenchman or a German, you must consider as a comrade." Capitalists, as such, will trade, not merely with a potential foe, but
with an actual enemy. The profit motive, in its purity, does
not bow to the flag.

With nationalism, many things are blended which in themselves are blameless, or even admirable. Good citizenship,
for instance, respect for the law, the tending of common
interests, the enjoyment of common habits, the cherishing
of common traditions, the struggle for common ideals. In all
of these, Zola and Jaurès were as good "Nationalists" as Barrès
or Maurras. But nationalism as a doctrine is something different: it is a faith, above material interests, above any formal
code or institution, above reason. It is the belief in the real
existence and sacredness of the *folk soul*. In the mind of the
man who first spoke with fervor of the *folk soul*, Herder, it
was hardly more than a beautiful romantic metaphor, a cor-
rective to the excessive intellectualism of the Enlightenment.

That poetic conception still prevailed in the fraternal, generous "nationalism" of Michelet, and of the men of '48 throughout Europe. For them, nations were families, and should live side by side as friends. The sentiment was lofty and pure; unfortunately, it was not in accordance with the facts. The essential activities of Europe, religion, science, art, could not be confined within territorial boundaries.

The Nation as a person was therefore a myth. After 1848, it ceased to be even a beautiful myth. It became contaminated with the silly quest for prestige and the Machiavellism of the old dynasties, and with the brutal power politics of Bismarck. Because these survivals of the pre-Revolutionary era were narrow and cynical, they were called "realistic." Nationalism, a child of romanticism, assumed an ill-fitting pseudoscientific garb. German scholars—aye, and Englishmen too—evolved a conception of "cultures" as organic entities, with a life of their own: a dismal fiction which still cumbers many minds. Such a premise could only lead to totalitarianism. If such "cultures" do exist, they are of immensely greater value than the lives of puny men. Within a "culture" or way of life, the duty of the individual is to conform, 100 per cent. Else he destroys the pattern; he is un-German, un-French—un-American, a traitor. Among the cultures, there is a constant struggle for survival. Alien conceptions attempt to force themselves upon us, insidiously or brutally, and undermine our integrity. As a result, the civilized world of the Enlightenment, the humanitarian world of the late Romantics, were both shattered. Egoism became "sacred." No universal law: the nation was an absolute, and a law unto itself. Every national culture became a fortress.

If the "national culture" as a spiritual entity were a fact, it would not be afraid of scientific challenge. Every hypothesis is freely open to criticism. Not so a myth turned into a dogma. Because it is only a distorted romantic dream, the National

Idea cannot stand discussion. The defenders of the National Idea must be invested with pontifical infallibility. The one institution that stands for the National Idea in all its purity is the Army. If the Army condemns Dreyfus, Dreyfus must remain condemned, "innocent or guilty." So, in 1898, we looked totalitarianism full in the face. When it appeared again under the names of fascism or nazism, we recognized it without a moment's hesitation. Pétain's "National Revolution," so pitiful on the material plane, was not a feeble imitation of Mussolini's regime, or Hitler's, or Franco's. It was their forerunner, the nationalism of Barrès and Maurras.

From that time, nationalism to me was the enemy. My ideal was that of George Washington, Victor Hugo, Charles Péguy, Wendell Willkie: "One World," "the great Republic of Humanity at large." I saw in nationalism a new incarnation of Voltaire's *"l'Infâme,"* that must be crushed if men are to be free: fanaticism, fierce, ruthless, unreasoning, imposing itself by methods of terrorism. Devil's Island, with its lone martyr, is infinitesimal compared with Ravensbrück or Buchenwald. But the principle is the same.

My uncompromising antinationalism, the heritage of my Dreyfus days, has led me, in several cases, to oppose my best friends. I have done so with deep regret, but without hesitation. I am a determined anti-imperialist, and I said long ago that all colonial empires should be liquidated. But I do not want that liquidation to release nationalisms of the narrowest, most virulent, most oppressive kind. This country was created through a War of Independence; so we believe that "independence" is a sacred cause everywhere in the world (except, of course, in the case of the Confederacy). But there is something that is greater than independence, or unlimited sovereignty: and that is freedom. What is to be liquidated is the spirit of pride and greed; what is to be guarded against is crude and fanatical totalitarianism, whether imported or home-grown. If those ends be achieved, I care little whether it be under the Dutch flag or the Indonesian, the Latvian or the U.S.S.R., the French or the Vietnamese. In each case, my test is not the shibboleth *independence,* but the more vital questions: "Which solution will best lead to the pluralistic liberal state? Which will best assure the dignity of all men? Which will best promote the World Republic?" And the answers are not quite so automatic as would appear in the pages of our liberal weeklies.

The most dolorous problem is that of Zionism. I repeat that for fifty years I have admired and defended the Jews. I am proud of counting Jews among my most valued friends. In 1898, our argument against the anti-Dreyfusists was: "The Jews are not aliens. They are good citizens, and good patriots. They have their family tradition; but they share our common heritage, and they enrich it abundantly." And we thought we had won the case. Then mighty voices arose to tell us: "You are wrong. The Jews are a people apart. They will not, they cannot, be assimilated. Wherever they live, they are dwellers in a strange land." Who said this? Hitler? Yes, but also Herzl, Weizmann, and—at random—Ludwig Lewisohn.

Israel, to me, was a forerunner of the pluralistic state. It showed the possibility of preserving a tradition, while taking a full share in the life of the multicultural community. Israel had escaped from territorial thralldom. From a study of the Jews in civilized countries, I had arrived at the conception which I found later in Otto Bauer and Karl Renner: *individual cultural autonomy.* Let a man be a Pole, wherever he may live, if he feels himself a Pole; or a Jew, if he acknowledges himself to be a Jew. This liberal conception alone will purify nationalism. It will make frontiers harmless, mere administrative boundaries, such as those between our counties. Nation-

alism is a religion? So be it. Then, like other religions, let it
be nonterritorial.

Then came that dream of a new Jerusalem as a super-
Ghetto, a dream arising tragically in the ghettos of eastern
Europe. If we are to be segregated, let it be in a land of our
own! The Jews of London, Paris and Berlin, safe and honored,
looked upon that yearning with profound sympathy. It was
an arraignment of Poland, Rumania, the Ukraine. But there
is an abyss between sympathy and approval. The First World
War came, and the Balfour Declaration. Balfour was bound
by a formal promise to the Arabs: independence. His promise
to the Jews was diabolically clever and ambiguous: a "national home in Palestine," which might mean anything from
a Hebrew Vatican City to sovereignty over the whole land.
Balfour was a great aristocrat, a statesman of the old school,
a scholar, a Christian philosopher; I must refrain from expressing my thoughts. Before the war was ended, the Allies
had committed themselves to the Wilsonian principle of self-
determination. Had Palestine been consulted then, its answer
would have been unequivocal.

So, when we had before our eyes the admirable example of
Israel as a world-wide spiritual community, men of burning
faith and narrow vision attempted to create the very worst
kind of nationalism, racial and sectarian, exclusive, fanatical,
terroristic, a pattern for what the Germans planned to do in
the *Lebensraum* they had conquered. We are told that the
Jews have planted beautiful orchards on ground that the
Arabs had been incompetent to use. No doubt, but good
agriculture is no argument; the Germans might very well
have improved the cultivation of Poland. We are told that
millions of Jews have set their hearts upon Palestine; well,
seventy million Japanese might yearn for California, and
America would remain obdurate. We are told the land is
theirs by right. It was theirs by conquest, and they left it

two thousand years ago. We are told it is their Holy Land. It happens to be also that of the Christians. We are told their plight as displaced persons is heart-rending: England, France, are suffering from man-power shortage; South America has enormous undeveloped areas; and our immigration quota has not been filled.

On the nationalistic plane, the situation created by Balfour's cleverness is inextricable. The British know it now, and it is time for us to learn. If a small Jewish state were created, it could be maintained only by the constant use of force. Zionism has bred hatred, and will breed more. I know there are Jews, and among them those I most respect, who think and feel as I do. But when it comes to using pressure, the fanatics have a tremendous advantage. I am aware that I am powerless. At any rate, as an old Dreyfusist, I have relieved my conscience.

Thus did the Dreyfus crisis sharpen my critical spirit, and focus my antinationalism. In a third way also it has marked me for life. It was in those years that I became a Socialist.

Our *petit bourgeois* radicalism had not prepared me for this development. There was in our family a faint tradition of sympathy with the Commune. But what appealed to us was its purely Parisian, autonomist, democratic aspect, not the cosmopolitan and proletarian spirit of its last desperate hours. The Commune, let it be remembered, had respected private property. The "crime" we resented (apart from the ferocity of the repression) was that provincials should dare to subdue the City of Light. We were not filled with that social pity that Hugo had manifested as early as 1834, in *Claude Gueux*, and which was to inspire *Les Misérables*. We lived too close to the poor to entertain any generous delusions. In those days, it was *almost* true that anyone who cared to work, and did not

drink, could be decently comfortable; and that anyone who
had intelligence and energy could rise in the social scale.
Almost: not quite. But true enough for us to believe, with
bourgeois self-righteousness, that the down-and-out deserved
their fate.

The Dreyfus agitation had its start among bourgeois; its
scope was tremendously widened by the "intellectuals." If
it reached "the people," it is not because they were proletar-
ians, but because they were the heirs of the Enlightenment
and the Revolution, because their fathers had passionately
supported the cause of Greece, Italy, Poland. Many a common artisan showed a freer mind and a more generous heart
than some members of the French Academy.

So, per se, the Dreyfus Case had nothing to do with socialism. Such was the conviction of Jules Guesde, the leader of
the strict orthodox Marxians. Guesde was the perfect sectary;
austere, disinterested, wholeheartedly devoted to his ideals;
a rigorous logician, he was unable to think except along the
party groove. Just as the Medical Faculty, under Louis XIV,
had rejected Harvey's discovery of the circulation of the
blood, because it was not in accordance with Aristotle, Jules
Guesde dismissed the Dreyfus Case as irrelevant, because
it was not mentioned in *Das Kapital.* In his eyes, it was a
quarrel among bourgeois: let them stew in their own juice.

Jaurès professed to be a Marxist, as Léon Blum did after
him. Both of them, however, were humanists and humanitarians. They combined the tradition of Descartes and the
Philosophes with that of Lamennais, Michelet, Hugo, and
the great democrats of 1848. For Jaurès, socialism was not
a complicated and creaking intellectual mechanism; still
less a fatalistic apocalypse, prophesying catastrophe, and,
beyond, a new heaven and a new earth. His socialism was a
constant quest for truth, freedom, justice. The Dreyfus Case
appeared to him as an episode in that eternal crusade.

I do not believe that Jaurès brought the masses to Drey-fusism. The masses, like the classes, went either way. At the height of the agitation, La Villette, a workingmen's district in Paris, returned a Royalist deputy. It was among intellect-uals that the influence of Jaurès was most potent. Some of them had a long way to go, like Anatole France, the delicate Pyrrhonian with aristocratic tastes, or Francis de Pressensé, a Huguenot who was writing in the ultracapitalistic paper *Le Temps*.

Jaurès is one of the noblest figures in modern history. A philosopher, a historian, a good Parliamentary tactician, a magnificent orator, he was deeply loved by all those who approached him. His murder was a disastrous loss, not for France alone, but for Europe and the world. None of the great leaders in our century, Wilson, Lenin, Churchill, Roose-velt, Stalin, De Gaulle, have offered the same perfect balance of rich qualities. He combined splendid ideals with practical sense; his shrewdness was free from cunning, his moderation from ambiguity and compromise, and his great fraternal love had no touch of bathos or mawkishness.

His figure haunts me like a remorse. I reproach myself for not loving him enough, when I owe so much to him. The truth is that I was adversely affected by mere externals. He was a peerless orator, but I happen to hate eloquence, and at times his Babylonian periods irritated me, as did the rhetor-ical passages in Victor Hugo. The printed page never does justice to an orator; but I saw and heard Jaurès in action, and was grievously disappointed. His honest burly figure struck me as heavy and commonplace. In his ill-fitting clothes, he looked at times the provincial pedagogue, at times the ward politician. His harsh brassy voice, with traces of southern accent, grated on my Parisian ears. My convictions and my taste were at odds. I knew that my convictions were my deeper self. But my taste refused to commit suicide.

Jaurès, as I said, converted many of us, young and old. He brought Zola, the typical *petit bourgeois* radical, at least very close to socialism, in a Fourierist-Proudhonian form which has its strong points. He did not affect Clemenceau in the least. Clemenceau remained to the last the most rugged of individualists. Although he never wrote anything so dramatic as *J'accuse!* and *The Proofs,* his activity and his influence were prodigious. I needed Clemenceau no less than I needed Jaurès. For I was convinced that generosity and the love of freedom are not antagonistic. There is an individualism that is founded on selfishness: "Every one for himself, and Devil take the hindmost!" That congenital meanness of the profiteer had no place in Clemenceau's heart. His individualism was first of all a manifestation of his courage: self-reliance, not self-seeking. He dared to be himself, with the crowd or against the crowd. He was of courage all compact, from the crudest, which is to face a sword or a pistol, to the highest, which is to face obloquy and defeat. My two guides pointed out the same way. Jaurès, although he submitted himself to Marxian discipline, remained a free soul. Clemenceau worked for the people, not for himself alone. Both men were servants of truth and justice.

In the First World War, many Americans came to like and admire Clemenceau; but they failed to understand him. There is a Clemenceau legend which had dire historical results. Because he was nicknamed "the Tiger," we thought on this side that he was tigerish. Because he had stood for *Revanche,* which means vindication or justice, we believed that he was vindictive. Because his wit was sharp as steel and pricked bubbles without pity, we called him a cynic. He was exactly the reverse of a jingo. All his life, he had fought the powers in his own country that stood for military prestige: the Second Empire, General Boulanger, and, in the Dreyfus crisis, the General Staff. On his deathbed, he was still fighting the ghost of Foch. He would have spurned to serve "France first, last and all the time!" or "France, right or wrong!": he served his own ideal of liberty and justice. He had no hatred for Germany; but he knew very well, in 1919, that the Germans would be very slow to learn the ways of peace. There are two dicta of his that deserve to be better known in this country. According to Lincoln Steffens, he told Lloyd George and Wilson: "Permanent peace . . . a beautiful thought. But do you mean it, with all it entails? The giving up of Empires? [He had always been an anticolonialist himself.] The renunciation of privilege? Free trade? Do you mean it?" Lloyd George and Wilson hemm'd and haw'd: "Why, not quite. At least, not yet." "Then," said Clemenceau, "you do not mean peace, you mean war." Could we meet his test today? When Pershing asked him, in the worst hour of 1918: "What would you do, if the Germans were to take Paris?" he replied: "I should fight on. Above Paris, there is France; above France, there is civilization." When he came to us after the war, we refused to heed his warning. We owe an apology to his angry, indomitable shade.

As a personal episode, the Dreyfus Affair ended magnificently; not in shameful defeat, as in the case of Sacco and Vanzetti; not in a grudging admission of error, as in the case of Mooney and Billings. Dreyfus was promoted and decorated on the very spot where he had suffered degradation. His heroic champion, Colonel Picquart, became general and minister of war. Zola's remains were transferred to the Pantheon.

But as a national crisis, it ended in frustration. The great waves of the crusading spirit finally expired in a dismal political swamp. I did not despair. Thirty-five years ago, a British reviewer called me "Mark Tapley"; I believe I am congenitally incapable of despairing. But Charles Péguy, Daniel

Halévy, André Gide, and many others, obscure or famous, felt intensely what seemed to them the sordid murder of an ideal. The mood is best expressed in Anatole France's savage satire, *Penguin Island.*

I had the same experience three times again: after the First World War, after the Russian Revolution, after the Second World War. Material triumph stood out in ironical gaudiness, against a background of moral failure. These repeated lessons, over half a century, seem to demonstrate a historical law.

But what is the law? I do not believe that a stern and ardent purpose is inevitably incompetent and futile. On the contrary, enthusiasm (and even its hateful shadow, fanaticism) makes for miraculous efficiency. America achieved the impossible during the war. The cautious trimmers, the appeasers, the compromisers, the profiteers, the cynics, were contemptuously swept aside. Great things were done in the name of great thoughts.

Neither men nor nations can remain constantly on a level of heroic strenuousness. But relaxation does not need to be moral laxity; "normalcy" does not necessarily denote timidity and meanness. I have known apostles in many lines who could keep up their energy, unflaggingly, for decades. And for the masses, a concerted effort is actually easier than listlessness or confusion. Americans would have been far happier if, after the surrender of Germany and Japan, they could have worked according to a farsighted and generous plan.

In three of these cases, there was no such plan. For this lack, no single element was to blame. Great crusades are waged by coalitions, in the name of very general principles, but for very definite ends. The end once attained, there is no loss of idealism; but the binder is removed, and the loose bundle of ideals falls apart. All Dreyfusists were believers in truth and justice. *My* Dreyfusism took the extreme form of

free thought, antimilitarism and socialism. But Abbé de
Bréon was at least as good a Dreyfusist as I, and no one could
expect him to become a freethinker. Captain Dreyfus, Colonel
Picquart, General de Galliffet, could hardly turn into anti-
militarists; nor could Clemenceau, a rabid individualist, be
converted to socialism.

Exactly in the same way, the French Resistance movement
during the Second World War united soldiers like De Gaulle,
Delattre de Tassigny, Giraud, Leclerc, Catholics like Bidault
and Thierry d'Argenlieu, Socialists and Communists. They
fought shoulder to shoulder. When France was liberated,
they paid a last unanimous tribute to the man who had stood
as the symbol of their common purpose. The very morrow
was unquiet, chill and gray. Men relapsed into the squabbles
of parties and the scramble of petty interests, not because
the worst elements had taken the upper hand, but because
men of good will no longer had a rallying point.

I am not satisfied with this fitful course of history. It dis-
courages men of little faith, and turns them into cynics. But
what should be done? In 1900, I should not have wanted my
"integral Dreyfusism" to establish and perpetuate itself in
power by dictatorial methods. I am glad France found a
Waldeck-Rousseau rather than a Stalin. We frittered away
our victory? What was the alternative? Suppose we had been
able to purge and liquidate everyone tainted with anti-
Dreyfusism (including Paul Valéry). Suppose we had "forced
free thought" (!) upon men for whom it is an abomination.
Suppose we had carried our antimilitarism to the extent then
advocated by Gustave Hervé (who lived to be a henchman
of Pétain) and "flung the flag upon a dung heap." Suppose
we had imposed socialism upon a country of artisans, small
shopkeepers and peasant proprietors. What would have been
the result? Immediately, and without question, civil war;
and, if we had not been crushed, an iron dictatorship to

achieve victory and preserve victory. Frankly, the humdrum Republic of Loubet and Fallières was better than such a fate.

Crises are wasting fevers; storms are destructive; wars and revolutions are disasters. Yet the plodding scholar, who must believe in the sanity of ubiquitous imperceptible gradualness, looks back wistfully upon the mad and tragic hours. I have worked faithfully, with moderate hopes and moderate success. But, in those few moments, I was fully alive.

CHRONOLOGY OF THE DREYFUS AFFAIR

ACT I   1894   *Oct. 15:* Captain Alfred Dreyfus, General Staff, Intelligence Section, arrested on charge of treason.
Dec. 22: Sentenced to life imprisonment by Court-martial.

       1895   *Jan. 5:* Degraded.
April 13: Arrives Devil's Island (part of Salvation group).

ACT II   *July 1st:* Lieutenant Colonel George Picquart appointed head of Intelligence Section.

       1896   Picquart discovers document incriminating Major Walsin-Esterházy.
Picquart sent on mission to North Africa.

       1897   *July 13:* Leblois, Picquart's friend and counsel, informs Senator Scheurer-Kestner of Picquart's discovery.
Nov. 14: Scheurer-Kestner's open letter.
Dec. 2: Esterházy asks permission to appear before Court-martial.

       1898   *Jan. 11:* Esterházy triumphantly acquitted.

ACT III   *Jan. 13:* Zola's letter *J'accuse!* in *L'Aurore.* Picquart arrested.
Feb. 7–23: Zola tried and sentenced. Appeals.
May 23–July 18: Second Zola trial, Versailles. Sentenced again. Leaves for London.
July 7: War Secretary Cavaignac reads to Cham-

ber documents decisive against Dreyfus. Jaurès, in *Petite République* (*Les Preuves*) demonstrates they are forgeries.

Aug. 13–31: Captain Cuignet discovers documents were forged by Lieutenant Colonel Henry, of Intelligence Section. Henry, arrested, commits suicide.

ACT IV   *Sept. 3:* Madame Dreyfus applies for new trial (*révision*).

Sept. 26: Government accedes.

1899 *Oct. 27, 1898–June 3, 1899:* Case before Supreme Court (Cour de Cassation). Revision granted.

Aug. 7–Sept. 9: Second military trial of Captain Dreyfus, before Court-martial at Rennes. Convicted, five votes to two, "with extenuating circumstances."

Sept. 19: Dreyfus pardoned.

1900 *Dec. 24:* Amnesty, extinguishing all prosecutions and suits arising out of Dreyfus Case.

1902 *Sept. 30:* Zola accidentally asphyxiated.

ACT V

1903 *Nov. 26:* New application for revision made by Dreyfus.

1906 *July 12:* Supreme Court quashes Rennes judgment *absolutely*, i.e. without ordering new trial. Dreyfus completely vindicated.

July 13: Dreyfus reinstated in Army.

July 14: Decorated with Legion of Honor.

1908 *June 4:* Zola's remains transferred to Pantheon. Dreyfus wounded by fanatic.

EPILOGUE:

1914–18 Lieutenant Colonel Alfred Dreyfus serves in World War I.

1923 *May 21:* "Count de Voilement" (Esterházy) dies destitute and an outcast at Harpenden, England.

1935 *July 12:* Colonel Alfred Dreyfus dies, seventy-five.

C H A P T E R   S I X

My England

=================================

WHEN I was well under sixteen, I decided that English, and the culture of English-speaking countries, would be my field. The word *decide* is at the same time accurate and misleading. My adolescent mind was perfectly clear; thenceforward, there was no room for hesitancy or drifting. Earlier fancies, for engineering or for the Church, have left an indelible trace; but they never caused me to swerve from my path. The details of my career—writing, teaching, international affairs, at home or abroad—I could not foresee; but the direction was set once for all. I had no misgivings, and I have no regrets.

Yet the decision was by no means inevitable, and it came without dramatic suddenness. There was no single overwhelming influence. We had no connection with England or with English people. My Chaptal teachers of the language were adequate and gentlemanly; but they roused in us no enthusiasm. Many tenuous threads happened to pull me in the same direction.

Of these, the most definite was Mabel—*The Mabel*. She was not a girl, but a ship, my favorite among those little cargo boats which plied between London and Port Saint Nicolas, at the foot of the Louvre. As I have noted, these humble little steamers were the romance of my childhood. They evoked the vasty deep and its perils; icebergs like ominous phantoms in Hyperborean twilight; tropical bights slumbering under their palms. They illustrated, not only Jules Verne, but Edgar Poe and Baudelaire. Those placid Victorian barges were my *Bateaux Ivres* long before I had heard of Rimbaud. They carried my fancy "from the Pathetic Ocean to the Ironic Sea." But, first of all, they drew me irresistibly to their home port, huge and mysterious, *London:* a name fraught with magic, which I pronounced, lovingly, with two French nasals.

The other influences, as I attempt to reconstitute them, form the oddest jumble. My mother spoke some English, "ful faire and fetisly," but decidedly not "after the scole of Stratford-atte-Bowe." She taught me a few ditties. The very first English words I remember speaking, or singing, were snatches of a song: "My little darling, I love you. . . ." As "the gist of the language," it was decidedly better than Figaro's equipment.[1] But the phrase was of no practical use to me for many years to come.

We had among our books a tattered, red paper-bound copy of *Les Aventures de Monsieur Pickwick*, which had then the same appeal for me as The Gumps or the late lamented Colonel Bungle had in later years. *Ditto: Jack Sheppard, ou le Bandit de Londres,* by Harrison Ainsworth, a horrific tale; and a well-illustrated Lord Byron. Only *Manfred* made a lasting impression upon my boyish mind: the puppet shows in the Champs Elysées, and *Les Pilules du Diable,* a perennial pantomime at the Châtelet, had made me familiar with the Faust theme. Somewhat later, when my predilection was be-

[1] *The Marriage of Figaro,* Act III, scene 3. Figaro: "Do I know English? Sure! The essence of the language: Goddam!" An ancient tradition: in the days of Joan of Arc, the invaders were known as *"les Godons."*

ginning to take form, I read many books about England, including the mild satire by Max O'Rell entitled *John Bull et
son Ile.*[2] I was given as prizes well-illustrated works of Sir
Walter Scott's, in the Defauconpret translation; but they interested me far less than the companion volumes of the
"Leatherstocking" series.

There was, of course, a vague Anglomania in the Paris of
my childhood: that element has been active in French life
for fully two hundred years. People turned up their trousers,
because it was raining in London: hence the absurd cuffs
which are still a receptacle for dust, and from which even the
Second World War could not deliver us. The right people
held their forks in the left hand, English fashion. Spurning
the old French *goûter,* they had their "five o'clock" every day,
religiously at four. They sent their laundry to London, there
to acquire that inimitable gloss which was a perfect imitation of celluloid. At one time, men raised their elbows for
shaking hands, because Albert, Prince of Wales, *arbiter ele-
gantiarum,* suffered from an edema under his arm. The walls
of Paris blazoned forth the merits of "High Life Tailor," which
of course we pronounced *iggliff.* Yet the Englishman, with
his monocle, check suit, large teeth and enormous feet, was a
figure of fun; and of the trio of clowns who convulsed us with
laughter at the circus—Footitt, Gugusse and Chocolat—
Footitt, with his English accent, was easily the most mirth
provoking.

Out of this welter of boyish dreams, desultory readings,
bits of songs, odd phrases, innocent snobbishness, there arose
the mighty shade of Taine. But his influence was not a decisive factor: he merely gave substance and dignity to my
growing inclination. His *Notes on England* and his *History of*

[2] Once a minor classic, not much worse than modern variations on the same
theme, like *With Malice Toward Some.* Probably inspired the title of G. B.
Shaw's play: *John Bull's Other Island.*

English Literature were my talismans, somewhat unwieldy for a fifteen-year-old, yet effective. Taine's great admiration for Lord Macaulay induced me to read all the *Critical and Historical Essays* pen in hand, as models of construction and style. I do not believe I have ever eliminated from my organism all the Macaulay I absorbed at that time. I still have his works on my shelves, in a compact, unattractive "Popular Edition"; I have not opened them for nearly fifty years.

In the spring of 1896, I won an interscholastic prize in French Composition; and when my mother asked me to name my reward (within reason), I unhesitatingly answered: "A month in London." She was rather taken aback. Our longest trips so far had led us to neighboring provinces, Champagne, Burgundy, Picardy, all within two hundred miles of Paris, and on *terra firma,* as ordained by Providence. My favorite uncle had served in the Navy: still the thought lingered that sane people do not, of their own free will, challenge the treacherous sea. There were other dangers too. The word "pickpocket," in its English form, had passed into the French language; and we were persuaded that pocket picking was one of England's basic industries. So I carried my few gold sovereigns in a flannel belt next to my skin. Only Jack the Ripper, who at that time was casting a sinister shadow over England, could have rifled this marsupial container; and Jack the Ripper's activities were confined to women.

I was to feel many times the capricious fury of the Channel. But my first crossing, from Dieppe to Newhaven, was tolerably smooth. I remember no discomfort, only the exhilaration, the wild surmise. For a boy of sixteen, it was a soul-stirring experience to see the continent fade and sink below the horizon; and although the white cliffs of Sussex are not very different from those of Normandy, they rose with a magical appeal out of the glaucous waves. I wish the world could be made up of islands, each country framed in silver and set like a jewel. A land frontier is a mere nuisance. Not even the desert is a proper substitute for the unplumb'd, salt, estranging sea.

It is unwise to dismiss a truism with a shrug; even more unwise than it is to pooh-pooh a paradox. A truism should be challenged. It may be dead, for all we know; but if alive, it may hold secrets behind its bland and common countenance. I was made to realize, at an impressionable age, that Great Britain was an island; and I have pondered that obvious fact ever since.

Insularity has been England's shield and England's pride; but every shield is also a burden, and pride is ever a flaw. In 1896, I was already very much interested in great public works. I had heard of the proposed Channel Tunnel. I was aware also that the British had risen mightily against that threat to their sacred insularity. The scheme had been denounced, not only by Field Marshal Lord Wolseley, with the inveterate conservativeness of the military mind, but by "daring" thinkers such as Herbert Spencer. A whole generation later, after the First World War, the project was mooted again; and British reviews, with dogged obstinacy, reprinted verbatim their hostile articles of the eighties. Today, aviation, the radio, the robot bomb, have destroyed Great Britain's physical insularity; but the psychological insularity it has engendered may long survive, a blind unreasoning fossil in a fast-moving world.

There is nothing spectacular about Newhaven. Harbor, station, rolling stock struck me as pleasantly old-fashioned rather than quaint. I was boyishly delighted with the toy-like, bright yellow locomotives of the London, Brighton and South Coast Railway. But the unobtrusive efficiency of English life impressed me at once. No bustling, no shrieking, no apparent order, and yet no confusion. In a few minutes, the little train glided out of Newhaven without a jerk and without a whistle. When it stopped gently under the dingy shed at London Bridge, I stepped easily onto the raised platform, and there was a cab waiting just opposite my car, not twenty feet away. A real hansom cab it was, with silk-hatted driver on his perch behind; and we sailed across the Thames, through the gloom of the gas-lit, deserted city, interminably, into the northern suburbs. Everywhere the gentle and pungent London smell, which I still have in my nostrils: soft coal, dampness, smoked fish, unfamiliar tobacco. Now and then, out of the murk, stalls and barrows fantastically lit with oil flares. Perhaps no other five-mile trip in the world could be so utterly drab; but I felt as though I were going deeper and deeper into the heart of romance. It cost me a fortune: four shillings and sixpence.

Of this first trip, I have no very distinct memory: my impressions were obliterated by repeated later experiences. We had picked out, in the advertisements of the *Daily Telegraph*, absolutely at random, a place offering board and room for a single gentleman, at the rate, not absurdly cheap at the time, of a guinea a week. It happened to be in Holloway, on the interminable and dismal Caledonian Road. Chance had not been unkind to me. I had a clean cheerful room, in a modest and very decent household—a local dressmaker, if I remember correctly. I was at once introduced to the boiled potato, boiled cabbage, boiled vegetable marrow of Old England; even at sixteen, I could find no romance in that aqueous fare.

For a whole month, I did nothing but wander in the streets, my whim the only guide. I felt no desire to visit the museums: they were not English enough. I was more curious about the Crystal Palace than about St. James's or Buckingham, and probably I was right. I explored the Metropolitan and District railways, then reeking and grimy, as though tunneled through a mountain of soot: a foretaste of the nether world, of infinite fascination. I reveled in the little paddle steamers that churned their way down the brownish Thames from Westminster to Greenwich; and what a thrill it was to pass under the Tower Bridge, opened a couple of years before, a triumphal gateway to the seven seas!

The one memory that still haunts me is that of beating helplessly against the shores of a second island, more inaccessible than the white cliffs in a storm: the beetling, jagged, impregnable English language. My teachers had fostered the delusion that I had some command of it; but for days I could not make out a single word I heard, and I am certain that no one could understand a single word I spoke. Yet my hosts, I feel sure, did not use the Cockney dialect, a bolder departure from God's own English than even Brooklynese in its most aggravated form. With great patience and courtesy, my interlocutors would repeat their sentences, putting them into words of one syllable, and for emphasis accenting them more and more forcibly, until they were positively barking. And the louder, the more explosive their speech, the greater my confusion. History has played a subtle trick on mankind. The most widely diffused language in the world, probably the richest, perhaps the most expressive, is also the most bewildering. Everything about it is a delusion and a snare. Its grammar, as touched up by Messrs. Ogden and Richards, may be reduced to simpler rules than that of Esperanto. What if it had no grammar at all? It is a writhing mass of perplexing idioms. Its pronunciation and spelling are jungles strewn with pitfalls. What of its boasted brevity? For international purposes, the sesquipedalian is far better than the terse. "Canine" is more intelligible than "dog," "organ of vision" safer than "eye"; and the American government was probably well advised when, during the war, it translated:

"Turn off the light" into "Illumination must be extinguished."
In other words, if Englishmen want to be understood, they
had better speak Latin.

Years later, I heard a story which struck a sympathetic
chord. It is a brief dialogue after the Battle of Waterloo.
Pious English Patriot: "God has heard our prayers!" *Skeptic:*
"But didn't the French pray also?"—*Pious Patriot:* "Bah!
Jabbering monkeys! Who can make out what *they* say?" By
the end of four weeks, however, the weird inarticulate sounds
began to assume some significance; and when the bus con-
ductor made a few Kaffir clicks with his tongue, I knew that
he meant *tuppence 'a' penny.*

But the language difficulty was accepted as a challenge. I
returned from my trip more definitely committed to my line
of study. I had fallen in love with England; all the more easily,
perhaps, because my French pride was reassured. The English were not supermen. Paris appeared luminous and orderly
after the dinginess and chaos of London. I remember, the day
after my return, crossing the Solferino Bridge: how modest,
how restrained, but how clean and harmonious was my beloved Seine! I evoked the Thames at its best, by the Victoria Embankment: beautiful gardens, handsome buildings
on one side, but, across the stream, mud flats at low tide, in
which barges wallowed messily, gaunt warehouses, breweries,
smokestacks. . . . And a dish of *épinards aux croûtons,*
smooth and creamy, brought forth a pitying smile, as I remembered my daily encounter with boiled vegetable marrow.

I have kept no record of my many trips to England; but my
first visit to Brighton, in 1900, deserves separate mention.
Brighton was a very pleasant town, quiet and dignified as
resorts go. Even on bank holidays, swarming with half-crown
trippers, it never looked like Blackpool or Coney Island. It

is the site of an exquisite architectural joke, the Royal Pavilion, erected by the First Gentleman in Europe, the Prince Regent: bulbous domes and minarets, like a bundle of Gargantuan vegetables smeared with yellow paint. Yet there is a smiling elegance to that absurdity, which compels indulgence and even sympathy. But Brighton means more to me than the Front, the Piers, the Aquarium, the Devil's Dyke, and the seagoing railway to Rottingdean. It was in Brighton that for the first time in my life I enjoyed—*en tout bien tout honneur* —the companionship of girls. I had no sister, no cousin of my own age, no friend of the other sex. The home where I boarded that summer was swarming with young ladies. They taught me—a rather somber youth, still fighting the Dreyfus Case in my soul—the sweet absurdity of girlish laughter. It reassured my scholarly conscience when I read that Erasmus, nearly four centuries before, had discovered that English girls were kissable. Young friends among our GI's assured me that Erasmus' testimony is still valid.

I had been taught (people in those days, following Alfred Fouillée, believed in that quaint folklore called "national psychology") that the English were cold, apathetic and infinitely proper. Brighton corrected that gloomy view. I the Parisian was the Puritan. Paris of the *Fin-de-siècle* period had not prepared me for Brighton in the gloaming. Every seat in the public promenades was occupied by at least two couples, entwined in speechless bliss. I believe this was locally and technically known as "spooning"; and dear old Dr. Spooner (mere coincidence), according to Julian Huxley was to mention in Egypt the charm of "minxes by spoonlight." As animated discussion had so far been my favorite sport, the Brighton conception of sociability struck me as commendably inexpensive, but a trifle dumb. Carlyle would have called it: "congruency with the unutterable."

At last came my great opportunity. I secured a fellowship to study for one year in England; and it was renewed without difficulty for a second year (1901–1903). The stipend was not munificent, but it was adequate. The academic conditions were marvelously liberal. I was simply to be a sponge, absorbing as much English life as I could hold. My sole obligation was to write a monthly report on my progress to my correspondent, Professor Baret, of the Sorbonne. To be sure, there were a few competitive examinations in the offing. But the prospect did not disturb my sleep.

I spent the first few months at Borough Road College, a teachers' training school in the vicinity of Richmond. The western suburbs of London are delightful, the fare to the city was reasonable, and my hostess had cooked for aristocratic families. But my relations with pedagogy, French, English or American, never were more than icily correct. My probation at Borough Road was, I surmise, indispensable; but it was a great relief when I felt that I could strike out for myself. Professor Baret, the most gracious and sympathetic of guides, gave me leave to do so. I had been lucky enough to discover Toynbee Hall, Whitechapel; and Toynbee remains, even more than Chaptal or the Sorbonne, my veritable Alma Mater.

Toynbee was a university settlement in the slums of the East End. It had a unique character. It was not a mission, although its starting point had been St. Jude's. It did not bring to the people any ecclesiastical or sociological gospel. It was not a democratic "Co-operative of Ideas," like the many "Popular Universities" which mushroomed in Paris in the sultry atmosphere of the Dreyfus Case. It was not a research bureau. It was not a community center of the American type. Its pragmatism, its ideological vagueness, were deliberate, and I might almost say systematic.

Canon Barnett, the Vicar of St. Jude's, believed that the masses could assume power whenever they chose. There were no legal obstacles to a democratic and social revolution, as was to be made manifest in our own days. He wanted the masses to use that power for their own good, not in a spirit of blind resentment. He believed no less firmly that the classes had evolved a pattern of civilized living that was worth preserving. If the culture of Oxford and Cambridge were to be destroyed, the common man would be the sufferer. Intelligent luxury does not mean conspicuous waste. There is more conspicuous waste in the saloon than in the library.

So Canon Barnett wanted to plant in his parish a small colony of decency and refinement. This may sound intolerably smug. It was not, because the canon himself was both gentle and simple. His aim was not to parade privileges and claim superiority, but to tell the people: "These things we have are yours for the asking." A man of very moderate means may read good books, discuss high thoughts, enjoy pictures and music, speak with quiet precision. Canon Barnett did not want to avert or even retard a peaceful revolution; he wanted to save refinement by abolishing privilege.

This modest faith implied fundamental democracy: the toffs and the toughs are men. It challenged the caste prejudice so deeply rooted in Barrie's symbolic butler, *The Admirable Crichton*. The "Great Unwashed," and those who "fattened on the sweat of the people" met, not only in intellectual discussions, but in social intercourse. Canon Barnett—and Mrs. Barnett, heiress to "Rowland's Macassar Oil"—believed in the gospel of tea parties. It is difficult to wax vehement over a cup of Oolong and thin slices of Hovis bread. The philosophy of Toynbee Hall was perfectly expressed in the subject of a debate which I heard George Bernard Shaw open before our usual Whitechapel crowd: "That the working classes are useless, dangerous, and ought to be abolished." The East End laborers saw the point, and cheered him vigorously.

No initiative was discouraged at Toynbee, and its activities were manifold. It rivaled the People's Palace, Walter Besant's Utopia on the Mile End Road. There were classes of all kinds, and university extension lectures of very high quality: I remember Philip Wicksteed's course on Dante with particular gratitude. There were debates, started by visitor or resident, and freely open to a very rough-tongued and nimble-witted public. A day or two later, small groups would gather informally around the fire, and discuss the same problems more quietly. There were social functions, a promenade concert, an amateur performance, a *conversazióne*. There were local committees in which the residents took part merely as neighbors. There was legal and professional advice. There was charity also, I surmise, but so unobtrusive that I never saw any trace of it.

In the main hall dwelt the Residents, all university alumni, mostly from Oxford and Cambridge. They were not all Anglicans by any means. One at least was a Jew. Two neighboring houses, Balliol and Wadham, were used by students, young business and professional men—a few doctors in particular—who could not afford to devote all their time to the work of the settlement. These houses had been built as "model tenements" ("model" calls for a question mark). As they were vaguely Gothic, they fitted in with the indigent collegiate architecture of the Main Hall. At Wadham, where I lived, we had a common room and good informal discussions of our own; but we had access to the whole life of Toynbee. The Residents were our elder comrades. One coached me heavily in German, without any thought of a fee; another guided my first attempts at literary English. One lived with us, and acted as our dean. We had dinner with them every Sunday; there I was initiated into the glories of roast beef, Yorkshire pudding, Oxford theology, and elusive Oxford chaffing (but no vintage port, alas!) Some colleges in the old universities may have better cuisine; but I doubt whether any had better talk.

Toynbee was changing in character in those days. It had been founded in a purely British slum; but the slum had turned into a ghetto. "Petticoat Lane" seemed to have been transported bodily from southeastern Europe. All the signs were in Hebrew characters; all the talk was in Yiddish. The open-air market teemed with stocky, strong-featured, gesticulating figures; some men had prophets' beards, a plait on either side of their face, long rusty frock coats with suggestions of the kaftan and the gabardine; older women wore smooth jet-black wigs. Here and there, incongruous in that bit of Kichinev or Jassy, a blue-helmeted bobby towered, blond, beefy and placid.

The first task now was to assimilate these hordes with haunted eyes, the subjects of Israel Zangwill's thorough and sympathetic work. They were extraordinarily eager and able. They swarmed to the classes, and they charged roughshod into the debates, undeterred by their linguistic disabilities. They were appallingly earnest: they had fled from pogroms, and they were impatient of Oxonian levity. I remember one of them chiding McGregor, the subwarden, who had spoken entertainingly of "the Celtic Fringe": "We are hard-working men, and we do not come here to listen to jokes." But they hailed George Bernard Shaw deliriously, for they understood his purpose, while the West End still thought of him as a jester. In my many months at Toynbee, I could not detect the least evidence of anti-Semitism; not even in the form of excessive courtesy.

My life had two centers, Toynbee and the British Museum. I can feel the atmosphere of the reading room just as I did forty-five years ago. The subdued light under the immense dome, the leather-padded desk that soon became a cherished friend, the odor which was learned and yet not musty, above all the rich velvety texture of the silence, all conspired to obliterate time and space. I do not know a place in the world —certainly not my own study—that is so fit for a tête-à-tête with the great of all the ages. I read ravenously, rapturously, without any self-centered thought of erudition or criticism. It was a glorious intellectual orgy; and the afterglow of those great months has not yet faded away.

But I did not limit myself to those two poles. The whole of London was mine. I attended political meetings, and heard Hyndman, John Burns, Keir Hardie, as well as the most gentlemanly Unionists. London to me was a living museum of religions; I could enjoy, on two different planes, the eternal quest and the ludicrous oddities. I heard Carlyle, of the Church Army, play the cornet from his pulpit; Felmingham, at odds with his bishop, defy hierarchy and orthodoxy at the South Place Ethical Society; Parker, at the City Temple, a weary old lion; Reginald Campbell (then at Brighton), with the face of a young archangel, and a theatrical light playing on his snow-white hair. I heard solemn services at Westminster Abbey and at Saint Paul's; and quiet evensong in the little church so quaintly named "All Hallows Barking by the Tower."

I went to the theater at least twice a week. I saw every play that was staged that season, except musical comedies (*A Chinese Honeymoon* was then in its fifth year, but I resolutely stood out). That was an extravagance; to indulge it, my French thrift had to rise to Scottish heights. I knew, for each article of food, whether the Aerated Bread Company charged a halfpenny less than Lyons's, and whether Lockhart's Cocoa Rooms gave you a more generous "mug" than the British Tea Table. I patronized Pearce-and-Plenty, Harris the Sausage King, and, in my more Spartan moods, vegetarian restaurants

which offered three courses for sixpence. A seat in the gallery
cost one shilling. To be in the front row, I had to wait an
hour: half of it outside, where minstrels tried their hardest
to make us forget the rain. Once I stood in line two hours for
a half-crown seat; but it was well worth it: a benefit performance of *The Merchant of Venice,* in which all the great
actor-managers in London took part, and the very last time,
I believe, that Ellen Terry and Sir Henry Irving appeared on
the stage together. That was at Drury Lane, that enormous
cavern, where I saw spectacular melodramas, and a dismal
Dante written by Sardou because of Irving's imagined re-
semblance to the great Florentine. The playwrights of the
day were Pinero, who could at any rate turn out a deft farce;
Henry Arthur Jones, who deserves to be forgotten, but not
quite so deeply as he now is; J. M. Barrie, whose fantasy almost reached the level of symbol. Ten years after his debut,
Shaw was still considered as a clever controversialist in
preface and dialogue, but no dramatist at all.

Over all, enveloping me, absorbing me, there was London,
which I loved hardly less than Paris, with a love at the same
time more conscious and more romantic. I could do in London
what I could never achieve in Paris: lose myself; for London
was then an amorphous mass, Paris had a plan. I would walk,
deliberately at random, through the evening mist and drizzle,
under the blinking yellow lights, deep into unknown districts,
the stately deserted West, the squalid East, the nondescript
North. I would chance upon a quiet garden, an ugly brick
church to which the mantle of night imparted a touch of
dignity, a brewery towering like a feudal castle; all without
a name and never seen again. I saw rows of identical houses,
self-satisfied, humble or despairing, losing themselves into the
murk; suddenly, a teeming thoroughfare, children dancing to
the metallic jangle of a mechanical piano. Then, when I was
quite sure I had lost my bearings, the game was to find my

way back home. Asking for directions would be cheating; anyway, ten to one, the Cockney answer would only deepen the mystery. Even in Limehouse, I never had any sense of insecurity.

There are lovely days in London; spring in the Temple gardens could be poignantly Edenic; and there is statistical evidence—absurd as it may seem—that the rainfall in London is not much greater than in San Francisco. Yet the London I remember is a city of night, brown fog and slanting rain. And the creatures I can see with my inner eye flitting for a moment and melting into the gloom are women: bloated slatterns in shawls and cloth caps, girls with fantastic flowery hats and haggard smiles. I did not analyze my mood then; I cannot account for it now. There was no morbid quest for the squalid and the perverse; there was no indignation, no horror, and, I must add, no compassion. Yet I felt strangely elated in that phantom world. Perhaps it was an unconscious challenge. Perhaps it provided just the bitterness I needed to season my intellectual feasts.

England for me was no mere tourist's paradise, still less a field for business activities; the career I envisaged was literally a vocation. I never was an Anglomaniac; I never desired for a moment to become a British subject; I was called to understand and love England, without any disloyalty to my French heritage. It was the most baffling, the most arduous, the most entrancing of all problems; and it has lost none of its perplexing fascination. To measure the difficulty of the task I had chosen, I must present, without attenuation, the inveterate Anglophobia that prevailed in France.

The decade when England was the center of my thought, from 1896 to 1906, was a perfect epitome of a history extending over more than eight hundred years. In those ten years,

I witnessed the most virulent hostility between the two countries, and also the dawn of a shy, tremulous *Entente Cordiale*.
Throughout the centuries England and France have been
linked, and I might say locked, in a close and angry companionship. According to Seeley, they have been engaged in
no less than three Hundred Years' Wars. No two nations have
expressed more sustained and more bitter aversion to each
other (unless it be England and Scotland: Lord Tweedsmuir
—John Buchan—was brought up in the feeling that "against
our little land there had always stood England, vast, menacing
and cruel," and the Irish too might have a tale to tell). Of the
three outstanding figures in French history, Joan of Arc and
Napoleon were martyred, Louis XIV was humbled, by the
English. The promising empires of the French in North America and India were wrenched away from them by the English. In my student days, the memories of these ancient
wrongs were kept alive by British policy. The British had a
valid case in the Fashoda crisis, and the final settlement was
not unreasonable; but they enforced their will by methods
which were frankly brutal, and with what seemed a sadistic
delight in inflicting humiliation. History is not a mass of dis-
connected headlines: there are permanent trends. The French,
not without justification, felt that no country had ever treated
a neighbor with such persistent and implacable hostility. That
bitter conviction I fully shared. Emancipated as I was from
French chauvinism, I was not ready to worship Rudyard
Kipling and Joseph Chamberlain.[3]

[3] The dismal tale did not end with the formation of the *Entente Cordiale*.
A common distrust of Germany brought the two countries together; but as
soon as Germany ceased to appear as an immediate danger, from the morrow
of Versailles to the Munich capitulation, England deliberately ignored the
interests and thwarted the policies of France. The French felt abandoned after
Dunkirk: the mightiest empire in the world could not spare a single plane to
mitigate an ally's disaster. The crippling of the French fleet at Mers-el-Kebir
was a brutal gesture, in the Copenhagen tradition; and there is no proof that
it was necessary. The same ruthless disregard for the feelings of a friend were

What rankled most in the French mind was the self-righteousness of the British. There are French *chauvins* to match English *jingoes;* but there are also many Frenchmen who condemn the spirit of prestige and power as manifested in Richelieu, Louis XIV and Napoleon. I have yet to meet an Englishman who takes the same view of Elizabeth, Cromwell or Chatham. England's foes are the enemies of the Lord, and must be destroyed. The French acknowledge the greater success of English arms, industry and commerce. But they see no moral cause for this material superiority. They would apply to England as a whole what Labouchère [4] said of Gladstone: "It was all right for Mr. Gladstone to have the ace of trumps up his sleeve. What was intolerable was his pretending that God had put it there." To change the metaphor, there is no better Englishman than little Jack Horner: he sticks his thumb in other people's pies, pulls out the best plums, and beams: "What a good boy am I!"

The French could not see that British policy had been consistently virtuous or consistently wise. England was proud of "muddling" abundantly; but Europe had deeply suffered in consequence. England herself had been spared the worst. Not through a special dispensation of Providence; not through the mystic virtue of muzziness; not through the heroic doggedness that refuses to admit defeat; but through two privileges of a purely material nature. England is an island: else Napoleon might have signed an imperial decree at Westminster, and Hitler might have entered London as he entered Paris—Churchill or no Churchill. England always had time finally to muddle out of her muddling; she could always afford to see her foes—and her allies as well—wear themselves out.

---

shown by Winston Churchill in the Syrian crisis. In 1946, the British, in control of the Ruhr, were much more concerned with the revival of German industry than with the bleeding wounds of the French economy.

[4] Henry du Pré Labouchère, in spite of his name, was not a Frenchman, but an English journalist, Member of Parliament and millionaire.

Then England is rich in coal, as France is not. From the beginning of the Industrial era to the Second World War, this
gave her a massive superiority. Facts are facts; but economic
geography should not be piously translated into the language
of the Psalmist: "Thou preparest a table before me in the
presence of mine enemies."

Such was the heavy and somber tradition with which I had
—and still have—to contend, and first of all in my own heart.
The facts cannot be altered or smiled away. But they can
be weighed against other facts. Within my memory, Franco-
British relations have been a chaos of heroic co-operation,
distrust, enmity, mutual admiration, mutual contempt, a
riotous confusion of ambivalent feelings which might at any
moment crystallize into hatred or into love. The two motifs
are inextricably intertwined: hostility, fascination. "That
sweet enemy, France," said Sir Philip Sidney; and in Paris,
Anglophobia and Anglomania were for ages equally rife.
From the Norman Conquest to the days of Horace Walpole,
Beckford and Gibbon, French culture has been an indispensable part of England's background. In return, it was in
England that Voltaire discovered himself, and he has been
aptly called "England's best gift to France." The whole Enlightenment was indissolubly Franco-British. While kings
fought, the mutual appreciation of the two countries went on
unabated, and British prisoners of war were great social
favorites. French Romanticism followed four masters, all
British and oddly assorted: Shakespeare, "Ossian," Sir Walter
Scott and Lord Byron. France's admiration for England has
always been at the same time reluctant and unstinted. Even
when folk tradition would have it that all Englishmen were
mad, it was acknowledged that at any rate they were sturdy
and generous lunatics. On the other hand, no nation could
receive warmer tributes of love than France did from George
Meredith, Swinburne, John Morley, George Moore, Patrick

Geddes, Ford Madox Ford, Oliver Madox Hueffer, Charles Morgan, D. W. Brogan. If all the elements of an eternal feud are there, so there are also the foundations of a "more perfect union."

This union, which Saint-Simon proposed in 1814 and Winston Churchill in 1940, I have realized in my heart. I love the countryside, the home life and the literature of England as though I were British born; and in the flaws of England —some of them distressing enough—I find no secret element of joy.

Perhaps the union was so complete because England did not revolutionize my thought. Her influences strengthened certain tendencies which were in me before I had crossed the Channel, and which remained with me after I crossed the Atlantic. Nationalism is vanity. The experience was decisive: neighbors could hardly be more different than the French and the English; yet very soon the differences appeared trifling. There is no French race and no English race. England is no more "Saxon" than France is "Latin." Both peoples are hopeless mongrels; they result from the fusion of numberless elements in unknown quantities. In both we find a mysterious substratum, an obscure Iberian layer, a dash of the Greek and of the Phoenician, a Celtic conquest, four centuries of association with Rome, Germanic and Scandinavian invasions. The year 1066 made the dynasty and the aristocracy predominantly French for several hundred years, until the language itself became a hybrid. England, like France and America, is a melting pot. As a result, there is no single English type, but an infinite variety of English specimens. If the Nordics be the sole legitimate Aryans, the race of the gods, then the English do not qualify for admission to their Walhalla: there is a large proportion of brown eyes among "the better classes." But the blazing red of the Kymri, or the flaxen blondness of the Scandinavian, do not seem alien either.

John Bull, stocky, choleric—Churchillian—is British to the
marrow of his bones; but so is the tall, slender, phlegmatic
Englishman. I have seen on London pavements swarms of
men who might be of the same breed as Sir Norman Angell
or the Duke of Windsor. National differences are not "in the
blood": they are to a very large extent sartorial and tonsorial.

As there is no single English type, so there is no standard
English character. Walter Bagehot was right: Un-English
is a perfect fallacy in one word. The teetotaler is no less English than the drunk, the pugilist than the aesthete, the agnos-
tic than the believer. There are English manners: at times
excellent in their restraint, at times execrable in their snobbishness. There are English traditions: John Ball, Wat Tyler,
the Levelers, the Chartists had their roots deep in English
earth, far more than the Italianized courtier, the merchant,
the banker. Neither Cavalier nor Puritan can be expunged
from English history. If Dissent be English, so is conformity.
The cream of the jest is that "old English" sentiment should
find its perfect representative in Disraeli.

I moved back and forth from the France of the Dreyfus
Case to the England of the Boer War. It was evident to me
that the English did not instinctively agree among themselves, any more than the French. Patriots in the higher sense
of the term could ardently condemn the course of their government, even though the battle flag was unfurled. Sir Henry
Campbell-Bannerman and David Lloyd George denounced
the spirit of the South African campaign and its "methods
of barbarism." They were not overawed by Lord Roberts or
by Kitchener, any more than Zola, Clemenceau and Jaurès by
the French General Staff. On the other hand, *chauvins* and
jingoes reasoned (?) surprisingly alike on both sides of the
Channel: there is no more international disease than rabid
nationalism. In terms which acquired currency years after-
wards, hundred-percentism is a totalitarian blasphemy

against freedom. Any man who glances at his daily paper is aware of these truisms. But we still shrink from the obvious consequences.

In the late nineties, I was inclined both to anarchism and to socialism. The two tendencies are by no means irreconcilable: even Marx anticipated the withering away of the political state. There is about both labels a flamboyancy which makes them red rags to the Safe-and-Sane. Yet neither necessarily implies violent methods: the most thoroughgoing exponent of brutal terrorism were the leaders in the anti-Communist crusade, Hitler and Franco. My own temper never was revolutionary or even Jacobin. I never believed in being soft; but I believed even less in getting tough. Toynbee Hall provided a political atmosphere more congenial to me than the *petit bourgeois* radicalism of my youth, or the truculence (verbal, at any rate) of the Extreme Left. The England I knew was still that of John Stuart Mill and Herbert Spencer: *On Liberty, Man versus the State*. It was already that of the Webbs, Bernard Shaw and H. G. Wells. Fabianism is not my Utopia by any means; but at the time it suited me perfectly. The climate of London receives but faint praise: it is moist, cool and dull. Yet I found that I could work more happily in London than in Honolulu, Marrakech or Los Angeles.

I am conscious that London pushed me a great deal farther to the right than Fabianism. It wrought in me a change which was at the same time permanent, yet not organic: a twist rather than a growth. It encouraged me to be, in some of my tastes, a Tory. Gradualism is not sheer sluggishness, timidity, dread of the dark. It springs from an instinctive reluctance to alter a past to which we are sentimentally attached. We find charm in the moldy, the mossgrown, the moth-eaten. Grime is transmuted into patina; absurdity into quaintness; superstition into "the wisdom of our ancestors."

It is a form—one of the lesser forms—of Romanticism. It is almost inevitably tinged with make-believe. Yet, even now, I would deal with it tenderly.

My mind reverts inevitably to architectural symbols. There is a definite gain in preserving, and even restoring, the monuments of bygone eras. When I saw the Tower in London, I regretted the Bastille. I have no taste for Wardour Street antiquarianism. The Gothic front of St. Pancras Station, although good of its kind, elicits a smile, like the even better Richardsonesque of the Union Depot in St. Louis: "Ye Olde Railway Shoppe" has no appeal for me. But I maintain that the historical styles are still valid for historical purposes. When the Church of England has discarded the creeds, the episcopate, the Thirty-nine Articles, the Authorized Version, the Book of Common Prayer, and the hymns ancient and modern, then it will be proper to have cathedrals designed by Neutra, Frank Lloyd Wright and Le Corbusier. In the meantime, I prefer Sir Giles Gilbert Scott's truly noble fane at Liverpool, or the nave of St. John the Divine. They are "functional" in the highest degree. Modernists sneer at the Houses of Parliament as a pastiche. But the keynotes were provided by St. Stephen's Hall and especially by Henry VII's chapel, back of Westminster Abbey. The pastiche has endeared itself to generations. It is as essential a part of London as St. Paul's. A Parliament from which a member cannot resign, but must apply for the stewardship of the Chiltern Hundreds, requires a medieval setting.

So I acquired a veritable attachment to the Established Church, in spite of her being so respectable. I had almost the same fondness for the Royal Family as for the Lion and the Unicorn, although Queen Victoria had somehow polarized all the Anglophobia of the French, and although Edward VII was a "Parisian" of the kind I could not approve. This mild Toryism of mine needed the mists of old England: in France and in America, it refused to strike root. Beer and whisky magnates turned into belted earls ("a barrel rampant on a field of gules") were part of the British show, a gentle comic relief, like the wigs of judges and barristers. In America, I could not muster the same amused tolerance. I have met Tories, in New England and in the South, and found them, not merely unconvincing, but slightly annoying. I can enjoy straight make-believe, within reason; but imitation make-believe is beyond my capacity.

Now I must sing a palinode. As I grew older, I felt that my Toryism was not a distinction, but a flaw. No one in the world has any feeling but respectful friendliness for the un-assuming and well-behaved family at Buckingham Palace. But the heraldic menagerie of Lion and Unicorn is not a harm-less luxury. A traditional monarchy preserves an aristocracy; and although both may be shorn of actual power, they keep alive the besetting sin of the British, so mercilessly exposed by Thackeray, snobbishness. It may be said that if the British like to be snobs, it is their affair. Not entirely. Class conscious-ness (not in the economic sense) operates beyond the fron-tiers of the realm. An Englishman is instinctively, uncon-sciously, as supercilious toward the lesser breeds—Continen-tals and "natives"—as a "gentleman" is toward the "lower classes." He may be flawlessly courteous, and kind as well as fair: but he is conscious, and makes you conscious, of dis-tances. He is most offensive when he is feudally benevolent. At this moment, the Armed Forces and the Foreign Office of democratic England are still officered by members of the upper class. I like the P. G. Wodehouse world of Butlers, Drones and pig-raising Dukes. But when these charming people attempt to plant little kings everywhere, even in the most uncongenial soil, I am troubled. If that export Toryism were to wind up as a *Prisoner of Zenda* operetta, the cost would be small. But this is not a world in which it is safe to

play such pranks. I am reluctantly compelled to pass upon
monarchy, peerage, nobility, gentry, squirearchy and butler-
dom the same verdict as Bernard Shaw upon the "working
classes": that they are useless, dangerous, and ought to be
abolished.

The most valuable training I received in England was in
clear thinking. This may sound like irony, in view of the
hymns the British have sung to the national virtue of "muzziness." "Logic" is left contemptuously to the frivolous Gaul,
along with millinery, cuisine and bedroom farces. The British
are muddled, and they know it: which is the highest triumph
of perspicacity.

Before we accept this admission, we shall have to discount
the element of British humor, which is quiet, at times almost
imperceptible to American ears, but with undertones that
are subtle, and even delightfully perverse. The cleverest
Englishmen boast of their stupidity, without the fair warning
of a tongue in their cheek; and we take them at their word.
Of course, few people, in England or anywhere else in the
world, really like to think: it hurts. Even professionals shun
the malady of thought: philosophers are eager to rig up a
system, chiefly because it will absolve them from any further
thinking. Particularly, successful people are satisfied to let
well enough alone; and compared with the experience of
other nations, the history of England, for two centuries, has
been a record of internal peace, expanding commerce, imperial sway. *Quieta non movere;* let sleeping dogs lie, even if
they be watchdogs. If you refrain sedulously enough from
thinking, you will be able to eat your cake and have it too—
for a while.

I did not expect my kind hostesses in Holloway, Brighton,
or St. Margaret's, Isleworth, to think. And, most emphatically,

they did not; I did not know that adult intellects could be so unruffled. But I happened also, at Toynbee, to meet university men and workingmen, not all from Kichinev. I attended meetings, and I read books. And it was impressed upon me that in spite of their solemnly humorous denials, the British thought vigorously and well. British stolidity is an elaborate hoax.

I am not alluding to professional logicians, of whom England has had her full share, down to Bertrand Russell and I. A. Richards. I do not believe that their formal logic, subtle as it may be, has in any way clarified their thought. Indeed, in many cases, it has created palpable darkness. I have in mind the very large body of educated men, and the vast company of writers, to be found in England. Somewhat to my surprise, I discovered that English literature was supremely intelligent.

The chief cause of confusion is that the English affect to reject "logic." But what they mean by that term is not clear thinking: it is simply a caricature of deductive reasoning. "All men are equal; Einstein and a drunken fool are both men; therefore Einstein and said fool are equals." If this be rationalism, it never prevailed in France, even in its alleged master Descartes; Montaigne, Pascal, Voltaire, were conspicuously free from it; and Molière derided "that reasoning which banishes reason."

The master of English thought is Francis Bacon; and, remotely, his namesake Friar Roger. Both were advocates of the experimental and inductive method. But the inductive process is the reverse of muddling, and the reverse also of irresponsible, romantic intuition: it is a severe intellectual discipline. Sheer empiricism unleavened by thought would arrest cultural development; it would lead to the automatic perfection of the beehive. Induction is exploration, i.e. a challenge to prejudice. The syllogism is but an instrument; if by logic you mean the art of conducting one's thought, so as to curb and guide imagination and passion, then the English are among the best logicians.

For if England has produced no formidable dream-castle in the German style, she has contributed more than any other country to the clarification and organization of modern thought. Most of the ideas upon which the West has been living for three hundred years were *elucidated* in England. Bacon opens the way; he was not the first experimenter, but he reduced the inductive method to lucid rules. No one could be more definite in his narrow line of thought than Hobbes, unless it be, at the other extreme, Berkeley. Locke provided the intellectual armature for the whole Enlightenment. Political economy had a long history, and the French among others could boast of notable pioneers; but it took Adam Smith to formulate the classical theory. Many people must have been dimly aware of the population problem: but Malthus was the first to focus it, with excessive definiteness. Everybody, for a century, had been groping for the concept of evolution; but it had to be finally clarified through English minds. Bourgeois liberalism could not be more cogently expressed than it was by Stuart Mill and Spencer.

The lamentable confusion of Britain's foreign policy during the last thirty years—almost as bewildered and bewildering as our own—does not give a true picture of the British mind. Diplomacy was left in the hands of the fossil classes, at a time of vertiginous change. In other words, England had to shoot the rapids with pilots who could only look astern. It was a tragedy, but not a death warrant. There was more than sunset splendor, more than an anxious prayer, in Kipling's *Recessional:* there was a prophecy of indomitable life. The captains and the kings shall depart, and the navies melt away. The imperial pomp that Churchill refused to liquidate already seems to us tarnished and wearisome. But the courage that is in Churchill and his people lives on; and it includes intellectual courage. There will always be an England.

PART TWO

My America

CHAPTER SEVEN

First Contact

I arrived in New York on September 15, 1906, after a stormy crossing on the old French liner *La Touraine*. Jules Romains, then just come of age, had already discovered "Unanimism," but I was not aware of it. Yet there was a soul of the ship, dwarfing our puny individual souls. What we felt cannot be expressed according to the canons of modern taste. The most humble among us were obscurely at one with the Argonauts and the Conquistadors. Our eyes and hearts were straining for a new heaven and a new earth. The realists and the sophisticates will sneer away these apocalyptic words as florid and trite. But the true can never be trite: only the pretentious, the conventional, the smart. After forty years, the anguish, the exultation, the wild surmise that filled those lonely hours are still vivid in my memory.

This is the truth, the plain truth, but not the whole truth. If the truth within the truth is to be told, America was not primarily for me the Land of Liberty, but the Land of Miss Wilhelmina Macartney. She alone was my "promise of American life": all that Herbert Croly had to offer in addition was accepted with deep gratitude, but did not determine my

171

choice. If my Golden Fleece had been hidden in Lhassa, Thibet, instead of Beaver Falls, Pennsylvania, my destination would have been Thibet. How we met, quite accidentally, in Paris; how we first discussed scholarly topics, the alleged monotony of Racine, the intricacies of the subjunctive; how we soared from these dusty fields into the Magic Land: these are factors in my Personal Equation upon which it would be futile to dwell. Whoso has received the baptism of fire will understand; the rest will raise weary eyebrows. Love is thickly coated with sentimental conventionalities. The society column of our local papers invariably calls the most commonplace engagement a romance. Whether our own experience was among the rarest, or whether it was quasi-universal, we shall never know. In either case, silence is the better policy. If the experience is unique, it cannot be communicated. If it is common, it may be taken for granted. It inspired poems meant for two pairs of eyes only. If, with advancing years, I lapse from Higher Seriousness into the looser ways of the fictionist, it may provide a theme for a novel. But I do hope I shall be able to make a living in a less questionable fashion.

So our love story will be kept out of this honest inquiry. Not so our marriage, for it raised all the problems, national, social and religious, to be discussed in this book, and a few others besides. Shakespeare, who, fortunately for us, was not afraid of the trite, wrote: "The course of true love never did run smooth." Some Spirit with a Mephistophelean sense of irony opened Polti's *Thirty Six Dramatic Situations*, picked out the choicest obstacles, and scattered them in our path. In retrospect, I enjoy the comedy; and although, at the time, I indulged in moments of despair, I must confess that nothing could actually shake my assurance, or, if you prefer, my conceit.

I was a very young man, but not absurdly young, in good

health, of sound mind and unblemished record. I had just
taken with first honors a coveted degree which seemed to
herald a successful career. According to the rules of the
French game, I could command a respectable dowry in the
matrimonial market, with prospects of more (technically,
des espérances, say a wealthy aunt, childless and elderly).
It was a rude shock to my *bourgeois* sense of established
values when I discovered that, in the eyes of my prospective
parents-in-law, I was thoroughly ineligible, on every possible
count. My proud title, *Agrégé de l'Université*, was meaningless to them, as it is to the vast majority of mankind. So far as
they knew, I might be one of those "French masters" who
are simply living phonographs, and can never aspire to pro-
fessorial rank; when an alien is hard up, and has nothing
left to pawn, he offers to teach his native language. To be a
Parisian was in my eyes a patent of nobility; in theirs, Paris
was the modern Babylon. And I wore a beard which permitted to surmise the worst. The Reverend John L. Macartney had a beard also; but his was orthodox, historical, snow
white, venerable; mine was unruly, of many colors, in a word
Gallic.

These minor difficulties might be adjusted: I did shave my
beard, and secured reputable jobs. But there was a far more
formidable obstacle: my future family belonged to the Reformed Presbyterian, or Covenanter, church. Now, the Covenanters are the Dissent of Dissent, the Puritans purified,
the Saving Remnant, the Salt of the Earth. A Covenanter
farmer, pioneering in the West, wrote to his friends in the
East: "Send me an upstanding Godfearing maiden to be my
wife and helpmeet. If possible, a Reformed Presbyterian; if
none is to be found, a United Presbyterian; but on no account
go lower than that!" Now I might have been defined at the
time either as a Romanist or as an infidel; and it was a grievous

problem for the Macartney clan to decide which was worse.

The contest went on for nearly two years. As was proper, the ardor and toughness of youth won in the end. Opposition suddenly collapsed; so suddenly that all the arrangements for the wedding had to be made in three days. I thoroughly recommend the method. Ours was quite the nicest wedding I ever attended. The elation of victory completely abolished stage fright, and I repeated the sacramental words with an intensified French accent, but without faltering. We were married in my bride's home, Fern Cliff, on the campus of Geneva College. No less than five Covenanter ministers took part in the ceremony, the leading role being assumed by my father-in-law. If a telegraph strike had not interfered, my four brothers-in-law would have been on hand, and ready to do their bit—all of them Presbyterian ministers. But five is a goodly number. I need not add that this fivefold knot has never slipped. We lived happy ever after. And that, as Keats so aptly puts it, is all ye need to know.

Four of the officiating divines were past or present presidents of Geneva College. I felt myself quite a Covenanter by marriage, and appreciated the piquancy of the situation, just as Voltaire did when he was made an honorary Capuchin. Geneva saw a gleam of hope in the fact that I was a compatriot of John Calvin; still, it watched the perilous experiment with misgivings. At the end of nearly three decades, as no catastrophe had occurred, Geneva conferred upon me an honorary degree, in acknowledgement of the miracle. This act of friendliness touched me deeply; and the silvery hood is particularly becoming. I once planned to dedicate a book to the most orthodox member of the family (for there are degrees even in absolute faith), in this form, which he had approved:

IN TOKEN OF BROTHERLY AFFECTION
AND TOTAL DISAGREEMENT;

but third parties were afraid that it might sound like Gallic flippancy. On the contrary, it seems to me a thoroughly American formula. I could extend it to all my Covenanter friends.

I felt so much at home among the Covenanters that I claimed the privilege of teasing them: was I not almost a son of the house? They insist on calling the Lord's day the Sabbath, without any scriptural warrant. They believe that the Psalms alone have been appointed by God Himself for His own praise, and that it is sinful to sing hymns not dictated by the Holy Ghost. They also reject instrumental music as pagan, prelatical, papistical and profane. I was tempted once or twice to quote the 150th Psalm, the very last: "Praise him with the sound of the trumpet: praise him with the psaltery and harp. Praise him with the timbrel and dance: praise him with stringed instruments and organs. Praise him upon the loud cymbals: praise him upon the high sounding cymbals." To my logical Latin mind, the instructions seemed explicit. But my suggestions were received with mild silent reproof.

The Covenanters taught me a lesson which they still have to learn: namely, that you cannot judge a man, nor predict his conduct, by his beliefs, however ardent and sincere. The *style* may be the man; the *thought* is not. There is today an overabundant literature ascribing our moral confusion to materialistic determinism. If the young and the not-quite-so-young eat, drink and be merry with such dire consequences, Haeckel, Fechner or Karl Marx must be to blame. None of the recent books in that strain is quite so cogent, or so readable, as *The Disciple,* by Paul Bourget, which appeared in 1889. Now, in spite of all quibbling, determinism, fatalism and predestination are three avatars of the same doctrine. All three deny the freedom, or at any rate the efficacy, of the human will. Man is but a pawn in the hands of Nature, Fate, or God. With man's liberty, his responsibility disappears.

Why should he not indulge his basest instincts? He is not his own master. Immediate pleasure is the one thing as certain as final doom. Logically, the argument is irrefutable. But it is contradicted by the facts. Men who did not believe in free will were on repeated occasions among the most resolute and austere in history: Stoic philosophers, early Mohammedans, Calvinists, Jansenists, scientists, and even certain types of Marxians. To be "determined" implies, paradoxically, the highest degree of will power. Napoleon considered himself as the tool of destiny. Why this contradiction? Perhaps because the man who feels himself the slave of an unknown, other-than-human force is thereby released from all thralldom on the purely human plane. I have known Covenanters to sin; but it was not because they believed in predestination.

Just as the Macartneys had thought of me, sight unseen, as the incarnation of stage Parisianism, so I had a definite image of them as the conventional Puritans. I pictured them as stern, even morose; ever inclined to admonish, rebuke and reprove, as enjoined by the Apostle; their daily talk punctuated with menacing scriptural quotations. To me, they were "the wrath to come." And this again was strictly logical. Puritans have no business to be amiable. The quest of beauty is sensuous even when it is not sensual; the pleasure of which beauty is the sign and promise is a snare laid by the Tempter. This world is a vale of tears. After having thus carefully taken all joy out of this life, the Puritans, as I constructed them in my mind, proceeded with great thoroughness to darken the life to come: certainly eternal punishment, infant damnation, and the small number of the elect can hardly be considered as doctrines of cheer.

There again, reality gave the lie direct to logic. I met *one* long-faced, lank, cadaverous, sternly rebuking, Bible-thun-

dering Covenanter: the type does exist.[1] But I have met
cantankerous people in all walks of life, under every sky,
and professing every possible philosophy. With that one
exception (and even he had gleams of kindly humor), I found
my Covenanter friends actually more cheerful than most
of my Parisian acquaintances. To be sure, they were debarred
from certain kinds of pleasure: they could play flinch or five
hundred, but not whist or poker. But I looked down upon
even flinch or parcheesi as frivolous: when I became a man,
I put childish things away. From all descriptions, parties
"thrown" by the sophisticates are lugubrious affairs; while
a gathering of Covenanter friends simply ripples with laughter.

I had the same experience with other people of secure faith,
even though that faith, to strict Covenanters, would seem
a ghastly distortion of the truth. I had it with the Mormons
of Logan, Utah, among whom I spent happy summer weeks,
ringing with music and mirth. I had it with the Ladies of the
Sacred Heart at Menlo Park, California. Father Garasse up-
held "a virtue called *Eutrapelia,* such humor not incompatible with saintliness of life, rather is it a mark of that inward
joy demanded by God of his servitors: *hilarem enim datorem
diligit Deus."* [2]

Like all true believers, like the Mormons, like the Roman
Catholics, the Covenanters are theocrats. They are consistent
and courageous enough to denounce and repudiate the Constitution of the United States as a godless instrument; they
take pride in their "political dissent." The constituted authorities, very properly, respect the Covenanters, who do not
respect them. As long as they do not conspire against law and

[1] So does the conventional Parisian: cf. Princess Pauline Metternich, Albert,
Prince of Wales, and Leopold II of the Belgians.
[2] Henry Bremond, *Literary History of Religious Thought in France,* Vol. I,
Devout Humanism (New York, 1928), p. 244.

order, they are allowed to hold and preach the most radical doctrines. This I considered a lesson in fundamental Americanism.

I was told of a Covenanter sermon which impressed me profoundly. The preacher was evidently affected by the optimism which is the essential tenet of the American creed; in the vulgar tongue, the booster spirit. This had caused the tonic pessimism of his traditional faith to fade and shrink almost out of sight. History would somehow end in reconciliation, not catastrophe. The Good would triumph, and bring the whole universe under its beneficent sway. The powers of evil would be relegated to the Pit in a remote and obscure corner of the cosmos. Then his Covenanter conscience smote him, and he added: "To be sure, that Pit is bottomless." I never had realized so forcibly before that one infinite may be infinitely greater than another infinite. We need not worry about the narrowness of the Pit: there will be ample room for all.

On this comforting assurance, I must leave my Covenanter friends. They have been generous to me, and I have not withheld my respectful affection in return. My own experience made me listen with great sympathy to *Abie's Irish Rose:* it may be rudimentary, but it deserves a place in American folklore.

I have been tempted to abandon for a moment the normal sequence of events; indeed the Covenanters have lured me to the morrow of Judgment Day. Let us leave them to their "total depravity," a doctrine in which they virtuously rejoice; and let us go back to Saturday, September 15, 1906, when I first beheld the Statue of Liberty. I must admit that my salute to this world-famous image was cool and perfunctory. I did not fall in love with the robust torch-bearing figure until

1919, when, on the transport *Zeppelin,* I returned from the First World War. In 1906, I was more concerned with the triple-headed Cerberus lying in wait for me—customs, health, immigration authorities—than with Bartholdi's grand and simple symbol. The lady wears a crown of spikes: it reminded me of the forbidding *chevaux-de-frise* on the crest of a wall.

In those idyllic days, when America took pride in being the refuge of the destitute, the persecuted, the downtrodden, the ordeal of entry was light enough. The doctor turned my eyelids for trachoma, and stamped approval. The customs officer glanced disparagingly at my brand-new canvas bag, and let it go. I had more trouble with the immigration authorities, but the trouble was entirely within my own mind. I was asked to certify that I was not insane, and that I was not an anarchist. I sincerely believe that I was fully as sane as my questioners. I know that at the time I was an anarchist of the strictest Herbert Spencer observance, *The Man vs. the State.* But I understood at once that it would not be quite safe to speak too plainly in this land of free speech. So I forswore myself (this belated admission may cost me my citizenship), or rather I used the good old method of the casuists, mental reservation: "I am not an anarchist (in the crude sense I guess you have in mind)." I suppose today a member of a Catholic religious order—the only true Communists in the world—would have to swear that he is not a Communist. So from the first my freedom of thought and speech in America was a game of hide and seek.

Coming to America, quite apart from my passionate pilgrimage, was a great joy and a great hope, but not a revolution. I knew the language after a fashion; not that of George Ade, O. Henry and H. L. Mencken, to be sure, but that of Professor Henry Wadsworth Longfellow, whose *Excelsior!* I cannot even yet expunge from my memory. Quite simply, I found in America the democracy for which France was still striving. It was as though the Dreyfus crisis, which I had just lived through, had borne all its fruit. No royalism, no militarism, no clericalism, no class barriers. It was familiar enough: not a new heaven and a new earth, but my old world with the nuisances removed.

Even the material aspects of American civilization gave me no shock. It was not a jump into the unknown, but a return to a regretted path. I had already found out that the daring, Saint-Simonian spirit of the Second Empire, transmitted to my generation through Jules Verne, had lost momentum under the stodgy petty bourgeois Republic. America, where people would rather create than save, delighted me; but it gave me no thrill of surprise. I had gone back to my normal world, a world which was not a slave to bureaucratic routine.

As a Frenchman whose adult mind had been fashioned in England, I found myself at home in America from the very first. That is why I felt so confident of winning my matrimonial battle, in spite of formidable odds. No one, in spite of my quaint tricks of speech and manners, has ever attempted to make me feel a stranger. I was thus spared the throes, but I also missed the tremendous release, that immigrants must have felt when they were born anew on Ellis Island.

But there is no perfect John Doe—that statistical figment, thirty-six years old, five foot eight inches, with a twelve-hundred-dollar income and two and three-quarters children. I was enough of an American not to be perfectly satisfied; for I took my obvious blessings for granted. The moment I landed marked the opening of a forty-year war, which I have finally won in my own heart: peace without victory, as Paul Verlaine said long before Woodrow Wilson. Of this protracted conflict, the rest of this book will be the record.

The conflict was almost entirely within. I came to America with unswerving faith in American principles, but I had to fight to preserve my faith. I firmly believed that democrats throughout the world were following the American and the French revolutions, twin pillars of fire. And the American Revolution was, in its doctrine and in its effects, the most radical that had ever happened in the annals of mankind. But to my dismay, I found that "Radical" in America was a term of reproach; that Thomas Paine was actually despised in the days of Theodore Roosevelt. Americanism did not mean the Declaration of Independence and the Preamble to the Constitution, pure and undefiled. There were at least two other types of American minds, the Tory and the Pragmatist or "Realist." The Tories caused me no mental anguish; after living in France and England, they struck me as imitation fossils. I never allowed the D.A.R. to deprive me of my legitimate heritage, the American Revolution.

What perturbed me was the sudden and unconscious shift from high principles to cynical realism. Hypocrisy or stupidity would not account for this bewildering phenomenon. Those in whom I detected it were evidently shrewd and sincere. They were the successful men, the acknowledged leaders. When pitting myself against their moral authority, I had moments of self-doubt. After all, I was not physically born on this side. I never played baseball in the sand lot. To the present day, I do not like corn. And I speak American with an accent reminiscent of Maurice Chevalier and Charles Boyer, only not so delightful. When I refused to accept the two official symbols of the American spirit, the youth in Longfellow's *Excelsior!* and President Calvin Coolidge, I might, after all, be the victim of my logical and Gallic mind. I might be tainted with those foreign *isms* which are the bugbear of every right-thinking patriot.

So, although I was uneasy from the moment I landed, I kept my counsel for years; and when I first raised my voice, I expressed myself diffidently. Strangely enough, I found very little opposition, not enough for a good fight. I cannot even complain of indifference. I am not a born speaker, and I am not a popular writer, but I have been listened to with sympathy and respect. The greatest ordeal was the very kindness and tolerance of my audiences. Evidently, they thought I was reciting my own version of *Excelsior!* It might not be very well done, but at any rate my intentions were unimpeachable, like those of my illustrious colleague H. W. Longfellow. I was being "idealistic," which is excellent in its proper place, so long as it does not interfere with business. So they applauded discreetly and missed the point altogether.

The problem was obscurely before me from the very first. But it was not fully focused until the close of the First World War, and it will be discussed when we reach that period of frantic "normalcy." In the fall of 1906, I had no thought of criticizing or challenging American ways: my only desire was to learn.

I did not stop a single day in New York, which I found unbelievably unkempt and noisy. I proceeded the same evening to my post at Williams College, which I had obtained on the recommendation of my Sorbonne professor, Emile Legouis. If I was already John Doe in my heart, I was John Doe pretty thoroughly disguised, and escaped recognition. When I reached Williamstown, I was not so buoyant and not so impressive as I might have wished. The housekeeper at the Faculty Club, where rooms had been reserved for me, inspected me with ill-concealed disfavor. I was disheveled, crumpled and rumpled after a night in the coach. My long narrow yellow shoes were dusty. I did not know why people looked at my canvas bag with positive animosity: it had cost me a dollar and a half. My dignity as an *Agrégé de l'Uni-*

versité suffered from the fact that I trundled a mattress on my back. I had been advised to bring "bedding," and "bedding" I had brought, being of a literal mind. "Arise, take up thy bed, and go unto thine house." I was assigned the rooms of "Pickled Smith," and did not fully realize the honor. "Pickled" is an ambiguous term, and it took me a little while to understand that it was a euphemism for "Preserved."

Fate (or Dialectic Materialism, or Providence) had served me better than I knew. The Williams campus was, and, I trust, remains, a delightful spot. The architecture was then most attractive in its simplicity. The absence of walls or railings around the houses was a pleasant novelty to me: both the English and the French feel compelled to fortify themselves against intruders. It looked as though the buildings were scattered through a lovely woodland. I had spent two years actually within the park of Saint-Cloud, more appealing to me than Versailles, for its majestic living architecture was not so formal and ornate, and I had enjoyed the proud melancholy of its autumn foliage. But I was not prepared for the richness of the fall in the Berkshire Hills. Russet and gold were familiar enough; the deep red tinges were new. Autumnal splendor was a grand finale rather than a dirge. Winter, after the sleet and rain of Paris, and the choking brown fog of London, was a revelation. The thermometer sank to depths I never knew: there were eighteen zero days in February. But the sky was blue, and the cold tingled like a bugle call. Some students wore heavy fur caps, others went bareheaded. For months, the carpet of snow was undisturbed. Not a wheeled vehicle in sight. There were no automobiles at Williams in those idyllic days; hacks and delivery wagons were on sleds; and the air was merry with the jingling of bells. Spring burst out like an ode to joy. Never again was the pageant of the year so gorgeously set before me: in the West, in the South, or in giant cities like Paris, London and New

York, the contrasts between the seasons are not so dramatic. And I could lift up mine eyes to Greylock, pensive but not frowning on the horizon; Greylock, whose summit I never reached.

Only four of us had rooms at the Faculty Club, with Professor Milham smilingly acknowledging the dignity of "abbot." Well over a dozen gathered regularly at meals, around one long table; and the historian T. P. Smith (*P* here does not stand for "pickled") was our very lively Autocrat. It was one of the very best seminars I have ever attended. There was a marked difference between Toynbee and Williams. When I was in a Toynbee mood, Williams sounded, not noisy, but somewhat metallic. When the Williams spirit was upon me, Toynbee, in recollection, seemed, not exactly dull, but somewhat muffled. All departments were represented, so the conversation never grew too technical. Thanks to T. P. Smith, it did not break into half a dozen clashing colloquies. Thanks to Milham, it did not turn into a monologue.

My chief, the head of the Romance Languages Department, was Professor Asa H. Morton, a very handsome gentleman, then in his middle forties. There was about him something of the academician, something of the minister, but, thanks probably to a black beard already speckled with silver, even more of the architect. He was fond of art, and so was Mrs. Morton. He was a great virtuoso on the Pianola, a pneumatic contraption in which the player could control the volume and the tempo; and he managed the pedals and levers with the airs of a Paderewski. I was slightly overawed by him, and I regret it deeply; for I believe we could have become lifelong friends, instead of remaining within the bounds of academic etiquette. There was a certain New England stiffness of manners at Williams in those days. People addressed each other precisely as Professor, Doctor and plain Mister, whereas, today, I suppose, every one is Hank, Tom or

Butch. And the faculty dressed even for small parties. As I had no swallowtails, I appeared in my severe pedagogical frock coat, the cut reminiscent of the Lincoln era.

My interest in religion, intensified at the time by my tussle with the Covenanters, found ample material at Williams. I could see that the place was in evolution; but it had retained traces of pristine rigor. Not so long before, professors had been officially reproved for taking unnecessary walks on the Sabbath. Chapel attendance was compulsory, and, for that reason, perfunctory. When I expressed my astonishment at such a regulation in a school not under denominational control, I was told that morning chapel was very convenient for announcements to the student body. It was then I first heard of the professor who, having forgotten an important notice, providentially remembered it in his closing prayer: "And, O Lord! in Thy great mercy bless Thy servant Professor Rumpelkammer, whose course Chemistry 15 will meet at nine o'clock instead of ten as heretofore, Amen!" I could see the cogency of the argument; but somehow it left a void.

On Sunday we had visiting preachers (if we had a regular chaplain, I must apologize to his shade, for I cannot remember him). Three in succession gave sermons on the Prodigal Son; and one of them offered a much-needed defense of that sacrificed character, the steady and thrifty stay-at-home. Professor Pratt was teaching the psychology of religion, and he let loose his students upon us, with pitiless questionnaires. Although I answered a few of them with scrupulous honesty, I was struck with the inadequacy of the method. No question of this nature can be answered by Yes or No; and no statistical table proves anything except that the religious spirit soars above statistics. It was my first encounter with the numerical fallacy, which I was to meet again, with the same profound distaste, in psychology and aesthetics.

Professor Morton had studied at Union Theological Seminary, and he held in his home a Bible class for seniors and members of the faculty. This group I eagerly joined. We gathered in the large attic of the Morton residence, transformed into a very handsome studio. In this connection, Professor Morton told us a parable which, I believe, is of very wide application. He wanted to have a heavy center post removed, as it greatly spoilt the convenience and effect of the room. "Impossible!" said the contractor. "The whole roof rests upon that pillar." Whereupon Professor Morton called his attention to the base of the post: it was a full inch from the floor. It was held aloft by the roof it was intended to support.

We made a comparative study of the Synoptic Gospels and of St. John's. The spirit of the inquiry was fearless and reverent: two admirable qualities, but so finely balanced that they checked and even canceled each other. This, I believe, is true of much liberal theologizing. A little later, Professor Pratt gave an address which created no little stir. He had allowed his fearlessness to outrun his reverence, to the consternation of the devout. Professor Morton was called to the rescue. He read before the Philosophical Union a paper on "New Wine and Old Bottles." I have just perused it again: its moderation, its sincerity, its clarity, are manifest. Blessed are the peacemakers. Yet there is something of the Laodicean in such well-meant efforts at compromise. On the strength of this address, Williams revived for Dr. Morton an old professorship on the Reconciliation of Science and Religion. Under his new title, he gave his excellent old courses, "Dante," "The Italian Renaissance." His wine was none too new, his bottles not so very old, and the combination was extremely reassuring. I expect that after this untoward agitation, the gentlemanly faith of Williams relapsed into slumberous peace.

I took one long step toward Americanization during that year at Williams: I was initiated into the American institution of after-dinner eloquence. It was a harder test than going through the health, customs and immigration examinations. I was staggered at first, but I recovered. At Thanksgiving, I attended a Congress for Social Education in Boston; at Christmas, a meeting of the Modern Languages Association at Yale. With these learned gatherings went banquets which were Spartan enough. But when the blob of ice cream and the anemic cookie had disappeared, a Walpurgis Night began.

Sober men (I verily believe they were sober) told stories which to my untutored mind seemed wholly immaterial, irrelevant and above all incompetent. Humbly, I ascribed at first the apparent absence of heads or tails to my incomplete mastery of the American dialect. Yet the words were plain enough. I had heard a few pleasantries in Paris and in London, even in academic circles. I had learned, and in a shy fashion practiced, the Horatian precept *Desipere in loco*. But I was not prepared for *desiperation* on such Gargantuan scale.

I do not know when the light came. Years later, I finally did appreciate after-dinner humor; I laughed at all the jokes I had missed before, as, with the regularity of the seasons, they paraded again before me. I learnt the vanity of the cautionary words: "Stop me if you have heard this one," for the latest anecdote about the Irishman and the Jew was minted among hod carriers on the Tower of Babel. Just as, according to the great folklorist Aurelio Macedonio Espinosa, the Tar Baby appears under every clime, so the Fuller Brush man (under a hieroglyphic name) convulsed the court of the Pharaohs. There are fewer basic jokes than there are dramatic situations. Age is not of the essence. The pertinent question is not: "Is it new?" but "Has it a point, and is it to the point?" If I thought it would illustrate my meaning, I would unblushingly quote what Queen Elizabeth said to Sir Walter Raleigh when he spread his cloak at her feet, or the minister of Coolidge the Taciturn, and his opinion of sin.

Folk stories of all ages and nations are interchangeable, for, as Wendell Willkie discovered, this world is one. But in details they have a local tang as well as a period flavor. Folklore, in the hands of a good psychoanalyst, would enable us to probe the subconscious and unconscious depths of national souls. And the result might be appalling. I was dismayed when I first heard of the guttersnipes and the fire on thoity-thoid Street: "There was a guy on the thoid story. We yelled: 'Chump! We have a blanket!' And the guy chumped. Chee! We had a laugh! We didn't have no blanket!" It made me realize that under the bland and at times vacuous countenance of my compatriots, there lurked abysses of cold-blooded ferocity. The Covenanters, with their belief in Total Depravity, are not so far wrong after all.

CHAPTER EIGHT

Stanford and David Starr Jordan

═══════════════════

ONCE AGAIN, Fate was kinder than I knew: I was called, unseen, unheard, unread, to Stanford University. My knowledge of American education was still nebulous. The New England colleges with which Williams played a weird kind of football had become familiar names to me; but I knew their yells better than their scholarly standing. Even in France, I had heard of Harvard; more vaguely, of Yale, Princeton, Columbia; and even of "experimental schools" called Johns Hopkins and Clark. In the western mists, there loomed an upstart institution, Chicago, abundantly blessed with wordly goods; it gave itself airs, although it never could rival the fame of the stockyards. Beyond, Cimmerian darkness.

I accepted the congratulations of my Williams colleagues with becoming modesty and secret misgivings. My fiancée, who knew California, was delighted with the prospect, and that was enough. The older generation was not so easily pleased. My prospective parents-in-law, still valiantly attempting to avert their fate, frowned upon Stanford. Its president, David Starr Jordan, had an ominous reputation. He called himself a member of the Church Universal, that is to say that his mind was a theological blank. He had come out brazenly in favor of evolution. Much later, the Macartneys were to discover the better side of Dr. Jordan. On the vital question of cigarette smoking, he was almost as sound as if he had been a child of the Covenant. When offered a friendly weed, he would blandly reply: "I haven't sunk so low as that"; and he used to preach a brief sermon on "The Future of a Cigarette Smoker": "He hasn't any." Still, this hardly made up for his skepticism about Total Depravity.

As for my mother, she had read horrific descriptions of the San Francisco earthquake and fire. That I should of my own accord migrate to such a Dantesque region struck her as compounded perversity. I assured her, on the best authorities, that such catastrophes occurred on the average only once in fifty years. But no one ever found comfort in the law of averages.

"O California, sweet and wild!" The West had still a magic for which glamour is no substitute.[1] The very name was romance. I felt as though my American adventure were at last beginning in good earnest. I had not been overwhelmed by the East. After all, for an untrained observer, New England still seemed a trifle colonial, and Boston culture derivative. I suspected that even Harvard was attempting to borrow respectability by calling its habitat Cambridge. I was not surprised that all educated people rushed to Europe *en masse* every summer, as a diver comes to the surface to breathe. New York—the New York a hasty visitor would know—was hideous in those days. The streets were democratically ill paved and unkempt. The four lines of the elevated filled the avenues with gloom and clangor. The brown-front houses stretched implacably in dingy rows. The taller buildings had

[1] It was only years later, when I had become a quasi-native son in the spirit, that I heard (misquoted) Sir Walter Scott's tuneful doggerel
O California, wild and worse,
Meet child for a strong-handed nurse!

not yet achieved the romantic power and the soaring grace
of the modern skyscrapers. New York was then no fantastic
eruption of towers, no Italian hill town on a Titanic scale: it
was rather, as H. G. Wells noted, a back yard cluttered up
with enormous packing boxes. There was brutal energy in
that chaos, but there was no grace. New York was still un-
tamed. The runaway metropolis has not yet been brought
under full control; at any rate, man today dares to face the
problem, and refuses to despair.

The old Northwestern Depot in Chicago, where we boarded
the Overland Limited, was aggressively squalid; and thanks
to the suddenness of our decision, we had been able to secure
only an upper berth. But who, on such an occasion, would
give minor discomforts a second thought? Perhaps "stout
Cortez," as he stood on a peak in Darien, was bitten by mos-
quitoes. And this was a peak indeed. Magic names—Omaha,
Cheyenne—pealed in my ears like joyous bells. From the ob-
servation platform, hand in hand, we watched the West un-
roll itself, illimitable as per specifications. We behaved with
the greatest decorum. Yet we were suddenly pelted with
rice. A messy and wasteful custom: but in those idyllic days,
world hunger was not gnawing our conscience.

Yes, the land ocean was more appalling in its vast and mysterious placidity than the turbulent waves of the Atlantic.
Vague childish memories hovered on the fringe of my consciousness: Buffalo Bill, Round the World in Eighty Days,
The Sign of the Four, the Fenouillard Family; but I did not
dream of swift melodrama. What I felt with greater intensity
than on the *Touraine* was that at last I had left Europe behind. A delusion: Europe is in the mind, not on the map. But
sheer magnitude, although stupid, is impressive. In a humbler
key, I could almost repeat the grand words of Pascal: "The
eternal silence of these infinite spaces frightens me."

We had a revelation of absolute solitude somewhere in

Nevada. The train stopped in the sagebrush. A young woman, a teacher, with handsome and somewhat Indian features, alighted. A rough wagon was there to meet her. Not a house in sight, not a tree: the sparse and dusty scrub stretched far away.

Then the sinuous descent, like a bird of prey wheeling, through the forest-clad Sierras; the huge ferryboat at Benicia carrying the whole mighty train on its four tracks; and at last, the bay, the Golden Gate, and San Francisco.

San Francisco is frequently cold and foggy in August, to the dismay of eastern visitors. But we were treated, on our honeymoon visit, to a sky of unbelievable purity, to a light in which every line and every shade stood out sharply, triumphantly, to a warmth and a coolness so exquisitely blended that each brought out the other's perfection. The waters were gay with white ferryboats, their great beams dancing on the upper deck, their paddles swathed in silver foam. Every boat was escorted by a welcoming committee of sea gulls.

The atmosphere of the city, sixteen months after the great ordeal, was that of a fiesta. In comparison, Paris, London, even New York appeared drab and morose. San Francisco, violently shaken out of its humdrum prosperity, seemed to have recaptured the spirit of the Argonauts. The streets had been cleared of rubble, and roughly repaved. As the central district was still under reconstruction, the great stores had opened emergency quarters on Van Ness Avenue: that is the wide artery where the conflagration had been stopped, by dynamiting the whole eastern side. Pretentious private residences, hastily enlarged with sheds, were now the Emporium, the city of Paris, the White House. The strangest sight was offered by the city hall. The whole baroque structure of reddish stone had collapsed; but the high dome stood, apparently intact, on its gaunt steel supports. It reminded me, incongruously, of a fantastic wickerwork *mannequin* or dressmaker's form, the kind that is found in every French bourgeois household, and that Anatole France had turned into a pathetic symbol.

To celebrate my entry into San Francisco, I resolved to have a real barber's shave, respecting, of course, the vari-colored goatee which I considered as the badge of my calling. It was my first experience of the kind. The shop was in a basement, with hints of mysterious depths. The barbers were short, fat and swarthy; a Negro was crouching in the background. Suddenly, my chair was tilted back, a wet towel stifled me, and someone seized my foot. I knew, by title only, that there were exciting tales about *The Mysteries of San Francisco* and *The Secrets of Chinatown*. I was, for a second, scared just enough to enjoy the thrill. In a miraculously short time, I emerged with that schoolboy complexion restored, and my shoes resplendent for the second time that day—a phenomenon as rare as a double sunrise. The experience cost me a fortune—at that time, the charge for a shave in London was threepence; it never was repeated.

Not even a Proust can probe the intricacies of psychological Time. Certain reflections came to my mind, I am ready to swear, in 1907; how definite they were, I cannot tell. They have grown with the years. They assail me today with greater urgency than forty years ago. I cannot disentangle the original impression from the slow enrichment of experience. I was then the prophet of my present self; I am now the fossil remains of my dead youth; and I have never ceased to be I. So I shall not attempt to date my thoughts. I am offering them, literally, "for what they are worth."

The first of these impressions, I have already noted, was the joyousness of an immense collective effort. It was a Renaissance feeling, a new springtime. The air is as bracing, the sun is as bright in San Francisco today as forty years ago: but that glory has departed. I am fond of quoting the words of Raoul Glaber, which break forth like a silver trumpet from the dimness of the eleventh century: "It seemed as though the earth were discarding the rags of its antiquity, to clothe itself anew with a white mantle of churches." Never was San Francisco so happy as in those noisy, dusty, makeshift, hectic years of reconstruction.

Such a dawn has ever been my Utopia: a full, hard day's work ahead, not merely to guard, not to scramble and squabble, but to build, each rejoicing in the other's achievement. To be young at such an hour were very heaven.

Modern society has known a few such moments of eager and intense energy. But, alas! almost invariably they had a tragic background: revolution, dictatorship or war. The Bolsheviks, the Fascists, the Nazis felt that great surge of will power; and so did we in 1917 and in 1941. This, and not sheer sadism, accounts for the fascination of a vast collective gamble with fate. In the morass of apathy and meanness, it brings that release which is the eternal dream of man. The selfish and the timorous (in their own language, the safe and sane) will never achieve security; at any moment, when mediocrity becomes unendurable, it will be shattered by the twin archrebels, Despair and Hope. There is only one way to avert catastrophe: to wit, that practical wisdom should learn to be as bold and generous as madness. Why should there be no virtue except in the powers of darkness?

When planners tell us: "Our cities are preposterous; they should be razed and built anew," we shrug our weary shoulders. There is not enough money to carry out minor, piecemeal improvements. In 1905, the substantial men of San Francisco would have considered a radical reconstruction of the city as "starry-eyed." Then Nature gave a kick; the impossible had to be done; and it was done.

It was done enthusiastically, swiftly, substantially: the new

San Francisco, whose growth I watched, is less flimsy than the old. I wish I could add: it was done wisely and well. In 1907, I was already deeply interested in city planning. To my dismay, I discovered that San Francisco went to work with tremendous energy, but with no plan at all. It was simply rebuilt on the old lines, in scorn of Nature and experience. The lots are too small for intelligent construction. The grid-iron layout remains rigidly imposed upon steep hills, without the least regard for their contours. Cars have to stop and start on eighteen per cent grades. Blocks do not follow the same pattern north and south of Market Street; thoroughfares do not meet, or else they come together at awkward angles. San Francisco took pride in rebuilding without a moment's thought; and the strong practical men of those days saddled future generations with disheartening handicaps. One can only dream of what a Haussmann up to date, a Patrick Geddes, a Burnham, could have done with such a magnificent opportunity.

London has perhaps learned the lesson. Europe as a whole has not; and Europe is only a little worse than India or China. Many things that were delicate and good were swept away by the Curse of God; but also the narrow lots, the gores and dead ends that invite congestion, the dangerous grades, the sunless courtyards, the surly blank walls, all the litter accumulated in the course of centuries by the dull, the short-sighted and the narrowhearted. Now they are to be carefully reconstituted, with a few absurdities added for good measure. We are able to plan for global warfare, but not for global peace. The "realists" keep closing their eyes to every reality that is constructive: "It is not cynical, therefore it cannot be wise."

I hate to darken with these disenchanted thoughts my early recollections of San Francisco. I saw the city rise again, solid and smug, the match, in most respects, of Cincinnati and Kansas City. Still, the dictatorship of George F. Babbitt could not obliterate Nature's magnificent gifts, or stifle altogether a spirit that is not of the countinghouse. Although the commercial aspect of pleasure is as obvious and as dismal on Market Street as in Times Square, there still is about San Francisco an aura of spontaneous cosmopolitan gaiety. The Orient is not beyond the Golden Gate: it has an outpost within two blocks of the financial center. Latin America is not wholly forgotten. The Italian and French colonies are proving their loyalty to America in the most effective way: they refuse to discard the gifts they brought from the old countries. Magnates of commerce still love to keep an expensive bungalow on the coast of Bohemia; the most prestigious club in town preserves a tenuous artistic tradition, and its high jinks in a romantic grove are attended by the very aristocracy of wholesalers. The flower stalls in the business district are not an empty symbol. If the Barbary coast is but a garish memory, it has, I am told, ubiquitous and more sophisticated successors.

From Telegraph Hill, eyesores, although flagrant, are but minor blemishes in an incomparable vista. The most conspicuous feature in the bay is Alcatraz Island, a grim federal penitentiary: it is exactly as if we kept a garbage barrel in the center of our drawing room. But the bay, and the hills, and the Golden Gate have a majesty that dwarfs the vulgarities of man. The civic center may be the very last ambitious group of buildings to be built in the classical French style; at any rate, it has spaciousness and dignity. The Golden Gate Bridge is not merely a record-breaking achievement: it is the perfection of functional grace. An energetic *joie de vivre* is still the spirit of San Francisco; but it is checked at every turn by the realistic question: "Is it good for business?" [2] I certainly do

[2] We have at present (1947) a clear instance of that inner conflict. San Francisco loves its cable cars. It is good fun to ride up Powell Street, hanging out on the running board; during the conference, I have seen admirals and generals enjoying the sport with boyish glee. Moreover, the cars, with their

not wish for another earthquake: San Francisco claims to be earthquake-proof anyway. And I have little faith in the permanent value of moral earthquakes. But I dream of a Declaration of Independence against a tyranny so plausible and insidious that it is the most "totalitarian" of all.

When we first beheld Stanford, we were struck with its strangeness rather than with its beauty. We were driven through a eucalyptus grove, along an avenue of palms; to me, a northerner, both looked exotic, but curiously ragged. More unfamiliar still was the architectural color scheme— buff sandstone arcades covered with red tiles; but it blended marvelously with the background of tawny hills and the bluish range beyond. The light had a metallic brilliancy, which was not of my world. From the parched and deeply cracked earth rose the pungent odor of the tarweed. Few roads were oiled in those days, and after five rainless months, dust lay thick on every shrub. We had the sense of being in an oasis: we could almost feel the hot breath of the desert. Today, familiar as we are with the Santa Clara Valley, its neat middle-class suburbs, its country estates, its opulent orchards, and the interminable string of dining places along the highway, this impression is hard to recapture. Yet the desert is not very far away: the range we can descry across the bay is as desolate, as unhuman as any part of the state. It is not far away in the past or future either: the slightest change in the climate would blot out our precarious civilization. Much of California is as artificial as Holland.

The strangeness of the sight was enhanced by the ruins we saw on every hand. The original Quadrangle—twelve

gaudy paint, their imperious bell, the brooklike murmur of their cable, bring out nostalgic visions of fabulous days "before the fire." But the cars do not pay. And San Francisco is trying hard to figure out whether their advertising value is equal to the deficit.

one-story buildings connected by a Mission-like cloister—
had stood the test very well; some of the taller buildings
were not badly damaged, and were already in full use again.
But the new library, the new gymnasium, barely completed,
were hardly more than mounds of rubble. As in San Francisco, a dome, in the shape of a Saracenic helmet, stood
bizarre and defiant on slender shafts of steel. The Memorial
Arch, perilously cracked, had been removed, leaving two
enigmatic stumps behind. The heavy tower of the church had
collapsed, and the resulting air pressure had blown out the
main front with its refulgent mosaics. The whole scene was
fantastic rather than tragic. The sharp sunshine effaced any
thought of human or cosmic disaster. It rather looked as
though some giant child had built a castle with yellow blocks,
and capriciously kicked it down. The catastrophe had displayed an uncouth sense of humor; and Dr. Jordan responded
to this seismic horseplay. He liked to talk with a twinkle of
these oddities. On a pedestal were found the name Guten-
berg and, neatly, an empty pair of bronze shoes. The "flying
buttresses" at each corner of the tower were the first to fly.
A marble Agassiz took a perfect dive into the pavement thirty
feet below, and remained there imbedded, head first, un-
damaged. "I knew his penetration into the abstract, not into
the concrete," said Jordan; as though the great and unphilo-
sophical naturalist had been Hegel or Spinoza.

In our first six years of Stanford life, we saw the debris
gradually cleared. Some of the most ambitious buildings,
flimsy and gaudy, were never restored. The church, however, was taken down stone by stone, and re-erected with a
steel and concrete frame, every rough-hewn block anchored
to that earthquakeproof core. The tower was voted unsafe
as well as unsightly. It was a heavy affair in the Auvergnat-
Romanesque so dear to Richardson, a somewhat questionable cousin of Trinity Church, Boston. It did not live on very

happy terms with the Spanish arcades and the Italian façade. A new mosaic front was imported from Italy, or rather two, for one was lost at sea. At the entrance are found the symbolical figures of Faith, Hope, Charity *and* Love, a distinction which might puzzle St. Paul. The whole is of incredible richness: it cost a million dollars to build and eight hundred thousand to restore. It greatly impresses the natives of Gopher Prairie and the citizens of Zenith. Loyal Stanfordites love it dearly, with a deprecatory smile. As one of the best said: "If architecture be frozen music, surely this must be frozen Sousa."

The students—at that time a thousand men and five hundred girls—tried hard to match the picturesqueness of the setting. Upper classmen wore corduroy trousers; the seniors had sombreros; the juniors had "plug-uglies," tall gray hats artistically hand painted, and smashed in a ritual encounter. I should like to see a picture of Mr. Herbert Hoover with such a battle-scarred monument. Senior girls gave the Quad an unexpected touch of old-world dignity by appearing in academic gowns: they said it saved laundry bills. A solemn tradition edicted that there should be "no queening on the Quad": the choice spot for "queening" was a cactus garden, now derelict, for the automobile has put it out of business. And there was to be no smoking under the arcades: else Mrs. Stanford would turn in her grave. All these "cultural patterns" are now with the snows of yesteryear.

After Williams, the West was breezy. Before I had got used to the climate,[3] a girl blew into my office, sat on my desk, and asked: "Say! Where's Allen's class?" I rose, bowed and answered icily: "*Professor* Allen's course is held in Room 244." There was a passing shadow of alarm in her innocent eyes.

Stanford's motto—in German until the First World War—

[3] People knew they were acclimatized when fleas ceased finding them interesting: it was a certificate of naturalization.

was borrowed from Ulrich von Hutten: "The wind of freedom blows." Other words from that knight-at-arms of the spirit might also have served: "O time! O Century! It is a joy to be alive!" But we could have found in the Renaissance another and greater patron: François Rabelais. Stanford University is the Abbey of Thélème. When he wanted to draw up an academic Utopia, the chronicler of Gargantua simply took the pattern of the medieval cloisters, as he had known them, and turned it inside out. This outrageous paradox, some three hundred and fifty years later, provided the blueprints for an institution of learning on the Pacific Coast. Who knows? Our wildest dreams of today may be realized three centuries hence, in Antarctica, after the ice cap has been removed by atomic power.

Like Thélème, Stanford is co-educational; and not a few of its "religious" discover their life companions in the study rooms or the social halls. Like Thélème, Stanford is situated in the country, a palace (if you are not too critical) within a pleasance. Like Thélème, it does not restrict itself to book learning, but stresses physical culture, games and sports, as well as the amenities of social life. It has been called a country club with a university attached, and accepts the description with a proud smile. Like Thélème, its essential rule of discipline is the honor code: in freedom and among friends, the right people are inclined to behave decently. The rod, in stupid hands, spoils the child; and autocratic hands are invariably stupid. *Fay ce que vouldras,* Do what you list, is no invitation to sloth, gluttony or lust. Rabelais himself led a sober life, and had a Gargantuan appetite for knowledge. It is simply the negation of servitude. There are countries in which the whole duty of man is: Do as you are told. America is not one of them.

As long as I have known Stanford, it has been a citadel of freedom. Before my time, there was one painful crisis. Ed-

ward A. Ross, Professor of Economic Theory, made utter-
ances which Mrs. Stanford considered as reflections on her
husband's integrity. I never knew the details of the affair. I
must admire Ross for his fearless stand. It goes against the
grain with me to say that, on certain occasions, valor might
profitably be tempered with discretion. Perhaps we might
say that "economic theory" might be sweetened with psychological sympathy. The situation was unusual. As long as
one of the founders was alive, the Farm, as it is affectionately
called even today, was still to some extent a family estate.
Mrs. Stanford had struggled valiantly to save the university
from financial disaster, at a time when Huntington advised
"stopping the circus." Through her faith, she founded the institution anew. For her, it was a monument to a great and
good man. Huge letters, across the whole front of the church,
testified that it had been ERECTED TO THE GLORY OF GOD AND
IN MEMORY OF MY HUSBAND.⁴ Jordan was too close to Mrs.
Stanford not to understand her feelings. He had to let Ross go.
The decision must have been hard. I know that many years
later, it still rankled in his mind.

As far as I know, the case remained unique. Veblen, it is
true, was told by Jordan: "Your marital relations are not
satisfactory to the Board of Trustees," and we can imagine
with what twisted smile he gave the historic answer: "They
are not satisfactory to me either." But no curb whatever
had been placed on Veblen's thought, which was fully as bold
as Ross's, if somewhat more cryptic in expression. I am not
"the spirit that ever contradicts," but neither am I meek as-
sent personified: my intellectual freedom has never been in
any way curtailed. I once received a letter expressing wonder that I could live "in the stifling atmosphere of Stanford,"
and it amused me greatly. No one, within the university, ever

⁴ When the church was rebuilt, the inscription was slightly toned down,
and made less conspicuous.

questioned our right to be rugged individualists in our own fashion. We formed a loyal family: always with the proviso: "but Truth is the greater friend." I challenged in my days the views of David Starr Jordan, as I shall relate; of my chief, John Ernst Matzke; of Lewis Terman and his intelligence quotients; of Ray Lyman Wilbur; and of Herbert Hoover, our Premier Alumnus. We all took such dissent for granted: I was deprived of the thrill of feeling myself a potential martyr.

There was at one time a slight tendency to intolerance— on the part of the student body. Most of the young people were fierce isolationists; "The Yanks are not coming" was their battle hymn. But a bare allusion to the Stanford spirit would suffice to secure a hearing even for the most unpopular views. I found that, away from the Farm, I could carry the Stanford name with me as a shield. People who may have found my opinions "subversive" listened courteously to me, because "it is a way they have at Stanford to say just what they please." If—Heaven forfend!—there were to be another witch hunt, state institutions might become the victims of political hysteria; but Stanford would remain a fortress of sanity. It would stoutly resist the most "un-American practice" of all, to wit, intellectual tyranny. I do not expect its proud Renaissance motto to be erased, and "Ichabod" to be writ in its place.

The Stanford spirit was that of David Starr Jordan. He was my great Professor of Americanism, and it is thanks to him that I have felt so profoundly at home in this country. He was American to the marrow of his bones, and even in those oddities which, abroad, might elicit a friendly but mocking smile. He was close to the soil and to the folk, a farm boy, a self-made man. He had in him something of Lincoln, of Whitman, of Mark Twain. Body, mind and soul, he was

built on a generous scale. He was a giant, stout as well as
tall. In a Japanese village a little maiden shyly approached
this walking mountain, touched him and cried: "He is real!
He is real!" Another called him Big Buddha, for even the
reticent Japanese loved him at first sight. But he was a
Buddha who could play baseball in his fifties. For he carried
his bulk, his learning and his message with careless western
ease. Naturalist, educator, poet, prophet, he had in him no
trace of conceit or pedantry. At times, this lordly indifference
was a handicap. In attire and style, he could be slipshod.
Witty and profound, he also rambled. The gemlike perfection
of a Gautier or a Heredia was beyond his reach. He forfeited
—gladly—the admiration of the supercilious. Yet I would
not have had him otherwise. His was a reassuring influence.
"Disturbers of the peace," like Gide, are needed, but they are
not enough. The man who does not feel anguish is a clod;
but the man who is satisfied to toy with his disquietude is only
half grown. Jordan was indomitably boyish, yet mature. His
sympathy with the perils and sorrows of mankind was not a
luxury, but a call to action. His unhurried gait was steadfast.
He liked to say, in homely terms: "The way out is forward"
and: "The world makes way for the man who knows where
he is going."

In one respect, the Jordan spirit was the lance of Achilles,
healing the wounds it had inflicted. For Stanford as he had
planned it was rigidly divided into watertight compartments.
A freshman chose his major subject on registration day; and
he was from the first a young specialist, trained by older
specialists "to learn more and more about less and less." A
great naturalist was held up as a model for devoting his whole
life to the study of a single sea slug. These excesses have
long been corrected. But they were checked first of all by the
example of Jordan himself, wiser than his system. He was a
specialist of the most orthodox kind; an ichthyologist of inter-

national repute, he had identified, described, classified more fishes than all other men combined, past and present. Had I known him earlier, the name Guérard would inevitably have been conferred upon some horrific denizen of the deep. But he was a biologist in the largest sense: Life was his domain. And the science of life as he conceived it embraced, not merely physiology and medicine, but politics and philosophy, poetry and religion: "that they might have life, and that they might have it more abundantly." He knew that no man can reach the summit where all ascending paths must meet; but he never doubted that such a summit was our goal. An indifferent classical scholar, he was in very truth a great humanist.

He taught me the healing virtue of American humor. Continental Europe has a background of tragedy, and not all tragedy is ennobling; it may lead to cynicism rather than to catharsis. As a young man, I could smile, but not without bitterness. Jordan's robust common sense was tinged, not with Irony and Pity—twin forms of superciliousness—but with the good spirit that is not afraid of rollicking nonsense. His jingles, with very clever drawings, are not unworthy of Lewis Carroll or Edward Lear. In his old age, in *The Higher Foolishness*, he could poke fun at pseudo science: fun that was pitiless without an atom of malice. Even toward the end, his body inert, his eyes half closed and glazed, his alert mind would still break through with a twinkle and a quip.

He was too large and too sane for envy or rancor. It was he who taught me that America was "the land where hate dies away." He confirmed my faith in the essential radicalism of the American mind. The ruthless struggle for life—the horrible "basket of crabs" described by Balzac—does not tell the whole story. This country is based, not on unreasoning traditions, but on principles, which are still dynamic today. The true America is constantly in the making.

And those principles, if we believed in them, would in-

evitably expand until they swayed the world. Like the Americanism of Washington, Jefferson, Wilson, Roosevelt and
Willkie, that of Jordan refused to stop at the border. He was
"a citizen of the great Republic of humanity at large." This
made him a pacifist: for no sane man will pin his faith to civil
war. In those days, the word "pacifist" denoted, not an advocate of absolute nonresistance, but a worker for peace.
Jordan worked arduously for peace, just because, realistically,
he knew that peace was threatened and had to be defended.
Si vis bellum, para bellum; si vis pacem, para pacem. This
thought gradually absorbed all others in his mind, scientific
research or academic administration. So, three years ahead of
the retiring age, in 1913, he was released from all other duties,
and, with the title of chancellor, "presented to the world."
The world rejected him, as it rejected Jaurès, with results that
our eyes have seen.

A fledgling assistant professor could hardly hope to associate on intimate terms with the world-famous president; any
more than plain ordinary saints can expect to hobnob in
Heaven with such celebrities as St. Peter and St. Paul. Yet,
across the chasm of years and position, a warm friendship
grew up between us. The way in which it started is so typical
of Jordan that it is well worth recording.

Stern realists—we always have them with us—were using
the magic formula Darwinism to sneer at those who dreamed
of peace. War, they said, is a "struggle for life," and it leads
to the "survival of the fittest." Peace (like hygiene and security) only encourages the multiplication of weaklings.

"Fittest," of course, is the most relative and loosest of terms.
On a particular plane, the germ that kills a man of genius is
evidently "fitter" to survive. Jordan, as a biologist, saw a more
fundamental fallacy in the argument. War is the reverse of

natural selection; it is eminently "dysgenic." It picks out the strongest, and sends them to slaughter; the race is preserved by those who were left behind. Jordan found historical confirmation of this view in the work of Otto Seeck, *The Decline of the Ancient World*. The German professor ascribed the downfall of Rome to the elimination of the best through prolonged warfare.[5] Jordan expounded his theory in many articles and lectures, collected as *The Human Harvest, The Blood of the Nations, War and the Breed*.

I felt that Seeck and Jordan greatly exaggerated the importance of that single factor. Had there been no political, social and moral causes of decay, it would have been easy for Rome to assimilate the Barbarians and rejuvenate the breed. Still, within narrower limits, the argument seemed and seems to me incontrovertible.

But Jordan, as a decisive proof of his thesis, offered the decadence of France, which he imputed to the formidable bloodletting of the Napoleonic wars. He forgot that the Germans fought as constantly as the French, and that in many battles there were Germans on both sides. The "decadence" he took for granted: had not the French themselves, in the nineties, admitted it, proclaimed it, gloried in it? It was nonsense, of course; but it is difficult to distinguish between universally accepted nonsense, and common sense. Jordan translated that popular prejudice into biological terms. The proofs that the French breed was going down were, first, the steady decline in the birth rate and, second, the decline in stature: the French army had been repeatedly compelled to lower the minimum for admission.

Backed by the authority of official figures and by Jordan's

[5] Havelock Ellis, in *The Soul of Spain*, adduces the same theory to explain the superiority of Spanish women over their men. He had apparently the curious notion that girls inherit nothing from their fathers or boys from their mothers.

scientific reputation, these propositions seemed unanswerable. Yet they failed to satisfy me. I was not impressed by the falling birth rate: I was already in favor of controlled, responsible parenthood. My ideal for the population of a state was not the maximum, but the optimum. I knew that professors' families did not compare in size with those of illiterate immigrants. I knew also that the Germans, who affected to despise the French for their lower birth rate, despised the Poles even more for breeding like rabbits.

As for the stature of the French, Jordan had drawn a wrong inference from an accurate fact. Even if there had been an actual decrease in size, it might have been caused by one strain among the many breeds of Frenchmen, say the Alpine, increasing faster than another, say the Nordic; and I had already fought the Gobineau-Vacher de Lapouge myth of Nordic superiority. But there had been no such decrease. France, in order to keep her army not too far below the numbers of the German army, was enrolling a larger proportion of the population; and in order to do so, she had to lower the height limit. But the average size of all conscripts had actually grown throughout the nineteenth century, and showed no sign of diminishing.

I hesitated before challenging Jordan's favorite thesis and illustration. Not because I was afraid of offending him and jeopardizing my career: I had already gauged the generosity of the man. The difficulty was different. The Dreyfus Affair had made me, for life, a determined antinationalist. I was still at that time a French citizen: my intervention would be ascribed to sheer chauvinism. My Berkeley colleague Lucien Foulet, hearing Jordan's lecture, had left the room with an angry protest; and his exit had been greeted with ironical smiles.

It was the first time I had to face that problem. I had to

encounter it again and again. I could not state even such a
plain fact as that *Revanche* does not mean *Revenge* [6] without
people raising amused eyebrows: "Ah! There speaks the retained advocate! *La Belle France,* right or wrong!" My conscience is clear, and so is my record. In all my books, I have
rejected the "greatness" which takes the form of arrogance,
the greatness of a Richelieu, a Louis XIV, a Napoleon. I never
believed in the "divine mission" of Joan of Arc, for that would
make God a Frenchman. In the causes I have advocated—a
new *Entente Cordiale,* reconciliation with Germany, a United
Europe, a World Republic, a world language, I have never
suggested the least privilege for France. The fact that France
was formally admitted among the Big Five at San Francisco,
and granted veto power, did not soften my protest against
that "realistic" betrayal of the world's hope.

Unconsciously, Jordan was working against his own principles, and offering a premium to militarism. France was
"decadent" and Germany "virile," because France could no
longer bully other nations; whereas William II boasted of
impressing upon the Chinese, for a thousand years, the terror
of the German name. It is the exaltation of the mailed fist. I
knew also that many Americans *wanted* to believe that France
was decadent, because in religion she was increasingly free.
If I were to judge nations (nations should not be judged, but
simply abolished), I should use other standards.

So I wrote to Jordan, protesting against his references to
France. I do not remember the text of my letter. I imagine it
was thoroughly undiplomatic, for very young men easily
confound firmness with angularity. Jordan overlooked the
faults, appreciated the intentions, and was impressed by the
arguments. He called me to his office, and told me: "If there

[6] Or that the word "Commune" had nothing to do with communism; that
Comité de Salut Public does not mean Committee of Public Safety; that,
in French law, an accused person is not presumed to be guilty until he can
prove his innocence. The list of such popular misconceptions is very long.

is a new edition, I want you to revise it." Thus began a friendship which death could not dim, but only transfigure.

The first fruit of our collaboration was whimsical. I had told Jordan about my experience in the French Army: a plain, very unsensational statement. It interested him; he had me write it down, and sent the manuscript to the *Popular Science Monthly* (as the *Scientific Monthly* was then called). It was my first appearance in American print. I wrote to my wife, then on a visit in southern California: "Joy! I have an article in a first-class magazine. Now you can buy that ostrich feather." She did. Payment came, in the form of fifty reprints. We still have the feather.

The second fruit was of decisive importance to me; it was through Jordan that my first book was published. A study of *Religious Thought in French Literature Under the Second Empire* [7] was manifestly a congenial worst seller. One of my brothers-in-law remarked, when he heard of the subject: "It should be as brief as the chapter on 'Snakes in Iceland.'" As a matter of fact, the original version ran to one hundred and sixty thousand words. Jordan himself sent the bulky and ponderous manuscript, with his personal recommendation, to all the American publishers he knew. And when the usual courteous rejection came ("This work is far too good to be exposed to the public gaze"), he would say with his infectious cheerfulness: "We'll try again!"

Finally, the book was accepted by T. Fisher Unwin, of London. Fisher Unwin was a delightful gentleman of the old school. His office on the lovely Adelphi Terrace was mid-Victorian in furnishings; but the house had preserved the delicate dignity of the Adam period. You had only to push a

---

[7] The final title, less austerely frowning, was *French Prophets of Yesterday;* and the book was properly streamlined.

padded door, and you passed from his business premises into
his private apartments, where Mrs. Unwin, the daughter of
Richard Cobden, had a cup of tea in readiness. Our relations
were ideal. Until he retired, he accepted every one of my books
without question, and asked for more, although I could swear
they never brought him any substantial returns. Without
effusiveness, he rejoiced at the favorable reception of my
work by competent critics. I could write only in my own way,
and it was not in me to seek popular success; without Jordan
and Fisher Unwin my first book, unpublished, would have
been my last. They saved me from "a-fate-worse-than-death,"
as they say in the old melodramas: lifelong frustration.

I shall mention only one other instance of my most happy
if unequal co-operation with Jordan. In the summer of 1913,
I was in Paris, to visit my mother, and to dig a few historical
nuggets out of the Bibliothèque Nationale. Jordan was in
Europe too, on a mission from the World Peace Foundation.
He asked me to join him as a sort of adjutant. I first went with
him through Alsace-Lorraine. It was an ideal trip in that
beautiful land; above all it was, to me, a revelation. I had
fought hard, in my student days, against Déroulède, Coppée,
Lemaître, Barrès, Maurras and their ilk. As the Alsace-
Lorraine problem was the sole obstacle to Franco-German
amity, I wanted to believe that it had faded to the vanishing
point. The German conquest, in 1871, was no doubt an act of
violence, a *Diktat* that the vanquished had never accepted as
legitimate. The provinces had formally protested, both in the
French Assembly at Bordeaux, and in the new German
Reichstag in Berlin: never was there a more unequivocal
plebiscite. But the conquest by Louis XIV was hardly a triumph of gentle suasion. The culture of Alsace was manifestly
Germanic. Even the divided and disheartened Germany of
1681 felt a tremor of sorrow and shame when Strasbourg was
lost. The Vosges seemed to me as "natural" a frontier as the
Rhine.

I was astounded to find that, forty-two years after its "re-union to the Fatherland," Alsace still refused to accept the arbitrament of the sword. The second and third generations had ceased to agitate openly for reunion with France; they had "to think with their heads, not with their hearts." They did not want a war of *Revanche* which, if successful, would first ravage their land, and in which they would have to serve under the German flag. Only if Germany could liberate herself from the Bismarckian spirit could Alsace be truly free, and a bridge between two great cultures. We met the leaders of Alsatian opinion, not merely the outspoken opponents of German rule like "Hansi" and Abbé Wetterlé, but businessmen who had to co-operate with the masters, and who sincerely admired the thoroughness and scientific spirit of German industry. We met German professors at Strasbourg, and German officials. They were courteous (so courteous that they told Jordan he was "a true German" and resembled Bismarck); their reticence was even more eloquent than the protest of the natives. All of them implied what a minister was to blurt out in the Reichstag: "Alsace is *Feindesland,* enemy country."

I never received a sharper lesson in the complexities of history. Sheer power, or "Might is Right"; expert studies in ethnology, diplomacy, economics; the self-determination advocated by Napoleon III and revived by Woodrow Wilson: these three methods, so radically different, have one point in common: they are too crude. To say that Alsace should be French, German or independent is an oversimplification; or rather it misses the point altogether. If we refuse to be blinded by doctrines or passions, we shall recognize that it is possible for traditions, aspirations and material interests not to coincide. It is possible for two neighbors to hold different faiths, to speak different languages, to cherish different loyalties, and yet to work together in peace, even perhaps in amity. Human souls cannot be reshaped by altering boundary lines.

At Strasbourg, in 1913, I first realized that the natural consequence of "freedom," "democracy," "consent," is pluralism.
To expect unanimity is naïve; to enforce conformity is tyrannical.

A little later, Jordan got me invited to a Norman Angell
conference at Le Touquet, a resort on the Channel coast. It
was a delightful blend of the week-end party, the expert commission, and the evangelical meeting. Morel, who had so
vigorously exposed the abuses of the Congo Free State under
Leopold II, was there—handsome, his dark complexion glowing as with an inner fire; and there were those fine representatives of the Cocoa-Quaker aristocracy, the Rowntrees. Angell
was abundantly right: war is not good business, except for a
handful of profiteers. The city of London, for generations the
nerve center of the capitalistic world, was steadfastly in favor
of peace. The most orthodox defenders of private enterprise,
the Manchesterians, were pacifists as well as free traders.
Homo Economicus, if he existed, would be too sensible to
fight: his sole desire is to buy in the cheapest market and sell
in the dearest. War is the violent release of primitive passion, and the collapse of human reason: it has very little to
do either with regimes or with interests. If, at the time I
write these lines, many Americans are loudly declaring war
upon Russia, it is not because they have oil claims in the Near
East, or want to open a branch house in northern Korea; and
there is no reason to believe that the communistic Russians
will be less bellicose than the capitalistic Americans. That
is why Norman Angell's demonstration was at the same time
luminous and futile. War does not pay? What of it? There
always will be an Alfred Tennyson to retort:

> Tho' niggard throats of Manchester may bawl, . . .
> We are not cotton-spinners all.

CHAPTER NINE

Houston and the Rice Institute

In 1906, I knew nothing of Williams College; in 1907, nothing of Stanford University; in 1913, nothing of the Rice Institute. My career has been a happy series of leaps in the dark. I trust that the next leap, which cannot be long deferred, will prove no less fortunate.

At his request, I went to San Francisco to meet the president of the Rice Institute, which had just been opened in Houston, Texas. I found Dr. Edgar Odell Lovett a most impressive and suave gentleman, a very Grand Duke among educators. The interview was extremely pleasant, but inconclusive. Dr. Lovett wanted first of all a teacher of Spanish; but, although I am very fond of sonorous Castilian, my mastery of the language was—and remains—limited to reading. And I was not nimble enough to keep, as he suggested, one jump ahead of my students. So I dismissed the matter from my mind; and the invitation from Houston came, if not as a shock, at any rate as a great surprise.

My wife and I both loved Stanford, work and people, climate and spirit. But man does not live by climate alone; nor, to be grossly materialistic, will the spirit of Rabelais and

Ulrich von Hutten meet one's grocery bill. In Babu English, "the wind of freedom butters no parsnip." Stanford was then in its second Stone Age. Making the buildings safe for academic democracy had been an expensive enterprise. I had just been promoted to associate professor, without increase in salary: a Barmecide feast. In some classical comedy, a master asks his valet: "How much am I paying you?"—"Nothing, my Lord."—"Very well: I double your wages." The Rice Institute did offer to double my salary. I had already given one hostage to Fortune. To use a formula familiar to all ministers of the Gospel, "I felt it my duty to accept a wider field of usefulness." But not without misgivings.

Of Houston, I knew nothing at all, not even the local pronunciation of the name, *Hewston*. An encyclopedia, hastily consulted, told me that it was "built on a bluff": a perplexing statement. Friends who had been in Texas informed me that Houston was an inland settlement, on a bayou, "somewhere back of Galveston." The word "bayou" evoked torpid waters infested with alligators. Galveston was decidedly on the map, because a tidal wave had done its best to wipe it off. I was in Brighton when it occurred, and heard a sermon on "the daily benefits of God": "Such catastrophes never happen on the Sussex coast." I thought the reasoning rather tribal.

My ignorance, although inexcusable, was not so shameful as it would be now. Those were the days when the Ship Channel was barely out of the Utopian stage; when Jesse Jones and Will Clayton were rising young businessmen, and not statesmen of international stature; when, to the general public, Colonel House was not even an enigma wrapped in a mystery. I saw Houston turn in a decade from a slumberous semitropical town into a dynamic metropolis, wrestling with historic New Orleans for the scepter of the gulf. Oil and transportation worked the miracle. When Marshal Foch went through Houston (December 7, 1921), I, as master of ceremonies, asked him: "Have you heard the noise of seventeen railroads meeting the sea? No? You are going to hear it now." And, inevitably, the president of the chamber of commerce did give the marshal a most impassioned amplification of Houston's famous slogan.[1]

What first struck me in Houston was the absolute, the miraculous flatness of its site. A suburb was known as Houston Heights, because it was a good eight feet higher than the center of the city; and the Country Club was voted delightfully picturesque, because it contained depressions of at least six feet. The prairie encircling Houston was as illimitable as the sea; and like the sea, it possessed a horizontal majesty more impressive than the hillocks of a crumpled landscape. Over that immensity, the sky was enormous. Nature was boldly simplified, reduced to a single line, stark, functional, yet smiling; for the sky was gay with lazily drifting white clouds, as it seldom is in California. If the humid heat of late summer was oppressive, the nights were luminous and soft, balmy with the steady and gentle breeze from the gulf, fifty miles away.

Houston, which had barely passed the hundred thousand mark,[2] sprawled indefinitely over the prairie. Only Main Street was fully paved, in rather uneven bricks. As the level area was hard to drain, and as the rainstorms were of tropical frequency and violence, the streets were lined with deep open ditches; every house had its little bridge of shaking planks,

[1] Orators were vying in their praises of the great Allied leader—and southern eloquence was in the grandiose and florid tradition. The American colonel who acted as the marshal's interpreter gave the pithiest and most adequate rendering of that splendid rhetoric: *"Comme d'habitude"*: same old stuff. The marshal nodded benignly. There was, however, another strong touch of local color. The marshal was told that, in the scheme of world history, the miracle of the Marne and the storming of the Siegfried Line were very well in their way; but they could not compare with the Battle of San Jacinto, now commemorated by a shaft taller than the Washington Monument.

[2] 78,800 in 1910.

soon decayed in the hot moist atmosphere. After a cloudburst, cars could be seen bogged in all the side streets, axle
deep in gumbo mud.

Houston at that time was purely southern. An excellent
quarterly published in Dallas is devoted to the *culture* of the
Southwest. *Cultures* would be more accurate, for there are
at least three. Dallas and Fort Worth are frankly outposts of
the Middle West, the vigorous young cousins of Chicago, St.
Louis and Kansas City. San Antonio still bears, more than
any single place in California, the imprint of Spain; the vicinity of Mexico is felt, in the buildings and in the people.
Houston was a colony of the old South.

I was unspoilt by literary prejudices. I had never indulged
in those nostalgic visions of the Old South which move so
strangely the natives of Keokuk, Iowa. Faulkner's nightmare
country was still *terra incognita:* we did not know what de-
lectable horrors we were missing. I had glanced at *Uncle
Tom's Cabin,* but purely in the light of a campaign document;
by 1913, only a few episodes survived as semihumorous bits
of folklore. O. Henry's story, "A Municipal Report," had
struck me as a very fine piece of work, a perfect epitome of
his smart, journalistic, yet very genuine art, all complete with
wisecracks, atmosphere, humor, pathos, and trick ending. It
happened that for the first few weeks of our Houston life,
we boarded in a house where the odor of aristocratic decay
was faint but undeniable. It created a curious association in
my mind between crystal candlesticks and cockroaches. Like
all growing cities, Houston had blighted areas which had been
the haunts of elegant society. Certain streets lined with once-
proud mansions, their pillars askew, their white paint blistered
and peeling, their lawns a weed patch, seemed a perfect setting for mournful tales of shabby-gentility. With a Hollywood sense of atmosphere (although Hollywood was but an
infant then), Nature draped the live oaks with the ragged gray

lace of Spanish moss, a Baudelairian growth which brings beauty and death.

But it would have taken a more determined sentimentalist than I am to linger in that sweet melancholy twilight. The essential fact was that Houston was conscious of a new day, and facing it with eager joy. I imagine we caught Houston at its delightful and evanescent best, when southern grace and leisureliness still held in check the bustle and the ruthlessness of the competitive market. Old families were growing rich again: but those who lagged behind in that race for wealth were still honored members of the best society. Genealogies —all our friends had delightful albums with ingenious little windows—counted for more than bankbooks. A very dear lady boasted (but the term is too coarse for such a true gentlewoman) that she belonged to "one of the First Families in Louisiana": First Families in Louisiana were transported, for the good of the old country; and Manon Lescaut, with a little better luck, might have founded one.

All this was Old Southern rather than purely Texan. For the original Texans were not aristocrats, but adventurers: sea pirates and land pirates. There were still faint traces of the heroic old days. The watchman at our bank—a particularly mild-looking citizen, with a shy and kindly smile—was reputed to be quicker to the draw than any man in Texas. The Unwritten Law was almost the only one which commanded universal respect: the Ten Commandments and the Constitution of the United States trailed a long way behind. A *gentleman* shot another *gentleman* dead through a door of the Rice Hotel. He was on the wrong floor, and apologized. But as the affair was between gentlemen, and there was a lady in the case, the jury promptly returned a negative verdict.

The Rice Institute was part of the new day for Houston; and it was welcomed with almost as much enthusiasm as the Ship Channel and the Humble Oil Field. There was a neat mystery story about the Rice bequest. William Marsh Rice died leaving a great deal of his property to his lawyer; but —through some ghost writer, no doubt—he also signed checks after his death. This unusual procedure aroused suspicion; and it was hinted that Rice had been poisoned by his valet at the instigation of the lawyer. This learned gentleman managed to save his neck, but not his legacy; and for many years, he kept up his practice in the West, the shield of widows and orphans. He must have been a very good criminal lawyer.

So the money went, as originally intended, to the Rice Institute. The name had been selected by the founder; no one knew exactly what he meant by it—probably a trade school. This uncertainty was embarrassing at times. I was asked: "How many *inmates* has the Rice Institute?"—a misconception justified by the fact that the great wrought-iron gates were kept severely closed at all times. When my colleague Colonel Blayney went through Indo-China, a French official told him: "We are awaiting with impatience the publications of the Rice Institute; for the rice crop is a matter of life and death in this country." Dr. Lovett added the comprehensive subtitle: "A University of Liberal and Technical Learning, Dedicated to the Advancement of Letters, Science and Art." He wanted to make it an institute in almost every sense of the term: on the broad foundation of a good college, a graduate school of technology, a research center, and also an Athenaeum, a place where visiting or resident lecturers could, without loss of self-respect, address an intelligent general public. It was his desire to keep Rice in close touch with the leaders of the city; and although the institute was built in the prairie, several miles from the center, Lovett managed to turn feasts of learning into brilliant society affairs. Country Club audiences, if you like, but the keenest, as well as the friendliest, that I have ever met.

Dr. Lovett, being an astronomer, had a lofty ideal. *Tout bien ou rien:* nothing but the best is good enough. He did not fully succeed: men have a regrettable way of being human, and the limits even of a generous endowment are soon reached, when prices begin to soar. There was in him the flaw which, according to Aristotle, often is the excess of a virtue. Lofty in thought and speech, he was also lofty in bearing, with the scrupulous courtesy of a royal personage. He could be frigid. Dr. Cook, the highly imaginative arctic explorer, exclaimed after meeting him: "At last, I have discovered the North Pole!" The folklike quality of David Starr Jordan was not in him; and his exquisite taste would not permit him even to attempt that which was repellent to his nature. He was aloof and lonely. Universally respected, he was also genuinely beloved; but no one would presume to let him know. I am now breaking the reticence of many years only because he and I are academic ghosts.

He set up his standard from the very first. The formal opening of the Rice Institute was a most elaborate ceremony; it attracted leaders of thought from many countries; Houston, for a few days, became the intellectual capital of the world. The celebration is commemorated in three magnificent volumes. The original faculty was hand-picked with the most fastidious care: I realized, when I met my new colleagues, what a distinction it had been for me to be selected, on the promissory note of a single book. The professor of English was Stockton Axson, Woodrow Wilson's brother-in-law; not a productive scholar, but one of the most effective lecturers I have ever heard. A perennial bachelor, a great society favorite, the gentlest of lions, Axson could have impersonated Mr. Micawber even better than W. C. Fields. The professor of Physics, H. A. Wilson, was a Fellow of the Royal Society, and later preferred Rice to Lord Kelvin's chair in Glasgow. In Mathematics, C. G. Evans was already on the highroad to

fame, Harvard constantly trying to lure him back. Biology
was taught by Julian Huxley, poet, essayist, traveler as well
as scientist, now secretary of UNESCO. His grandfather's
renown rather frightened the orthodox, for Texas nearly followed Tennessee in voting that the earth is flat. A neighbor
explained to us: "I don't mind; my daughters have been well
brought up; they can listen to him all day, and not believe a
word he says." In Philosophy, our mentor was Radoslav
Andrea Tsanoff, the liveliest and kindliest spirit that ever
sprang out of Bulgaria. He made us love that country, in
spite of its unfortunate habit of backing the wrong horse. He
has wrestled with *The Nature of Evil* and *The Problem of Im-
mortality* without losing his indomitable cheerfulness. But I
cannot transcribe the early faculty list of the Rice Institute:
all valued colleagues and loyal friends. Their careers proved
that Lovett from his Olympian heights was able to discern,
not achievement merely, but promise as well.

There were a few exceptions to mar that fine record; some
tragic—three at least of my Rice acquaintances committed
suicide—one infinitely pathetic. At seventeen, William James
Sidis was a graduate assistant in Mathematics. Evans vouches
for his ability in that field. I can certify that he had unusual
gifts as a linguist. The boy was healthy, sane and, I believe,
normal in every respect. He was the victim, not of the in-
tensive education given him by his father Dr. Boris Sidis, not
of the romantic curse called Genius, but of the thoughtless
cruelty of the public. He was treated like a two-headed calf.
His boyish singularities—and what lad of seventeen is a pattern of mellow wisdom—were mercilessly exposed and ampli-
fied. Because he blurted out that he had never kissed a girl,
he was made the butt of endless practical jokes. Then he committed the crime, in common with G. B. Shaw, Julian Huxley,
H. G. Wells, Henri Barbusse, André Gide, Romain Rolland, of
becoming interested in the Russian Revolution. That was long

before the time when Messrs. Wendell Willkie, Joseph Davies, Eric Johnston, made an attitude of intelligent sympathy respectable. In the dark Mitchell Palmer era, he was positively hounded. He broke down; he tried to forget his learning, and to do penance for his torturing notoriety. He lived on for a quarter of a century, obscure, resentful, wasted: a crime on our collective conscience.

In architecture also, it was Lovett's desire to set a standard. He could do so with a clear conscience. Stanford, I noted, had to go through the ordeal of a second Stone Age; but in the spacious early days of Rice, the income was adequate both for decent salaries and for elaborate buildings. The object of this architectural perfection was not conspicuous waste: the high standard was a discipline, a costly but effective lesson. The school, in that easygoing southland, was to be faultlessly attired, like Lovett himself, and like the legendary British engineer who, the only white man in a Bolivian mining camp, would dress correctly for dinner. The lesson was taken to heart. I left Rice twelve years after its opening: the careless youngsters had taken no liberties with its beautiful walls.

The designing had been entrusted to Cram, Goodhue and Ferguson. That famous partnership was dissolved before construction was well under way; Cram remained in sole charge, with W. W. Watkins as his very able local representative. From the aesthetic point of view, the institute raised many problems. Cram was an artist, which is the supreme way of being a functionalist: I am not sure that the converse is true. He believed in poetry, music, painting, statuary: the beauty that exists for its own sake, on its own merits, not as a byproduct, or as a premium for efficiency. The Rice Institute is a work of art, that is to say a luxury: like Solomon's Temple, the Parthenon, the Pantheon, the Sainte-Chapelle and the Taj Mahal. Cram refused to consider a university as a factory for the "processing" of young minds.

When I first beheld the institute, I was struck by the perfection of its color scheme. It has the same quality as that of the Grand Canyon; in description, it might seem brilliantly bizarre; in reality, it is a tapestry, rich but subdued. White marble framing the great archway, tinted marbles for the columns and the ornamental slabs, stand out without violent contrast against a background of tawny brick, which on certain days has a salmon tinge. At all hours, but especially in the evening, the walls absorb the light and make it a part of their own texture: Cram had drafted the sun as his co-decorator. To me, the effect was not gorgeous, but friendly: the buildings offered themselves as a bouquet of welcome.

The administration building, which is the key of the whole scheme, produced on me an impression of strangeness. It was like one of those arresting faces that cannot be deciphered at a glance. The thing was too perfectly in harmony with the atmosphere to seem exotic. It was not defiantly dramatic, like a Piranesi, a Gustave Doré, or the Pittsburgh jail. Nor was it willfully picturesque, like the Zwinger in Dresden, the Brighton Pavilion, or the dear old Trocadero. With strong, simple lines, it was restrained, and reposeful. Yet it would not tell its whole secret.

It had, manifestly, a style, which was not that of the sheds at the turning basin. Cram loved Gothic, and could use it with the freedom of a master; but he had felt it would not be suitable to Houston's subtropical climate. There was no local tradition, either Colonial or Spanish: Houston never had been a Mexican city. Connoisseurs would tell you that the whole had a Venetian, or more accurately, Dalmatian character, with a tinge of the Byzantine and hints of the Persian. Of course, it was absurd to erect a Dalmatian monument in the Texas Prairie, and the Rice Institute had no desire to foster a Byzantine turn of mind, especially with Persian overtones. But this orthodox objection was valid only for the erudite, who could trace the details to their distant source. For Cram himself, the work was not a pastiche, but a free creation in a chosen key. Faculty, students, visitors, did not worry about the origin of the motives, any more than, in common intercourse, we fret about etymologies. Let theories bury their theories! (They inevitably do.) I lived for nine years in and with the Rice Institute, and Cram's symphony in brick and marble was to me a constant source of joy.

Houston society might have "taken up" the Rice faculty, with all the patronizing that the ugly phrase implies. What did happen was very different. The Rice trustees were among the leaders in the city; and it seemed to them that trustees and professors, associated in a great new venture, might very naturally be friends. We were not lionized: a very pleasant circle widened itself to admit new members. They were not overawed by our alleged learning any more than we were by their reputed wealth. I felt myself transported back to my Utopia, the eighteenth century, the age when sociability was the supreme art. In such a world, shabbiness is a sin, but not so deadly as vulgar display; dullness is a crime, but more venial than the brilliancy that demands the spotlight. No topic is barred—I talked socialism and racial equality without being tarred and feathered; but pedants must leave their erudition in the cloakroom, cranks their pet nostrum, prophets their righteous anger. Within the charmed circle, the first rule is courtesy, which means, not etiquette, but kindliness. That circle, I knew, was not the whole of life; beyond it were found the deeper concerns and the higher values: work, fight, and solitude. But a man whose inner life is austere is entitled to his modicum of luxury. And there is no luxury that can compare with good company. There certainly is none that is so hard to find.

I must not give the impression that the Rice faculty were engaged in a maddening pursuit of pleasure. Our lives were sedate, provincial and suburban: formal parties were rare enough not to be burdensome. And our city friends likewise were righteous and sober—within reason. Only the debutantes, poor things, were worked to death in the service of Society. It was easy in those days not to be a recluse without being hectic. There were so many hospitable homes that night clubs were unnecessary; and, before Prohibition, there was nothing smart about hard drinking. Our associates were not drones or butterflies. Indeed, in comparison, we were the gentlemen of leisure. Lovett, walking up to the institute, would cross Will Clayton walking briskly to his office downtown; for in that prehistoric epoch, men found it possible to use their legs on the sidewalks, and not exclusively on the golf links. The ladies were busy and competent housekeepers: supervising a large colored staff is no sinecure. They all had their church and civic activities.

The drawing rooms and the Country Club were not our only meeting places. Most of our amusements were family affairs, such as American folk enjoy throughout the vast continent: drives and picnics. If we had our unobtrusive place in Houston's social life, our friends in return had academic interests. They religiously attended our public lectures, and there was nothing formal about the cordial smile that greeted the speaker. The Art League, the Philosophical Society, were familiar meeting grounds. We had a delightful Town and Gown dinner club. We shared with the chamber of commerce the privilege of welcoming distinguished visitors—Marshal Foch, President Taft, President Lowell, Sir Auckland Geddes. I remember driving with Lorado Taft throughout the city, in hopeless quest of a monument that would pass muster. We finally took him to "The Spirit of the Confederacy," with broken sword and drooping wings. Alas! It would not do: the wings were not properly attached. We entertained Maurice Maeterlinck, his young countess and a motley retinue. I never met a man so intensely and aggressively bored. He had come to loathe *The Blue Bird*, which, in the public mind, had devoured all his other works; and, ineluctably, the dining room had been turned into a teeming aviary of paper blue-birds.

I am perfectly conscious that these southern memories, although honest and real enough, are not realistic. A vanished Arcadia has a poignant charm, even though, at the time, it was more than half a dream. Talleyrand said in his old age: "Whoever has not lived before 1789 does not know the sweetness of life." He was mourning for a dead world, but above all for his dead youth. Before 1789, in his episcopal days, he may have been harassed by debts, intrigues, squabbles and shady love affairs. The tenor of our life in Houston was commonplace enough, which, for a resolute optimist like myself, is no reproach: the pleasant routine of teaching, the youngsters growing, with all the ills that young flesh is heir to, and acquiring a southern drawl. There was also the constant fight against a leaky roof, a balky furnace, irrepressible insect hordes, and a basement determined to turn into a swimming pool. In a landscape, it is possible for every detail to be ordinary: all that matters is the quality of the light. The light of friendliness in Houston was sufficient to create a very pleasing picture.

I am an inveterate and unrepentant fellow traveler: I have repeatedly found myself associated with people whose prejudices were in contradiction with my principles (no, the terms cannot be reversed). I am not totalitarian enough to condemn a man *in toto* because his pronunciation of "shibboleth" is not the same as mine. On a partisan basis, my Houston friends and I were on opposite sides of the barricade. We should have been sniping at one another. At times, it is excellent to leave dummies, with wooden guns, to watch the barricade; whilst "the common man," on either side, takes time off and goes on a picnic. It might lead us to the simple and profound thought: "Why should there be any barricade at all?"

Of all the barricades that should not be there, the most formidable was the race question. I came to Houston in 1913, with very definite convictions; I left in 1924, with my convictions confirmed. The verdict was all the clearer in my mind because it was untainted with any animus. The people whom I condemned were my friends. I knew, not only how charming they were, but how good. It was a second case of deep affection coupled with total disagreement.

I soon realized that, on one point, the southerners were right. They claimed that they liked the Negroes, and they did. This undeniable fondness is an essential element in the problem. Cram suggested once the logical solution: since the South refuses to treat the Negroes according to the letter of the Constitution and in the spirit of Christianity, it should let them go. When it was propounded, the plan seemed fantastic; with the experience of the Second World War, it appears feasible. Within a generation, perhaps within a decade, ten million colored people could be shipped across the Atlantic. Liberia failed miserably only because it was an experiment on too small a scale, and starved from the beginning. After two centuries of training in the house of bondage, the returned Africans could be the leaven of their homeland, and turn it into a mighty nation. For every black man leaving our shores, there would be two Nordics eager to enter. From the economic point of view, it is well known that cheap labor is a drag on a nation's economy. If we are in a position to flood the world with goods, it is because we pay the highest wages. All this, in strict logic, is irrefutable. The magnitude of the scheme is not the final objection: the southerners could not bear to see the colored people go. They want to keep them, not to torment them, not to exploit them, but because the Negroes are an indispensable part of their southern life. Without them, the South would be mutilated, a mere "colorless" extension of the drab and practical North. The culture so tenaciously defended by the conservatism of the South includes both races.

So the South wants to keep the Negroes, and claims that it is treating them well. I am not familiar with the factories and the cotton fields. But in domestic service, I can testify that colored help in Houston received better treatment than the corresponding class in London and Paris. Their little houses in the back of the lot were less dismal than the garrets I had seen in my native city; even the shacks of the Negro districts, undrained, unkempt and ruinous as they were, compared favorably with the "Bidonvilles" (Tin Can Alleys) that formed a zone of squalor round the City of Light. For sheer degradation and horror, the slums of Liverpool are unsurpassed. I remember the days when a Paris *bonne* had one day out every month; Houston cooks and maids had a day and a half free every week. I saw in Texas nothing of that studied arrogance affected in Europe by employers, especially the *petits bourgeois;* an arrogance too often matched by the studied and sullen servility of the servants. In the South, even a scolding had a touch of human warmth. It might be sharp, yet it left no wound, for it was "in the family." Southerners are accused of treating their retainers as though they were domestic animals: I have often thought what a Heaven this world could be, if only we behaved to our fellow men as we do to our dogs.

I had not expected harrowing scenes in the South, and I saw none. The colored proletariat was manifestly well fed and cheerful. Yet I felt from the first that the whole idea of racial discrimination was damnable; and my smoldering indignation did not abate with the years.

As you know, I am historically minded. I have an invincible fondness for quaint survivals; and Le Corbusier's plan for the reconstruction of Paris would have filled me with horror, even if it had been technically sound. So I enjoyed in the South, as I did in London, associating with people who were steeped in the past. My Houston friends might be very up to date in their business transactions; in their thought, they were delightfully unreconstructed. They were admirable period pieces. They still cherished, undimmed, their vital myth. For them, the delicate and harmonious culture of the South had been crushed and almost annihilated under the brutal weight of the North; but it remained lovelier, in memory and defeat, than the coarse power by which it had been overwhelmed. Like Germany after 1919, they refused to endorse in their heart a "Guilt Clause" imposed by the sword. And they were not satisfied with noble and melancholy memories. If only they kept true to their tradition, they might, like Greece of old, civilize and conquer their savage victors. They had not forgotten what the North had attempted to substitute for the gracious pattern of southern life: the grotesque carnival of the Carpetbaggers. Myths are more potent in history than material realities: it is not for facts, but for dreams, that men fight and die. This southern myth, thirty years ago, still ruled the most generous minds in the South; and strangely enough, in spite of the healthy growth of the Lincoln legend, it had conquered the North. There is no more striking example of *Revanche* in the spirit than the ultimate and decisive victory of Lee over Grant. We are apologetic about Grant; but every one of us feels himself a little more of a gentleman for being a worshiper of Lee.

But ghosts, fossils, museum pieces—House of Lords, Jacobites, D.A.R., Confederacy—can be enjoyed with a clear conscience only if they are harmless; and the spirit of the past is welcome in the present only if it breathes noble thoughts. When tradition is used to bolster injustice, no sentimentality should blur our sight or stay our hands. And, although some of the best southerners are callous to the implications of their creed, race prejudice is not a wreath on the tomb of the Lost Cause: it is a curse. Even if it did not affect the material interests of both races, it would inflict upon both incalculable harm. It is not good for a ruling caste to pin its whole faith to an idol which is, at bottom, a lie. It corrupts politics; it paralyzes thought; it fosters that unreasoning arrogance which we found so unbearable in Imperial and Nazi Germany.

Even if the Negroes were as well paid, as decently treated, as the white proletariat is in many parts of the world, the fundamental injustice would still rankle in their soul. We are told that they are happy and thoughtless; that religion, love and song are comforts which no Jim Crow law can take away from them; that if it were not for northern agitators, they would be perfectly satisfied with the southern way of life. Even if only a few were sensitive to the stigma imposed upon them, inflicting it would still be a crime. In my youth, I struggled against an injustice suffered by a single man, Dreyfus, because he was the symbol of our common dignity. If there were but a single Negro tortured in the Devil's Island of our contemptuous prejudice, we should not cease from mental fight. To acquiesce in such an evil is degrading.

But it is too easy to declare that the Negroes do not suffer, because they are carefree and childlike. There must be in thousands of hearts moments of nameless despair and revolt. Resentment seldom flares into violence, not merely because the oppressed are cowed into submission, but above all because they are truer Christians than we are. Religion is not merely an escape into a less cruel world: in this world, it strengthens their patience, and makes it more difficult for them to hate. But their meekness cannot be our excuse; and our oppression is none the less cruel, when it uses invisible chains, and a whip which spares the body and lashes the spirit.

We were served for a number of years by a whole tribe, one member after the other. The matriarch, old Lou, born in slavery, illiterate, was in bearing, speech and soul a true aristocrat. She had brought up her daughters to the best of her ability, and they were fine girls, elegant, clever, loyal and gentle. Yet we could see the curse falling upon them. No truly independent position could be theirs; they could not have moved away from their ramshackle neighborhood. Inexorably, the low standard forced upon them by the contemptuous indulgence of the whites had its effect. How difficult, when you are branded as a "nigger," not to behave like a "nigger!" So they began to pilfer, as they were expected to do; and to divorce with the facility of famous heiresses and Hollywood stars. We could see the true nobility that was in their mother fade and crumble in them. And I felt convinced that this silent, barely conscious tragedy was repeated all over the city, all over the South, all over the nation.

I came in the South to a conclusion which at first was startling, and very soon appeared irrelevant: that the race problem did not exist as such. "Race" is a misnomer: the question is not anthropological, but social. The southerners, I repeat, are right: blacks and whites do not instinctively hate each other as cats hate dogs. There is no repugnance to the closest

Houston and the Rice Institute

physical propinquity. Talk of segregation! Southern homes are swarming with colored servants. It would be intolerable if a Negro preacher should erect his house next to a white man's; but there are servants' quarters in every back yard. No one objects when a Negress sits with the white folks in a streetcar, if she is escorting a white child.

This does not rob the problem of its tragic character; it simply tears off a flimsy pseudoscientific mask; and it reveals that the difficulty is universal. The barrier, I repeat, is social, not physiological. The attitude of the southerners toward their Negroes is scrupulously the same as that of the nobles under the ancient regime toward the commoners. It is that— and it survived at least as late as the First World War—of the officer, a gentleman, toward the enlisted man, presumably riffraff. In a well-organized society, a properly integrated "culture," everyone has his status and knows his place. The classes are not fluid: they seek to attain the rigidity of castes. To break down the barriers between them would cause the whole edifice to topple. Religion, in days not so very remote, gave this hierarchical arrangement its blessing; in return, the clergy, in most countries, formed the first of the privileged orders. Free thought, science, democracy, blew down these artificial distinctions. Within the same decade, Jefferson proclaimed the equality of all men as a self-evident truth, and Figaro sneered at those noble lords who "had merely taken the trouble of being born."

But men and nations, tormented by a secret dread of inferiority, will not be satisfied with an equality that would compel them constantly to prove their worth. They seek the security of a definite status, irrespective of their own questionable merits. A true aristocracy is equalitarian: because it has no fear, it demands no favor. A spurious aristocracy must seek the protection of shibboleths, customs, laws, and, as an ultimate argument, terror. It seems as though the most precious

right of the citizen were that of despising others. Aristocracy
was supposed to be "in the blood": the race feeling is but
aristocracy democratically extended, and vulgarized. Not all
Germans could be members of the *Junker* class; but every
German is a *Junker*, a member of the master race, compared
with the surrounding hordes of Latins and Slavs: Nordic
blood is noble blood. The British or Welsh miner on the dole
for years, the slum dweller, accepted the social privileges of
nobility and gentry with surprising meekness. But he held the
gorgeous East in fee; he was a lord himself, when he thought
of those dusky heathens who displayed big diamonds and
called themselves rajahs. Color is not the test: the British
overlords had that feeling for the Irish, the Prussians for the
Poles, the French colonists for the Berbers. The same gnawing desire for inequality is found in our democracy. We are
aware that there are privileged groups, and that their lives
are freer, more ample than ours. We seek compensation by
drawing an even sharper line below us. So the sharecropper,
the common laborer, the very small shopkeeper in the South,
will restore his self-respect by "keeping the nigger in his
place." And the contagion spreads North and West. There
have been race riots in Detroit; union men struck in San
Francisco to maintain the color line, and high school students
in Los Angeles. It is human, but it is not civilized.

Color, of course, is a godsend to those who spurn equality,
because it is indelible. All other tests might fail. In *Pygmalion,*
Shaw attempts to prove that to be a lady is a matter of pho-
netics. Commoners may amass wealth. Beauty and genius
are often found among the "common people." All the pitiful
little shibboleths of the old aristocracy—etiquette, good
clothes, the classics, horsemanship—may prove inadequate.
What a blessing it is to have a "lower class" that cannot break
its bonds! And how jealously we must guard the one way of
escape, the open and legitimate mingling of the races!

After a decade in the South, it was not the South I blamed most for the blight. There were historical extenuating circumstances. It is impossible for the patient to cure his own disease, when he cherishes it with pride. What I could not, and cannot, condone is the apathy of the country as a whole. We accept with resignation, and even with relief, the fact that we have morally lost the Civil War. We even attempt to persuade ourselves that slavery had nothing to do with the conflict, and that Lincoln became the Emancipator by sheer accident. The unsolved problem weighs on our soul. We refuse to acknowledge remorse; but our sense of guilt is there, and makes a mockery of our crusading attitudes. Eloquent voices are urging a return to religion: but no religion is worthy of the name, if it places an arrogant idol above brotherhood and love. We are the self-appointed champions of liberty; but there is no genuine liberty without equality of status. Among the competing "ways of life," that one will deserve to win that evolves the most generous solution of the race problem. In that contest for moral leadership, we have lost our lead. We could easily regain it, if only we believed in our own principles.[3]

[3] I am quite conscious—but it is melancholy comfort—that in this respect we are far from the worst. South Africa under Boer leadership, and with the blessing of grand old Marshal Smuts, far out-Herods our own South; and Kenya, on a smaller scale, goes to even greater lengths. The most caste-ridden country in the world is, of course, India. Had England used her long period of domination to batter down the caste prejudice, she would deserve to rule still. But she only added one caste, the most arrogant of all, on top of the others, and thus forfeited her claim to Empire.

CHAPTER TEN

I Become an American

FOR THE first seven years of my American life, at Williams and at Stanford, I had taken no active part in public affairs. Not that I ever felt a stranger in this hospitable land. My coming here was not an exile, but a family reunion. I never swerved from my decision to make America my home. My restraint was not due to any lack of political interest: It was inspired, I believe, by a very natural scruple. Even the friendliest of cousins, if brought up abroad, had better not obtrude his opinions about home affairs until he is thoroughly acquainted with conditions in his new land. Although France and America are "sister republics" (in every platitude there is a kernel of truth), there are on either side innumerable oddities and apparent absurdities to master. A very useful dictionary helps us protect ourselves against "False Friends," those delusive words and phrases which are closely similar in both languages, but with very different meanings. How could a Frenchman guess that a man might accept a *clerical* job, without any taint of clericalism? That a Republican is not democratic, and a Democrat is no republican? That, in very definite cases, Bourbon and Democrat might be synonymous?

That, by God's holy ordinance, *public* utilities should be in private hands? That a giant *collective* enterprise like General Motors is a monument of rugged individualism? That the party which believes in a free market, the ineluctability of economic laws and the wisdom of *laisser faire,* is also the one that advocates protection? That there are no classes in America, but that, although nonexistent, they should co-operate on friendly terms? That party loyalty is a virtue, and the party spirit a vice? That the Eternal Verities of the Constitution are as luminous as the sun in the heavens, but that four out of the Nine Old Men most learned in the law may fail to see the light? And so on ad infinitum. The vocabulary of politics, even more than that of philosophy, was given man so that he might conceal his thought. I could not express an opinion on American affairs until I had solved those riddles—or discovered they were insoluble.[1]

There was another excuse for my abstention. Thélème, as I like to call Stanford, is an admirable institution, but with the aloof charm of an Ivory Tower. We were not absorbed in our selfish pleasures and concerns; but, beyond our intimate circle, we could see nothing without either the telescope or the microscope. The problems of San Francisco and California remained in a blur. For an object to engage our scholarly attention, it had to be very far away, very long ago, or else infinitely small.

The perspective changed altogether when we moved to Houston. We were at once in close touch with the city. I may, at one time, have dreamt of a modern religious order, seeking perfect freedom in the service of science, and rejecting all other bonds as unworthy. But, as the husband of a very

---

[1] Few Americans, of course, have found their way through the corresponding intricacies of French public life. A generation ago, a Liberal was a conservative, a Progressive a reactionary, a Radical a trimmer and time-server, a Radical-Socialist the sworn enemy of socialism, while Traditionalists like Maurras wanted to reverse violently the immemorial course of French history.

American wife, the father of two exceedingly American children, I allowed that monkish Utopia to fade unregretted. I still believe that a university teacher should have world-wide principles and a cosmopolitan experience. But it is possible to serve the Common Cause and sympathize with the Common Man everywhere in the world, to enjoy Bali, Montparnasse, Chelsea or Salzburg better than Muncie or Grand Rapids, and yet to have a land that you fondly call your own. Southern friendliness performed the miracle. I was no longer detached. I struck root in the land of cotton. I felt with pride that "the eyes of Texas were upon me."

Yet my position, without being ambiguous, remained hard to define. I was asked to speak; I spoke with the utmost freedom, for I had been accepted as a child of the house. But if my heretical views were not resented, it was because my friends would make allowances for my foreign birth. I was a privileged character, like a king's jester. My cosmopolitan upbringing robbed my subversive opinions of their sting, and also of their efficacy. Every privilege has to be paid for in the end. An American voice with French—or Esperanto—overtones may be listened to with amused tolerance, but does not carry conviction. In all essentials, I insist that I am the standard American citizen although I cannot forget my Renan.

In August, 1914, we were at the seashore in southern California—at Long Beach, I believe—when big headlines caught our attention:

ANGELS DEFEATED

and, less obtrusively:

WAR DECLARED

It took me a few minutes to realize that the ill-fated Angels were not the heavenly host so staunchly supported by Disraeli,[2] but a local baseball team.

The war dispelled the last shadow of ambiguity that might have lingered in my mind. I received the news, not as a Frenchman, but as an American. I had been very comfortable as a hyphenate. My chosen task was to present to American students the civilization of my native country; in this activity, I served both lands, and was loyal to both. My position, although less prominent, was similar to that of Kuno Francke at Harvard. It would have been easy for me to remain, first of all, the interpreter of France; and at times there is but a shadowy difference between an interpreter and an advocate. I do not believe my friends would have taken it amiss; indeed it was expected of me. I had only to swim with the tide; for, from the very first moment, our hearts went out to France. I was not laboring under the same handicap as Hugo Münsterberg who, ably, honestly, courageously, offered himself as the champion of the unpopular German cause.

For the verdict of America, after the march through Belgium, was instantaneous and unequivocal. How difficult it is to write history! All this was plain and palpable a generation ago; but the old have forgotten, the young never knew; controversialists have befuddled the issue, and scholars have only made the confusion more learned. No campaign from abroad was necessary. Later, the most outrageous propaganda was of purely American origin. It told us what we wanted to believe; the Allies could not keep up with our demands. We thought that the British carried too far their old habit of reticence and understatement. The French ambassador, Jusserand, was wise enough to keep very quiet. The Germans, for nearly three years, had a free field; I was deluged with pro-German propaganda in English, in French,

[2] "I, my Lord, I am on the side of the angels. . . ." Disraeli, 1864.

in German, and even in Esperanto. Münsterberg, George Sylvester Viereck, and a host of others, took full advantage of their opportunity.

That overwhelming decision against Germany was not the result of any hostile prejudice. On the contrary, before 1914, no country had enjoyed greater favor in America. There were still traces of anti-British feeling, which the Irish did their best to keep alive. The French expedition in Mexico had left long and unpleasant memories. But the policy of Germany had never openly clashed with our own. America took it for granted that German philosophy, German music, German science, ruled the world. Our higher education was Germanized to an incredible degree—even the departments of Romanic Languages. We admired the efficiency of German industry, which ours was only just beginning to match. Our respect was not tinged with fear; it glowed with sympathy. The antics of the Kaiser jarred on our nerves at times; but we refused to take him tragically. It seemed as though he were playing, none too well but harmlessly, a part in a Wagnerian opera. We forgot the spiked helmet and the spiked mustache of the figurehead; we remembered that we had millions of excellent citizens who had come from Germany. Americans visiting the *Vaterland* returned with reports of a clean, hardworking, orderly, good-natured folk. We liked the Germans then, as we still do. We had not realized, and we are in danger of forgetting, that there are brutal depths in the nature even of the most cultured people; that, for over a century, German philosophy, literature and history had willfully attempted to release and exalt the primitive, that is to say the barbaric; that, if the beast within, thus encouraged, should break loose, the civilized forces would be at a disadvantage, through their very gentleness; that the wisest would be silenced, not through cowardice, not even through a lifelong habit of dis-

cipline, but through the most fatal and sacrilegious of fallacies: "My country, right or wrong!"

I was not even tempted to turn propagandist. I was requested to give a series of lectures on "The Problems of the
Great War," and many of my friends were chilled by their
studied objectivity. My London publisher, Mr. T. Fisher
Unwin, asked for the text, liked it, and even announced the
book; but British censorship demanded so many alterations
that I withdrew the manuscript. In other lectures, which appeared as *Five Masters of French Romance*, I criticized un-
sparingly the nationalism of Maurice Barrès, and endorsed
Romain Rolland's gospel of Franco-German reconciliation.
This was not done in obedience to the plea of President Wilson for absolute neutrality. He had the right, through proper
legislation, to curb unneutral acts; I never recognized his
right to abridge my freedom of speech or thought. Neutrality
has a definite and legitimate meaning in diplomacy; in the
case of individuals, it would imply indifference, which is
contemptible. History, which it was my business to study and
to teach, is not neutral: it should be objective. Judges and
juries are not neutral: they strive to be impartial.

Partisanship and neutrality were the classic Charybdis and
Scylla; there were other perils ahead. The Dreyfus Case had
made me an antinationalist and an antimilitarist. Naturally
enough, under Jordan's influence, I had become a thoroughgoing antibellicist. I fully believed that war pays neither
material nor spiritual dividends. Nothing can be proved,
nothing settled, by war alone. I knew that besides irreparable
devastation war leaves unquenchable hatreds behind. It was
tempting to side with David Starr Jordan, William Jennings
Bryan, Frederick Libby, and other "Advocates of Peace."

If only we could follow, unswervingly, one clear, absolute
command: "Thou shalt not kill"! But it was plain to me that

all the efforts of appeasers and pacifists could have but one result: the triumph of German militarism. They paralyzed the law-abiding nations, and did not affect the aggressors. Even a "white peace" would have been a victory for the Kaiser. Because they had spurned the law, the Central Powers had wrought destruction in Serbia, Poland, Belgium and France, and suffered very little damage themselves. The plain lesson of a White Peace would have been: "Be sure to strike the first blow." The predominance of *Junkerdom* in Europe would have been unchallenged, and German nationalism exalted to a new pinnacle of frenzy. As an antimilitarist, I did not relish the prospect.

There was in my mind a deeper reason for rejecting pacifism in its logical form of nonresistance. I have asked many friends—John Haynes Holmes in particular: "What would you do if you saw a wild beast crouching to attack a child?" "But man," they answered, "is not a wild beast! Man is the image of God!" Man, maddened by drink or despair, pride or lust, becomes an unreasoning brute; and if no other means avails, a would-be murderer should be shot down like a brute. The beasts of prey are no less to be resisted if they gather into packs and if the packs obey a rigid discipline. Firemen have the right to fight fire with fire; the police are empowered to use their guns on gangsters.

I knew that such arguments could be invoked, were invoked indeed, on both sides. In 1914, "cultured" Germany waged preventive war in order to protect, not herself alone, but Europe, from Tzarist tyranny; just as, a generation later, Hitler nobly laid down his life and that of his people to save the world from communism. But no principle is proved wrong because hypocrites, madmen or criminals use it as a cloak; else all religion would have perished from the world long ago. If self-righteousness is a pitfall, so are indifference and cynicism. The only clear lesson is that we should not act without submitting our motives to the most rigorous criticism. But if, after searching our hearts, our purpose still stands, firm and pure, we have no right to hold back.

Thanks to Wilson's restraining hand, America had time to probe her conscience. It could be said, as in 1776, as in 1861: "These are the times that try men's souls." It was for me a second Dreyfus Case, on an enormously larger scale; and men were not ashamed of being swayed by justice rather than profit.

In this great controversy, two elements affected me very little, because I took them for granted: the first was the atrocity stories; the other the tradition of isolationism.

I believed the atrocity stories, on the whole, even though I surmised that many were exaggerated or fabricated. How trifling they now seem, compared with the undeniable realities of the Second World War! But I could not blame the Germans for deliberately using *Schrecklichkeit,* for frightfulness is the very essence of war. We all know that Sherman was right; and the most telling cartoons of Raemaeckers were mild compared with the old etchings of Callot or Goya. "The laws of war" might have a meaning when battle was the sport of kings. When it became a life-and-death struggle between nations, the supreme law, the only law, was that of survival. What is the purpose of war? To inflict torture upon your opponent until you have broken his will to resistance. If by starving millions of women and children—the aim of the British blockade—that end can be achieved, starvation will be resorted to without a qualm. President Truman's very good average conscience was unruffled, when he ordered the atomic bomb to be used. To seek humanity and compassion in war is a romantic absurdity; there is no curb to man's fiendishness but the fear of reprisals. The result of confused thinking is to mitigate, not the horrors of war, but the hatred that we ought to feel for war. Militarists may grow sentimental about "chivalry." Chivalry indeed! The highest triumph of strategy is to trick your opponent into a position where he has no fair chance of hitting back. "Humane" war is a shoddy idol, like "glory." Civilized men ought to be of tougher fiber, and look war full in the face.

It may sound paradoxical, and even perverse, but I was and I am in full sympathy with Isolationism. Not because it is a tradition: we use Tradition as an argument only when Reason fails us. Not because I believe in the inerrancy of the Founders: the Declaration of Independence and the Constitution are full of flaws, and the development of industry has played havoc (as he foresaw) with Jefferson's economics. But I, as an immigrant, shared in the common American experience: all of us had turned our backs on the absurdities, the abuses and superstitions, the jealousies, intrigues and hatreds of old Europe. If Isolation meant parochialism, "Ourselves Alone," ignorance—willful or stupid—pride, "splendid" or silly, it was beneath the contempt of an educated man; and I could not deny there were such isolationists in every land, just as there are fetishists in every church. I had not yet come across Washington's formula, sharp and noble as new-minted gold: "As a citizen of the great Republic of humanity at large." But I knew that both he and Jefferson were men of the Enlightenment: that their thought and their heart embraced the world. I did not disown Europe; America to me was Europe, but a healthier Europe, Europe purified. I repeated in 1914, and could repeat today, the weighty and irrefutable words of the Farewell Address: "Why forego the advantages of so peculiar a situation? Why quit our own to stand upon foreign ground? Why, by interweaving our destiny with that of any part of Europe, entangle our peace and prosperity in the toils of European ambition, rivalship, interest, humor or caprice?" And I felt confident that Woodrow Wilson was, and did his utmost to remain, an "isolationist" in the spirit of Washington and Jefferson: no "entanglements" ("My allies, right or wrong!"), no commitments in contradiction with our principles, no return to a past against which we had rebelled.

The reader may think that between these conflicting impulses, I was left in utter bewilderment. I condemned the Germans and refused to hate Germany; I abominated war, and was not resigned to nonresistance; I was a world citizen, and a believer in American isolation; and, to cap it all, I spurned compromise and could not tolerate confusion. Yet through the complexities of the situation, I never ceased to hold a guiding thread. If I wanted to be impressive, I could make a show of Hegelian dialectics; if I were a preacher, my text would be: "Let the dead bury their dead!"; I prefer to use David Starr Jordan's unpretentious formula: "The way out is forward."

A mere accident enabled me to put my faith into words, and to submit it to the criticism of my fellow Americans. In 1915, I delivered a high school commencement address at Palestine; and (being thrifty) I repeated it verbatim at Texas City. I used to my heart's content—for once in my life—the artless rhetoric which is permitted on such occasions, and which was still greatly in favor in the Lone Star State. It was called "The Land Where Hatred Expires," a title inspired by Dr. Jordan; and it professed the pioneering spirit, the dynamic radicalism, which to me was the soul of America.

It was not an attack on tradition. Inherited wealth should not be frittered away: in the vast domains of sentiment and aesthetics, tradition is beyond price. Indeed, I pleaded for increasing to the utmost our store of tradition. We immigrants did not reach these shores as spiritual paupers. We wanted to add our own heritage to the common hoard. We might in time come to appreciate and enjoy freely the legacy of New England farmers and Virginia planters; but it could never be our very own. I knew full well that I had come on *La Touraine*, and not on the *Mayflower*.

When a tradition is exclusive and oppressive, it does not merely destroy other values, which may be inestimable; it ruins its own vitality. The curse of nationalistic Europe was the attempt to impose cultural loyalties: Germany believed, in 1914, that she had the right to cudgel a man from Strasbourg or Posen into feeling himself a German. The result of enforced spiritual conformity—hundred percentism—is undying hatred. America is "the land where hatred expires" because it offers, not a common past, but a common future. American life is infinitely richer than any single strain. It welcomes, enriches, transmutes, and transcends them all. We are proud to have among us Daughters and Sons of the American Revolution. We should be still better pleased if they would dress the part, like the hostesses at Williamsburg: living relics, well preserved, are more valuable than period furniture. But the Revolution is not a gene transmitted with the blood: it is a spirit. What we need is a "Society of the Friends of the American Revolution," ardent and determined. The true America is for ever ahead. The wisdom of our ancestors is meant to guide us forward, not to hold us back. The promise of American life is a constructive vision, not a slowly fading memory. *E pluribus unum* is a constant process, not of repression, but of expansion.

"Sons of the discoverers, the conquerors, the pilgrims and the pioneers! The task is not done. There are more strange and lonely seas for your ships to plough. Never have such infinite horizons been revealed to the eyes of any generation. Go forth, in the spirit of high adventure; discover for yourselves and organize for all future generations the new America, the promised land that we, your elders, dreamed of and shall never see, the universal commonwealth founded on justice and love."

My young Texas audiences applauded with polite relief, their minds absorbed in the festivities to come. But, to my surprise, this modest outburst of eloquence, first published locally, caught the fancy of the American public. *International Conciliation* distributed it for years by the thousand, in slightly garbled form.[3] I received hundreds of letters— from President Charles W. Eliot, from Davey the Tree Surgeon (with a treatise on arboriculture), from soldiers, shopkeepers, schoolboys. My fan mail was extensive and varied enough for a Gallup poll. This response assured me that I was no recalcitrant oddity, no alien presuming to criticize his hosts. My Americanism had stood the test. This was my veritable certificate of naturalization.

From the principles set forth in "The Land Where Hatred Expires," a definite policy could be derived. It had no claim to orginality: it was the one which the American conscience demanded. It was also the one which Woodrow Wilson was painfully evolving in his scrupulous mind.

The crisis had found country and President mentally unprepared. Both struggled anxiously against the logic of their own thought. Neither could accept with a light heart the responsibility of going to war; but neither could face the worse responsibility of craven acquiescence in a crime. Unable to think their way out of this tragic dilemma, people and leader attempted to throw the responsibility upon each other. Prudent men urged: "Not a word; not a move; leave it all to the President. Through his advisers, he knows: private persons only guess and feel. He alone has the right to speak in our name. Through him, let us present a united front to the world." But Wilson refused to act without a clear mandate from the people. We were reminded of the notorious Kansas law: "When railroads cross at grade, each train shall wait until the other be passed."

[3] No. 98, January 1916. Reprinted in full in *Beyond Hatred*, 1925.

Hotheads and partisans accused Wilson of flabbiness and pusillanimity. Preacher and pedagogue, he was no Rough Rider, no red-blooded he-man. They called his precarious neutral attitude "the peace that passeth all understanding." They were hoping for an incident that would force his hand: the *Lusitania* bade fair to be another *Maine*. Still Wilson wrestled with his conscience. He might be driven to the necessity of fighting; but he would refuse to fight for the wrong reason. He had first to educate the Allies and our own people to the full meaning of those perilous paradoxes: the war to end war, the victory pure enough to spurn victory. H. G. Wells speaks of "the race between education and catastrophe": Woodrow Wilson *almost* won such a race.

Not quite. When the war finally broke out, we did not fully know what we were fighting for, although "three-minute men" were telling us at every street corner. Because Germany had dared to knock a chip off our shoulder? Because England and France were our friends? Because they had retained the ablest lawyers? Because we had invested billions in their support? Because we were tired and ashamed of sitting on the side lines, and had grown at last "too proud not to fight"? Because we had to show the Huns how crazy they were to think themselves the Master Race, while we were around?

Everybody was using the formulas of Wilsonism, and most people were unconscious that they did so with their tongue in their cheek. In 1917, Wilsonism was not yet strong enough for the role it had assumed. It was widely diffused, but still unorganized. It strove to serve a peace ideal through warlike means. Both the bellicists and the pacifists, being cruder, were more effective. The bellicists now exulted. All that they saw in the new policy was: "Force without stint!" "They asked for it: let them have it!" Wilsonism to them was a martial tune with unfamiliar words; but who cares for the words, if the tune be stirring enough? We, the orthodox Wilsonians, could see the show stolen away from us, with flag waving (new glory for Old Glory!) and the blare of military bands; while the pacifists, with whom we agreed at heart, went to jail with a last reproachful look that meant: "Did we not tell you so?"

Thus the apparent unanimity created by the declaration of war was delusive; the moral situation was actually more confused than before. Confused, but not hopeless. With his new prestige as commander in chief, Wilson continued his campaign of education. I believe he was regaining the lost ground, and even advancing; but there is no way of gauging, both in diffusion and in depth, the state of public opinion. A very simple policy was appearing with increasing definiteness through the clouds of wishful thinking. World solidarity. Liberty for the individual: government by consent, democracy. Liberty for the peoples: self-determination, the illegitimacy of conquest, the liquidation of empires. Justice, not force: no power politics, for "power" is but a brutal threat. Above all, no secret diplomacy: for any deal that shuns the light is a shady trick. All this the common man could understand. It translated into concrete terms his deep-seated horror of war and intrigue. It harmonized the American tradition and the American ideal.

I called myself "an unrepentant Wilsonian" at a time when Wilson's repute was at its nadir. I still believe that he was, for a few supreme moments, the conscience of America and of the world. He came very near success. Had he died on Armistice Day, his fame would have been as pure as Lincoln's. Had he lived to the vigorous old age of Clemenceau, he might have emerged from his Valley Forge and led us to victory. I did not resent his coldness, his stiffness, his occasional smugness: he was great enough to make us forget these blemishes. But he had deeper flaws: I never thought, as he did, that he was defeated solely by the conspiracy of a few willful men. A Christian and a gentleman, he could not fully rise above personal antipathies. The servant of a nonpartisan ideal, he remained a party man in the narrow technical sense. He tried to keep the Machine clean; but he believed that Providence had to use the Machine. His most fatal weakness was not his "idealism," but his cleverness; not that the truths he proclaimed were too lofty, but that too often—and as a rule, unconsciously—he equivocated. Could any man become President of the United States, or, for that matter, president of a university, if he were not something of a politician? His favorite text must have been Matthew 10:13: ". . . be ye therefore wise as serpents, and harmless as doves." Clemenceau smiled at his "holy simplicity." I was struck rather by his unholy duplicity. Alas! None but "clever" men can reach the top; and at the top, cleverness is a curse.

I kept in close touch with opinion in England and in France; and I am persuaded that Wilson was more successful abroad than at home. He was leading us from apparent security and prosperity into the dark pit of strife, and it was only too natural that we should have misgivings. What he had to offer Europe, on the contrary, was clear gain. After three indecisive and torturing years, the old continent had come to hate war with a fierceness we could hardly gauge. For some of us, war could still be something of an adventure, "fresh and joyous." In England and France, that false dawn had long faded; martial glory was bogged in the mire of the trenches. Europe realized that she was sick unto death, because she was filled with unburied corpses: obsolete institutions, absurd frontiers, classes which were medieval ghosts. She craved salvation even more than sheer victory. Wilson promised, not the end of a nightmare merely, but a saner world. America brought everything: supplies, fighters, a moral justification for the struggle, and a constructive ideal. And America spoke with the voice of Wilson: the discordant murmurs, the equivocal interpretations, and above all the

bewildered or disapproving silences of which we were conscious at home could not cross the Atlantic.

The war raised a personal problem which I could not shirk.
My convictions and my physique were glaringly "unmilitary."
My ten months in the French army I had considered as a
term of penal servitude. My one desire had been not to be
court-martialed. I was delightfully surprised when I found
that I had gone through my 309 days (how we counted them!)
in good health and in good spirits; that I had positively enjoyed the rough comradeship of the barrack room and the
drill ground; and that—most outrageous paradox of all—I
had actually struck up a friendship with my top sergeant. Such
a record would hardly stamp me as a born soldier. In 1917, I
was thirty-six. I knew I would be virtually of no use as a
private, and a questionable asset as a company officer. In this
biography of ideas, I shall not dwell on my strictly personal
affairs, but it is pertinent to mention the fact that I had a
very happy home life. And I had work to do: not merely
classroom routine, or the Ivory Tower of research, but my
share in building up that which alone could make victory
secure: the sense of world citizenship.

Yet I could not be satisfied. The policy I had supported
had led to armed intervention. I felt my share of responsibility;
I did not want to be among those older men who send boys
to fight, and applaud from their safe and comfortable homes.
Then, in 1914, I had, without hesitation, ignored the sum-
mons to the French colors. In the eyes of the French authorities, I was simply a draft evader. Now I felt I owed a double
debt. I did not rush ahead without a thought; but there was
no period of anxious debating. The final decision came, literally, in a flash. One night, one of those tropical storms so
frequent on the Gulf coast did its very best to imitate a battle

scene; and after a thunder clap more deafening than the rest, the still small voice told me: "You must go." My wife did not place the slightest obstacle in my path: we thought and felt alike. The trustees of the Rice Institute, of their own accord, agreed to make up the difference between my salary and my military pay. The whole thing was freer from fuss and worry than the arrangements for a summer trip.

After all these years, I must at last confess to myself that I had another motive, not determinant, but very real. I have been, from infancy, "normalcy" personified. I have never gambled. I have never indulged in dangerous sports. I thought of myself as middle-aged. Yet even the most sedate bourgeois and scholar has in him an infinitesimal hankering for adventure. Here was—I blush to write the words—a magnificent show, the greatest and perhaps the last of its kind in history, which I could not afford to miss. Strive as we may, we cannot destroy the fascination of war, even when it is tinged with horror. *All Quiet on the Western Front* sold by the hundred thousand in Germany; Hitler had fought in the trenches; yet the Germans' "Never again!" proved to be a drunkard's resolution. William James was right: war cannot be disposed of by frontal attack. We must evolve an equivalent: some activity at the same time disciplined, passionate and disinterested; some way of enhancing the value of life by spurning it; some wager magnificent beyond the dreams of plodding success; some release for our ancestral instincts as well as for our noblest desires; in cynical terms, some way of going to the Devil for the greater glory of God.

I had been told, by friends in the War Department, that my natural place would be in the Intelligence Service, and that I could be given a commission immediately; but they advised me to go through an officers' training camp, so as to know the Army from within, and to get in the best physical

condition. This struck me as very sensible, and I immediately
sent in my application. In the meantime, we spent the early
summer in Estes Park, Colorado. Few experiences are so
vivid in my memory. The keen air, the sharp sunshine on
peaks and meadows, the jolly primitive housekeeping with
the youngsters, then aged seven and three, the companionship
of two stray burros which had belonged to William Allen
White, the hikes through the infinitely varied and smiling
mountain scenes, with my little boy on my shoulders—all
that loveliness and peace stood out sweet and clear on the
angry darkness beyond. I was summoned for physical examination. My eyesight was found hopelessly defective; but,
on a word from Washington, that disability was waived, and
I entered the officers' training camp at Leon Springs, near
San Antonio.

There began a story of confusion and frustration which
lasted throughout my military career, and beyond. It is a
dismal and all too familiar tale, and I wish to remember only
its humorous aspects. I was qualified for intelligence work;
my chief instructor, a promoted sergeant, could not, of course,
take this into account. His business was to drill me like the
rest, and drill me he did, through and through. My experience and degrees were beyond his purview. All that he could
see was that my stoop and my pince-nez—with a neat black
ribbon—were scandalously unmilitary; and when the pince-
nez was replaced by goggles, the effect was more disastrous
still. I do not accuse him of animosity or unfairness; but my
presence in his company was a stench in his soldierly nostrils.
I presume his presence in my lecture room would have had
the same effect upon me. For a hundred days, he tried to
eliminate the obnoxious civilian who, even when bayoneting
dummies, still was every inch the professor. He used no un-
fair means, and I used no pull. Nearly half the company were

"canned"; but I stayed to the last. Finally, with a heavy heart, he had to recommend me for a commission as second lieutenant, *summa cum misericordia*.

The colonel in command of the camp did his best to correct what he thought was a mistake. But the Army was a huge and improvised machine. In the assembly line, a rivet which has missed its appointed hole is out of luck. I got into the right places—the War College, General Headquarters at Chaumont—but always in the wrong way. Heads of sections wondered what this middle-aged second lieutenant was doing in the company of captains and majors. They were too gentlemanly to shoo me off, and too busy to inquire; so they had me sit in a corner until I could be ordered somewhere else. I remained "unattached" to the very end; I never belonged to an "outfit." On that account, my orders invariably were subtly wrong. The only communication I received that was faultlessly addressed informed me that my missing bedroll had been located, and was waiting for me at Vierzon. Only I never had a bedroll. I was finally promoted by mistake in the Interpreters Corps, to which I never belonged, and against the angry protest of its commandant. The imbroglio was cleared up two years after the war when, for the sake of regularity, the mistake was officially confirmed. The formula "snafu" had not been coined in those days; it would most accurately have defined my status. Ah well! War is a rough-and-tumble affair; it cannot be run with the smoothness of a well-established peacetime factory. The machine creaked, but it functioned, with unexpected efficiency. A sizable percentage of waste is inevitable. Fortunately, it was my time only, not my life, that proved "expendable." My fate was annoying and ludicrous, but not tragic. I have a thick volume of war memories which might be entitled "Casual Remarks of a Casual Officer," with the consoling reflection as an epigraph: "Better be a casual than a casualty."

I have no desire to pose as a Sad Sack or a Private Hargrove.
I had not a few weary hours; but I was seldom caught without a book; and my Blickensderfer, a weird but light and
sturdy portable typewriter, was a most sympathetic confidant.
In barrack rooms, billets or offices, I managed to dash off a
very full diary, properly sprinkled with poems, a book on
city planning, and one on French Civilization. Although
hopelessly astray, I had a good time on the whole, and did
some good work. A casual is drafted for the strangest jobs.
In the Postal Express Service, I saved thousands of our letters
from going to the Congo; for, if our mail had to go through
French hands, A.E.F. was interpreted not as American Ex-
peditionary Force, but as Afrique Equatoriale Française. I
hope I did not disgrace the Rents, Requisitions and Claims
Service when I flitted through it at Toul. For a whole delirious week, I impersonated a lieutenant in the Military Police,
without the knowledge of the provost marshal. A lady of
well-seasoned age and virtue, bloated, frizzled, whitewashed
and charcoaled, with deep blue circles around her eyes and
dabs of vermilion here and there, came to protest against our
placing the red-light district out of bounds. In the most matter-
of-fact tone, she explained that it interfered with legitimate
business and favored the black market. The scene had a rich
ironical and naturalistic flavor reminiscent of Guy de Maupassant, Henry Becque and Octave Mirbeau. With equal
gravity, I assured Boule-de-Suif of our profound respect for
private enterprise; but we wanted our men to concentrate
their efforts on driving out the Boches. I do not know whether
this appeal to her patriotism consoled her for the loss of the
American market. There were unexpected windfalls. I was
for a week or so on General Harbord's staff at Tours, while
the incumbent was on leave. Colonel Bush, on my confessing
that I had never tasted Vouvray, took me to Vouvray itself,
where we had a bottle between us. Colonels, of course, are

far more human than first lieutenants, and generals are most human of all. For a casual particularly, the war was Looking Glass House. You never knew what would happen next, and you soon ceased to wonder. If a dray horse had stood up on his hind legs and addressed me, I should have come smartly to attention without batting an eyelash.[4]

For several months, at Angers, I had very active and very important duties for which I was well prepared. This miracle, of course, was all wrong. I was doing liaison work without belonging to the Liaison Service (a superb outfit composed almost entirely of international bankers); and I was an infantry officer astray in a regiment of engineers. I simply had the luck to come across Colonel Roger D. Black. He thought I was the man for the job he had in mind, and requested me with no regard for the Tables of Organization. Angers was an important center in our lines of communication. There were in the vicinity stores, repair shops, transients' barracks, a large hospital, a training and replacement depot. Without any official title, I was put in charge of our relations with the French authorities, civil and military: Prefect, Deputy, General, Mayor, Police, Church, and Society. My sidecar was constantly dashing through the streets of Angers, and I was a familiar figure at all official ceremonies. If one of our trucks ran over a dog, I brought to the bereaved family the regrets of General Pershing; and I had to act more than once as a de-liaison officer. For the good Angevines, I was the mouthpiece of the American army, for I was the only officer whose French they could understand. It never ceased to fill them with wonder. An old cobbler told me: "My! but you speak dandy French! Almost as good as mine!" With the prefect, Paul Bouju, who became a lifelong friend, I exchanged sonnets in parody of Mallarmé. Angers seemed to believe that my gold bar outranked all silver insignia. A French ad-

---

[4] "You haven't any." (Wife's note.)

ministrative officer was greatly distressed because the large and handsome Desjardins Barracks had been turned over to us without a scrap of paper to register the transaction. I wrote him a receipt in pencil, signed with a flourish, and he was satisfied. I was involved in bread coupons for our men in French restaurants, and greatly concerned with garbage disposal. I escorted Madame Cointreau, of Triple Sec fame, in a collection for the wounded. I was doing nondescript but essential work and having the fun of a masquerade.

Oddly enough, this "return of the native" was for me a voyage of discovery. My knowledge of the French provinces was bookish, and blurred by prejudices. In Anjou, I found provincial life at its most provincial, and at its best. The city, of some eighty thousand inhabitants, was a little capital. It was more lively than my old quarter, the Faubourg St.-Germain. At every turn of its narrow streets, you discovered some enchanting monument of the past: quaint houses, lovely residences of the rich *bourgeoisie*, the ruins of an abbey, a cathedral of an unfamiliar type, very effective on a bluff overlooking the placid river Maine, and the mighty stump of the ducal castle. The region had enjoyed quiet, full-flowing prosperity for centuries. Not only in wealthy homes, but in village inns and in peasant cottages could be seen masterpieces of ancient crafts. Society itself had been little disturbed. As in England, there were "county families." The list of the General Councilors [5] read like a page from the Social Register. The officials of the Republic, when they could not be completely ignored, were treated with distant courtesy; the primacy of the bishop was unchallenged. There was a healthy cultural life: five museums, learned societies, a Catholic university whose chief ornament was the novelist René Bazin. Some provincial accents sound like a caricature of standard French.

[5] The General Council is the local assembly of the department (in this case Maine-et-Loire) with very little political power.

Not so in Anjou: the speech of the region is soft and slow, with singsong inflections, racy of a deep generous soil. In the air, clear but moist with western breezes, in the countryside, in the mellowed architecture, in the smile and the tone of the people could be felt what Joachim du Bellay, in a nostalgic sonnet, calls *"la douceur angevine,"* the gentleness, the sweetness of Anjou.

Anjou is gentle, not weak; easygoing, not easily led whither it does not want to go. The people are like their excellent wine: not pungent when first tasted, but of unexpected strength. Our soldiers were fooled by it. General Pershing had permitted the use of "light wines" and Anjou seemed to answer the description. Some were unguarded enough to gulp a few glasses in quick succession, and had to be carted home by the police.

Angers did not receive us with that delirious enthusiasm which is thrilling, uncomfortable and transitory, like a storm. The joy of the population at our coming was deep. It meant the end of an interminable nightmare; it assuaged misgivings which had been tormenting even the stoutest hearts. Even in the late spring of 1918, the Germans were still on the offensive. Refugees were still flocking from Picardy and from Paris. But there also came up from Brest and Saint-Nazaire the mighty American tide.

Those people had been starved even for the simplest social pleasures, and they had borne the privation with stoicism. Now it was patriotic to entertain the new allies; and what "duty" could be more delightful? There was no hypocrisy in this, only the lifting of a heavy restraint. The Angevines could at last follow again their friendly, hospitable nature. Everybody wanted to adopt us: the prefect and his generous-hearted wife, aristocratic families like the Contades, bourgeois great and small, down to the factory girls of the Bessonneau works and the modest corner *bistro*. A conservative community, Angers preserved a curious sense of social distances. A very neatly dressed lady came to inform me that her dog had been run over; but she would drop all claims if I could let her have two noncommissioned officers to exchange lessons with her daughters. In the generosity of my heart, I told her: "Madam, I could send you two officers." And she replied: "Oh no! We are only *petits bourgeois*." I had two fine young sergeants in the office, and it turned out to be a very successful bargain.

When I saw our doughboys play with the children at Angers, I was confirmed in my conviction that xenophobia is a disease as learned as its name, and not a natural instinct at all. It is kept up by pedants, doctrinaires and fanatics, not by the common man. Between the unassuming, unaggressive, cordial people of Angers and our men, all barriers ceased to exist. When it comes to friendship, articulate speech is of far less importance than a smile: we frequently entertained French officers, and, a couple of times, British missions, and we felt then much closer to the French. This perfect honeymoon between the two nations could easily have become an unquestioning, indestructible understanding. I saw that light fade away, amid squabbles and recriminations. We should find a term more sorrowful than "tragedy" for an ending which is not ennobling, but sordid.

But the first signs of estrangement were not perceptible until after the Armistice. Even then, they might have betokened an inevitable but transient mood. The sudden lull had caused a sharp reaction; all nerves were frayed; discomforts cheerfully accepted the day before became irritating. Both sides were cocky: the Yanks knew, and let it be known, that their intervention had been decisive; the French were conscious that they had suffered more. It was all over, and we wanted to go home.

Had the victors remained united for a generous, farseeing

peace, this *Katzenjammer* would have passed away. In November and December, if our manners were no longer at their best, our hopes were still untarnished. Old Clemenceau himself, in the hour of victory, had spoken nobly, in terms of humanity and not of France alone. And above Clemenceau, we believed, there was Wilson.

I was in Paris on Armistice Day. The joy of the people moved me deeply; a joy tremulous at first, rising in a mighty crescendo, until Paris, fantastic in the dim blue lights, was singing the "Marseillaise" with one tremendous voice. I loved also the bits of comic relief, the kids dragging German guns from the Concorde, the *midinettes* breaking into sobs in the middle of the "Marseillaise," and shifting gaily to "Madelon," the "kiss-in-the-ring" dances around every American uniform. (I was the only American left unkissed that night: a scholarly bearing has its drawbacks.) But in impressiveness and significance, Armistice Day faded compared with Wilson's arrival in Paris, on Saturday, December 14.

December in Paris has innumerable ways of being disagreeable: fog or icy rain, biting wind, snow, sleet or slush. At best, when the sky is clear, the cold is intense. So it had been seventy-eight years before, almost to a day (December 15, 1840), when, in the most elaborate pageant Paris had ever seen, the remains of Napoleon were brought back to his capital. "Day as dazzling as glory, as cold as the tomb," wrote Victor Hugo.

This time, we were miraculously fortunate. The weather was mild; no rain; a pleasant haze; in the gentle gray sky, there was even a hint of blue. As, from the balcony of Madame Georges Porgès, I was watching the Champs Elysées rising so harmoniously to the massive Arch of Triumph, I could not help contrasting the two men and the two destinies: Napoleon, Woodrow Wilson. Our American heroes too had arisen out of war, but they stood above war. Washington, Lincoln, Wilson: for them victory was but a painful necessity, and glory a vulgar show.

A confused noise arose in the distance, crackling like a fire, growing into a roar. The poilus lining the curb shifted uneasily, waiting for orders. The noise, as it approached, seemed to be made up of acclamations, jeers, hoots and laughter. The object was a little yellow dog, rushing headlong down the Champs Elysées. Frightened by the howls on either side, he kept strictly in the middle. He must have run through the whole official route, straight into Wilson's appointed quarters, the residence of Prince Murat.

At last a boom of guns, a bugle call, a roll of drums. The poilus, so human, so unheroic, so unsoldierlike when at ease, snap to attention, present arms, suddenly formidable, rigid, yet quivering with life. Wilson, bareheaded, waves his hat, and smiles as I did not know he could smile. I had caught a glimpse of him at Cornish, New Hampshire, sad, stiff, almost cadaverous. Today, he is curiously boyish in his radiant happiness. It is his one brief holiday between the crushing burden of war and the arduous task of peace.

I had seen many such pageants in the incomparable avenue: long ago the Tzar, King Edward VII; recently, George V, Albert of the Belgians, Poincaré, Clemenceau, Foch. Paris, with a fine sense of shades, had expressed courtesy, interest, gratitude, admiration and even affection. The vast inarticulate clamor that greeted Wilson included all that as a matter of course. But above the traditional tumult and shouting, there soared a unique note of religious fervor. Others had helped victory; Wilson was bringing justice. He was the man who had left politics and diplomacy behind. He could feel at that moment that through his heart and lips spoke the voice of the people and the voice of God. The instant was fleeting; in my memory it is eternal.

CHAPTER ELEVEN

The Great Refusal

AFTER sundry alarums and excursions, and a ten-day leave spent in my dear Angers, I was again stationed in Paris, from February until my return to America in July. A most enviable position! My official duties, in the Postal Express Service, were not exacting. They took me to many different points of the capital, which was clear gain. My living conditions were excellent. I had a pleasant room in remotest Montmartre, back of the Sacré-Cœur, with fine people who made me at once a member of the family. I took my meals wherever whim or duty happened to lead me. I even had snacks of roasted chestnuts or French fried potatoes in the teeming street, in a manner unbecoming an officer and a gentleman. I had many friends in the city, American as well as French. I was living in two worlds, and making the most of both. At times I felt as though twenty years had been rolled back, and I were a Paris student again. Yet, in the cherished place of my birth and upbringing, I had a sense of infinite loneliness, a yearning for my family, my country and my people across the sea. Above all, as an obscure witness, I was living momentous hours.

"The battle of Paris"—in the A.E.F., the term had ironic overtones—was fought halfheartedly, in a dense fog, and proved indecisive. It was, as Toynbee, I believe, said of 1848, "a turning point in history where history failed to turn." My French friends almost unanimously, and a few of the Americans, were ardent Wilsonians like myself. Day after day, we saw our great hope grow fainter. All that I remember of these five months now is a feeling of nervous irritation and mounting anguish. When the treaty of Versailles was signed, I entered in my pocket diary: "Despondent." I might have written, like Harold Nicolson: "To bed, sick of life."

To account for this failure is a delicate task. The world has attempted it for a whole quarter of a century, without reaching an acceptable conclusion. There is nothing so baffling as a dull, incoherent, amorphous tragedy; yet it may have longer and deeper consequences than a clear-cut, spectacular catastrophe. No crude explanation will avail. It is constantly repeated that the Armistice caught the victors unprepared. *Undecided* would be more accurate. Thanks to Wilson, war aims and peace principles had been discussed more thoroughly than in any previous conflict. If victory had not come ahead of schedule, if the Allies had had more time for reflection before Germany's collapse, they would simply have been better equipped to disagree. The ambiguities and contradictions were deep in their own minds.

The problems were so overwhelming that the efforts of individuals seemed futile. Heroes and villains catch the light for a moment, as they ride the crest of the wave; but it is not they who cause or direct the tide. I refuse to cast Clemenceau, Lloyd George or Henry Cabot Lodge in the part of Iago. Each worked strenuously according to his light, and his light was not darkness absolute. Nor am I inclined to place the blame on Wilson. I have become increasingly conscious of Wilson's shortcomings. My thoughts were finally focused by Stephen Bonsal's *Unfinished Business*. This matter-of-fact record brings into pitiless relief the limitations of the President, and, incidentally, of Lord Robert Cecil as well. Léon Bourgeois, whom they thought a great bore, had a far clearer view of the situation. Had Wilson been free from the notorious flaws in his intellect, his character and his bodily frame, the setback might have been less sharp, and he might have led us into the right path, again, years later. But in 1919, I doubt whether the treaty could have been made much better, or its fate more favorable. The forces of the past, which were hostile to Wilsonism, had, through the very process of war, regained power and prestige. The forces of the future, on which Wilsonism had to rely, were not represented at all. They hovered darkly beyond the precincts of the conference, vast but loose, to all appearances disturbing and even ominous rather than constructive. If Versailles is to be condemned, it is not for what it did, but for what it ignored.

The war, in spirit and method, had been revolutionary. If it had not been, the French and the British would have rebelled, and America would not have joined. Still, the masters of the ancient crafts, the diplomats, the military leaders, remained in control of the indispensable tools. Victory redeemed, and even enhanced, their reputation. Although they had failed to understand the issues, they were automatically entrusted with the settlement. A people's peace was tacitly ruled out. To diplomats and warriors, Wilsonism, i.e. the abolition of diplomacy and war, could only seem the most fantastic and the most dismal of Utopias.

We felt, of course, that Wilson should have insisted on an open conference, in which both military force and secret treaties would have been rejected as irrelevant, in which victors and vanquished would have freely discussed the implications of the Fourteen Points. Note that if such had been the case, the material result would not have been radically different. It is not the actual clauses of Versailles that are in contradiction with the Fourteen Points, but the spirit, that of a dictated peace. That spirit was borrowed from Germany. The Allies gave Germany a taste of her own medicine. But they had to swallow it themselves, and it was poison.

In this great trial, the assizes of a new world, the old nationalistic and military conceptions ought to have been the accused, and the people the jury. We had instead Allied pots calling the German kettle black. The confusion of two sets of principles, belonging to entirely different epochs, created a sense of hypocrisy. A peace dictated by the professionals, military and diplomatic, would have been cleaner. These people, left to themselves, do not indulge in sanctimonious nonsense about *guilt*. They think in terms of *mistakes*, not of *crimes*. They play a game, as hard as they can; as soon as it is over, they are ready to shake hands with their opponents. Indeed they like their opponents, who belong to the same class as themselves and observe the same code, better than they do the civilians and laymen on their own side. The Wilsonian idea of guilt was incongruously tagged on to the tradition of Machiavelli, Frederick II, Napoleon, Bismarck: force, deceit, *realism*. But under the new Wilsonian dispensation, Germany could not be convicted by Bismarckian means. She could not be convicted at all unless she were judged. And she could have been judged, for with the Fourteen Points, she had accepted the new law.

To me, an impotent, ill-informed spectator in Paris, history in the making was a crazy series of ill-focused dissolving pictures. It was taken for granted at first that the Inter-Allied conference was only a preliminary caucus: after a common programme had been hammered out, the real business would be to establish the peace, on the basis of the Fourteen Points, through discussion with Germany. But the point was not clear; the opening ceremonies had been too elaborate for a mere caucus. As the preliminary stage continued indefinitely, the idea that the main conference was to come later receded, and finally faded away altogether. As far as I know, the responsibility for this shift cannot be pinned upon anyone; and yet it was to ruin the whole settlement. Lloyd George, Tardieu, Shotwell, Harold Nicolson, Bonsal, have no clear explanation to offer. It simply happened. People were growing weary of the eternal wrangling. If alleged friends were in such a hopeless snarl, what could be expected of a discussion with the enemy? The world was yearning for peace—any peace. So, in dull despair, a clumsy hybrid of force and justice was agreed upon. A composite picture of Wilson and Bismarck could not be very convincing. Each element destroyed the validity and efficacy of the other.

This Wilson must have realized, although power is apt to blur the sharpest sight. We believed he stood for the right, and had the people of the world behind him. We were constantly hoping that he would assert himself. He had a few fits of petulance, but on the whole, he gave way. He thought —mistakenly—that he was not yielding in essentials. I cannot probe his soul. I believe he had a great capacity for self-delusion. I am now convinced that if he had stood firm, he would have been openly, decisively defeated in the spring of 1919: the odds were too heavy against him. If this possibility came to his mind, he shrank from it. He did not have the greatness of William the Silent, of Washington biding his time, of Lenin accepting the new economic policy frankly as a setback, of De Gaulle admitting: "France has lost a battle," in order to affirm: "she has not lost the war." If he had insisted upon fundamental Wilsonism—a conference applying principles impartially—he would have been branded as a pro-German, as he had been during his neutrality period. And America at that time was drunk, far worse than France, with anti-German passion. General Pershing, and all the professional officers with him, thought only of a crushing victory, unconditional surrender imposed in the ruins of Berlin: the policy which was adopted in 1945. In England, Lloyd George had just won his khaki elections, in reality on his war record, but apparently in support of a fierce Carthaginian peace. In France, the military were at the pinnacle of their prestige; Poincaré and his friends were accusing the Tiger himself of turning soft.

Wilson had against him a force which was narrow but deep, with the momentum of centuries: the military and diplomatic tradition. He had against him a force which was superficial, but, in the immediate present, ubiquitous and intense: the resentment of the victims against the aggressors. What was there on his side? The common sense and good will of the world: an enormous reserve of power, but so unorganized as to be impotent. Demos has no articulate voice: he can only reject or ratify the pronouncements of small, conscious, organized minorities. Were there such minorities in support of Wilson? He had with him a number of intellectuals; not by any means the majority of the educated, for education is in most cases the acquisition of fashionable prejudices. The Wilsonian intellectuals—Herron may be considered as a fair sample—enjoyed very scant prestige among the masses. American public opinion is a pachyderm, admirably protected against the slender shafts of original thought. In Europe, the determined Wilsonians were far more numerous, probably because Europe had suffered more tragically from the ills that Wilsonism was attempting to cure. But the traditionalists likewise were more formidable than with us. The *educated* meant the *bourgeoisie;* and the *bourgeoisie* was conservative.

In France, the largest group of thoroughgoing Wilsonians was the Socialist party. On the day of Wilson's arrival, there was an admirable number of *L'Humanité,* hailing him and pledging support to his cause. *Le Figaro,* which calls itself "the paper of the elite," retorted in an editorial: "The Socialists consider our guest as 'an apostle of international justice,' 'a messenger of justice and peace': *words devoid of meaning and value.*" The only Germans who had frankly rejected the Bismarckian gospel and fully endorsed the Wilsonian ideal were Spartacists like Liebknecht or Communists like Kurt Eisner. And beyond them, there were the Russian Communists, or, as they were then called, the Bolsheviki, "the enemies of mankind."

They too had been pleading for a people's peace. Wilson was not to be swerved from his path by discovering Lenin and Trotsky among his fellow travelers. Perhaps there is no more striking proof of his true greatness than his daring, almost alone among respectable statesmen, to plead for justice to Russia. The sixth of his Fourteen Points might still be our guide. "The treatment accorded Russia by her sister nations in the months to come will be the acid test of their good will, of their comprehension of her needs as distinguished from their own interests, and of their intelligent and unselfish sympathy." Such an appeal fell upon deaf ears; after nearly thirty years, we are still pretty hard of hearing.

What could Wilson do? He felt that the welcome he had received in Paris was, morally, a plebiscite. But how could he turn this amorphous mass of good will into a definite, active force? By appealing to the people everywhere over the heads of their governments, against their governments? Had he been followed, that would have meant a revolution, in which the Socialists alone could provide the dynamic, disciplined element. I do not believe that such a possibility ever crossed Wilson's mind: he had in an uncommon degree the common gift of never following through to the uncomfortable end of his thought. If the temptation had come to him, he would have recoiled, as Napoleon did in 1815 when, in Lyons, he was acclaimed by a revolutionary mob. Can anyone imagine

Wilson, the quiet scholar, the orthodox Presbyterian, a gentleman even by the most exacting southern standard, making
himself the leader of the social revolution everywhere in
Europe, in order to secure more equitable treatment for Russia and Germany?

So we had to accept, not defeat, but a mutilated victory,
half blind, her wings soiled and clipped. I did not despair.
If the Wilsonian ideal had suffered a check, the powers of
the past, the empires of prey, had experienced a disaster.
Leadership had passed from Europe, with its heritage of
hatred, to America, the land of hope. When I arrived in New
York on the U.S. transport *Zeppelin,* the Statue of Liberty,
which I had greeted before with cool, half-supercilious friendliness, assumed for the first time its full significance.

This military interlude had been a protracted Sabbatic. I
returned with renewed zest to my pleasant life and work at
the Rice Institute. Yet a change had taken place. I realized
that, although scholarship must not be neglected or warped,
the most pressing task was to work for a world of freedom
under law. All the evils that can torment a people in time of
peace are trifling compared with those that attend even victorious war. No extravagance could bring such abysmal
waste. No political reaction could be so frankly tyrannical as
conscription. No crime wave could cause as many deaths as a
single battle. No campaign of hate could lash men to the same
primitive fury. Until we had stopped international anarchy,
it mattered little whether we called ourselves Republicans or
Democrats, individualists or socialists, Catholics, Protestants
or Jews. This was the key problem, or, as Borgese was to call it
twenty years later, "the Common Cause."

We are apt to forget that, in 1919, such ideas were axiomatic
in this country. They were preached from every pulpit. They

were an immemorial American tradition focused at last into a clear-cut policy. For the sake of brevity, I call that policy Wilsonism; but it was not peculiar to Wilson. Neither was it partisan: a League to Enforce Peace, not as a remote ideal, but as a proximate goal, had first been mooted by Taft and Lowell. Sobered by my experience in Paris, I did not expect a sudden flight into Utopia. We should be "perfectionists," as we are told in the Gospel; at the same time, we should be resigned to imperfection. The Articles of Confederation and even the Constitution were by no means flawless instruments. Let us be satisfied with one short step at a time, provided it be in the right direction. And there was not the slightest doubt in my mind that America knew her way.

So, just as I had not been utterly discouraged by the inconsistencies, the ambiguities, the hypocrisies of Versailles, I did not despair altogether when I saw the political confusion in 1919–1920. I had long been convinced that party politics offered the clumsiest, most devious and most hazardous method of reaching a wise decision; but we had no other tool at our disposal. I did not despair when the League won a majority in the Senate (forty-nine for, thirty-five against), short of the required two-thirds. To the present day, and against most of my friends, I believe the two-thirds rule is wise. A treaty is no ordinary law; it binds the country both at home and abroad; and it should not be entered into without the most mature deliberation. The feud between Lodge and Wilson was lamentable. The collapse of the President's health was a serious loss to the cause (Wilson was far more of a martyr than Lincoln, for he knew the risk and faced it deliberately). But these were only unfortunate skirmishes. As long as public opinion, on the whole, remained solid, there was no cause for dismay.

And, as far as we could judge, public opinion was unshaken. As Samuel Flagg Bemis, a very conservative, frankly isolationist historian, puts it: "The rejection of the treaty amazed the nation and the world." [1] Had "a solemn referendum" on the question been taken, the answer would not have been in doubt. The elections of 1920 were nothing of the kind. The question was not definitely put, divorced from all other problems. Warren Harding himself was vaguely in favor of some League and Covenant. People voted on twenty issues, pell-mell. They had "had enough" of war strenuousness, and craved "normalcy." The interests and the machines indulged in their customary tussles. A fresh team was substituted for one that had fumbled, lost its captain, and was manifestly weary. Personalities played a part in the contest out of all proportion with their merits.[2] In spite of Wilson's request, the people passed no decisive verdict on World Law. All this meant delay, and delay was regrettable, in the convalescence of the world. Still, there was nothing to show that the will of the country, so manifest a few years before, had radically changed. Very slowly, very haltingly, groping and stumbling, the politicians finally do heed the people's behest.

What I was not prepared for was the collapse of the public will. It was not a spectacular revulsion of feelings, but a slow deflation, an inglorious oozing out of energy. Cartoonists have made us familiar with the picture of Uncle Sam "sternly resolved." There was nothing of the kind in 1920 and after. Uncle Sam's expression simply became vacant. After a time, it grew stubbornly vacant, "grimly determined" not to see, not to think, not to act, upholding neutrality, not virility, as the highest national virtue. This capitulation without a mental fight was the bitterest experience in my life. There is something exhilarating about facing a vigorous opponent. But to

[1] *A Diplomatic History of the United States* (New York, 1942), p. 654.

[2] The inestimable privileges of democracy were pithily expressed at the time:

> We repair to the ballot box
> And vote for Harding or for Cox.

struggle against a gluey mass of vague prejudices and un-
formulated fears is more disheartening than a sharp defeat.

A great country slinking away from its own ideal is not an
edifying sight. The ideal, denied three times and with an oath,
remained in the back of our minds, a silent accusation. "Normalcy," Republican prosperity, two cars in every garage,
hooch, jazz, sophistication, could not make us forget. We
rigged up a number of alibis to evade the plain question:
World Law or Anarchy? Some of them were most virtuous,
and professed to transcend Wilsonism. "It is vain to seek im-
provement through institutions: let us first change the individual." "We need no law to keep the peace: the only way is
to give up war." And this was ultimately written into the
nerveless, sightless, toothless Kellogg Pact. "It is not men
or nations that are guilty, but armaments. The wicked guns
corrupt the harmless gangsters. Had no stick or stone been
left within Cain's reach, he would never have slain Abel."
Some were red-blooded, and proudly dynamic: "We must
remain the masters of our fate! We shall never rescind the
Declaration of Independence! Security is an ignoble ideal:
virile nations love to live dangerously." So the lamb bleated,
and the lion roared, in unison, their rejection of World Law.

Most of these alibis to excuse our defection were retrospec-
tive. They attempted to show that our Wilsonism had been
based on false premises. All the talk about "the war to end
war," and "making the world safe for democracy," was clap-
trap. Everyone not incurably naïve knew that we had been
snared into war by the Merchants of Death, the international
bankers, and their hired propagandists. Followers of Harry
Elmer Barnes demonstrated luminously that the aggressive
Belgians were poised to sweep through Berlin. While the
Extreme Right invoked Washington and Jefferson, the Extreme Left quoted the prophet Karl Marx. War is inherent in
capitalism. Liberty, justice indeed! Dialectic Materialism, the

Economic Interpretation of History, explain every move in the tortuous and sordid game. Wilson is every bit as guilty as Ludendorff: the one may call himself a scholar and the other a soldier, but they are both the obedient servants of the bourgeois regime. And the stern realists added: "Come the Revolution, and the lion shall eat straw like the ox, and the weaned child shall put his hand in the cockatrice' den."

Right, Left, idealists and realists, bourgeois and Marxians, pacifists and flag-wavers, united in damning every clause of the Versailles Treaty, although in our separate peace with Germany we had explicitly endorsed it. Poland was a sorry fiction, an invention of the vindictive French to annoy the Germans. Reparations were economic nonsense, but war debts should be paid on the dot. Oswald Garrison Villard denounced France, who was supposed to have dictated, and was vainly endeavoring to enforce, the treaty of Versailles, as "the enemy of mankind." The official thesis was that innocent, peace-loving Germany had been attacked, abused, betrayed: a thought which became incarnated in a man named Adolf Hitler.

The most outrageous paradox in this paradoxical situation was that the abandonment of the American ideal became known as "Americanism." I knew my Europe well enough to consider it as "Europeanism" of the worst type, the most foreign of all *isms,* the rigidly imposed conformity and the dull resistance to progress from which the ancestors of our present citizens had fled. At the core, it is *totalitarian:* 140,000,-000 with but a single thought. It is less cruel than its European counterparts because it is more self-assured and more insidious. A man's essential freedom is in greater peril when, instead of jailing his body, you inveigle him into saying: "Let us make the vote unanimous."

Now America was to me the Land of Liberty; the land where dissent was not per se disloyal; the land where men were bound together by their agreement to differ in peace: which is the key to David Starr Jordan's fine definition: the land where hate dies away. *Un-American* is a fallacy rounded and complete in a single word.[3] Whatever an American chooses to do is American, provided he does not actually break the law. (Breaking the law, by the way, is quite an "American" tradition too: witness the evasion of the Constitution in the South, the open flouting of antitrust measures, the successful rebellions against Prohibition and the Office of Price Administration.) *Un-American* should therefore have but one meaning: illiberal, intolerant; and the Martin Dies Committee was to provide the perfect example of Un-American Activities. From 1920 to the present day, I have had to wrestle with that incubus. Well-meaning people have tried to teach me the patriotic virtue of the stampede: to make me love my mother on one particular day, eat more prunes in one appointed week, read at one time *The Winning of Barbara Worth*, at another *The Egg and I*. Their Utopia was a land where thought enjoyed perfect freedom, provided it flowed in the common channel at the common speed. Once I was told, after I had expressed opinions not of the strictest Hooverian orthodoxy: "Why aren't you a rugged individualist *like everybody else?*" Well, I took my inborn Americanism seriously enough to be an individualist in my own way.

So, in the name of the American ideal, I have steadily declined to be an orthodox, a regular, a passive follower of the Line, by whomsoever the Line may be traced, Moscow, Wall Street, Tammany Hall or Greenwich Village. I could never accept the literal inspiration and inerrancy of Adam Smith, the Federalist Papers, Karl Marx, Arthur Rimbaud or the Book of Mormon. I have remained a born nonconformist, a traditional dissenter. Because I am an American, I have obstinately refused to bow before the idols of the tribe: race

[3] Cribbed from Walter Bagehot, who said it of *un-English*.

prejudice, the pursuit of happiness, advertising, the profit motive, party politics and conventional religion.

When I was attacking that witless and formidable monster Hundred-percentism (no head, a thousand tentacles), I was not singling America out as a horrible example. I was aware that all countries, and above all those I knew and loved best, France, England, Germany, had their "vital lies," their tribal paganism, which they identified with their national spirit. But I had a different standard for America. This was the country where titles, privileges, prejudices, were to be left behind at Ellis Island, as undesirable immigrants. It was the nation conceived in liberty, and born of the Enlightenment. So superstitions which in Europe might have struck me as quaint, in America seemed to me absurd. We find it delightful that an Englishman, in true P. G. Wodehouse style, should call himself Marquess of Stoke-Poges. But if one of our compatriots should call himself Duke of Conshohocken, the order of our universe would be deranged.

So I was far more exacting for my own country than for the "benighted" continent I had left behind. I resented intensely anything that seemed to hinder, and even to cloud, the great American experiment, the hope of mankind, a society founded upon liberty and justice. I felt it as a personal wound that, in this country which had been so generous to me, there should be such a strange, such an unaccountable worship of meanness. I could not understand that admirable citizens like Charles Beard and Herbert Hoover should use "starry-eyed" and "do-gooders" as terms of reproach. The America I had sought, the America in which I still believed, was not a community of "fish-eyed evildoers."

This became my chief problem: why should good men—aye, even ministers of the Gospel—sneer at the good? I found the clue in a poem which had been cluttering my memory ever since I was thirteen, Longfellow's *Excelsior!* The curse of America's spiritual life has been American idealism, by which I mean the complacent assertion of sentiments so lofty that they evidently have no practical place in this world. We listen with pious approval to the strains of *Excelsior!* But we nurse the invincible conviction that the fellow was crazy.

Idealism of this kind is not harmless, like a fairy tale. For it inevitably begets Realism, which to me is *l'Infâme*, the Eternal Enemy, as Fanaticism was to Voltaire.[4] "I am a Christian; I am a patriot; no one could be more devoted to high ideals than I am. But America's business is Business." Here we put our finger on the Great Heresy, or the Great Refusal. Because Idealism is not the whole of human nature, we politely exile it to the empyrean, and we proclaim that realistic meanness should be our only rule. We start with Don Quixote: "Let us make the world safe for democracy"; we end with Calvin Coolidge: "They hired the money, didn't they?"

I like Uncle Sam: even in the crudest cartoons, he has clear-cut features and a resolute, kindly, humorous cast of countenance. He is an uncle after my own heart. Why must he constantly be wearing one of his two conventional masks, neither of which actually fits him: the inane beatific smile, the unseeing uplifted eye of the knight-errant, the sordid furtive leer of the profit seeker? Why should the solemn chords of *Excelsior!* invariably be resolved into: "Now let's make a deal"? Is there nothing in this vast country between the unscalable heights and the smoke-filled hotel room?

This dissonance runs through the whole of our brief history. We assert too much, perform too little, and call this

---

[4] Just as I was writing this chapter, I came across this passage from Georges Bernanos: "*S'il n'y avait que des salauds dans le monde, le Réalisme serait aussi le Bon Sens, car le Réalisme est précisément le bon sens des salauds.*" *Salaud* is an admirable word for which I can offer no English equivalent. Laval was the perfect *salaud. La France contre les Robots* (Paris 1947), p. 16.

contradiction "striking a happy medium." We affirm as a self-evident truth that all men are created equal; but this need not interfere with our having helot races and underprivileged classes. We proclaim that governments derive their just powers from the consent of the governed. But we teach the young that the Civil War was fought to preserve the Union, not to abolish slavery; and preserving the Union could only be done by force, not by consent. Woodrow Wilson, a truly great soul, was a master at shifting masks. No one could be more perfectly the *Excelsior!* youth: "The devils had taken me up to high mountains, to be tempted of them, but I had forced British and French statesmen (I do not trust them) to sign an Americanized treaty. I am compelled to be sincere if they are not. I can stand defeat. I cannot stand retreat from conscientious duty." [5] But the man who uttered this splendid assertion of rectitude was also the one who, autocratically, against a strong majority, had vetoed the proclamation of race equality in the Covenant. I have already mentioned how, according to Lincoln Steffens, Clemenceau, a fearless thinker, had called Wilson's bluff. In the same manner, sharply divorcing principles from policy, we advocated disarmament (in the belief that we were impregnable) without collective security. We signed the Kellogg Pact, but were careful not to provide it with teeth.[6] Oswald Garrison Villard urged that we resist the Nazis "by all means short of war and that will not lead to war." We condemn Franco on the highest ethical grounds; but we make sure that this condemnation will remain on the *Excelsior!* level, and not interfere with politics or private interests.

President Roosevelt was simply bewildering in his masterly manipulation of the two masks. He signed the Atlantic Char-

[5] Quoted by Josephus Daniels: *The Wilson Era, Years of War and After* (Chapel Hill, 1946), p. 461.
[6] The teeth were to show through at the Nürnberg trial; the delay in dentition cost many millions of lives.

ter, and lived to shrug it away. He faced war unflinchingly, in the defense of high principles, knowing that he was send-ing hundreds of thousands to their death; and he made a deal with Darlan, the embodiment of all the evils we were seeking to destroy, "in order to spare American lives." He made secret agreements which were not quite secret and not quite bind-ing. It was rightly said that he had a rendezvous with destiny, but on the way stopped to talk it over with Jim Farley. Presi-dent Truman closed the San Francisco Conference with simple words which were movingly sincere. Thereupon he hurried to Potsdam to play the most cynical game of power politics and secret diplomacy. I do not believe he will ever realize the absolute contradiction between his speech and his deeds.

Thus our constitution, our history, our politics, and above all our religion, all have about them the same shimmering mist of unreality. When we hear those deep organ tones, liberty, democracy, Old Glory, the service of the common-wealth, the golden rule, we glow with sacred emotion. We too find "unspeakable comfort in the blessed word Mesopotamia." But the glow can be switched off at will. This is a practical world.

"We contradict ourselves? Very well: we contradict our-selves. Is it not foolish to expect of a great people that con-sistency which is the hobgoblin of little minds?" I know that we should not be the prisoners of a rigid formula. I do not desire that Uncle Sam and the innumerable John Does his nephews should be simple in any sense of the term. Simplicity even when it is holy is indigence. We are not children, and we are not primitives. There should be room in our purview of the universe for pundit Irving Babbitt, of Harvard, and realtor George F., of Zenith; for Mr. Thomas Stearns Eliot, from St. Louis, Missouri, and for Mr. Samuel L. Clemens, likewise from Missouri. Why not have Jumping Frogs in the Wasteland? I have made it quite plain that I hate conformity and uniformity. I believe in pluralism: interpenetrating worlds with a strict minimum of traffic rules to avert dangerous collisions. But there must be, in the individual and in the nation, a persistent core, even though it cannot be expressed in logical terms. Else man and city would dissolve into chaos.

I am not among the sophisticates who revel in chaos. Still, I can sympathize with a divided personality, at war with itself. Many Germans and Russians are mad, and they know it, and they are insufferably proud of the distinction. It gives them, in their own conceit, a tragic appeal and a disquieting glamour. A cool, clear, analytical spirit like Stefan Zweig strained every nerve to reach the shadow land of unreason, which ever eluded him; like those wealthy Philistines who love to dwell on the coast of Bohemia. But that business of the two American masks implies no abysmal depths, no tragic conflict. I cannot forgive pleasant, sensible men, without a particle of Dostoevsky, Baudelaire or Nietzsche in their well-ordered minds, for having two parallel consistencies, two incompatible sets of principles, and using one or the other without a qualm. Above all, I cannot forgive them for being so evidently satisfied with themselves in either role. When duality becomes too profitable, it bears an unpleasant likeness to duplicity. It may be an exceedingly convenient trick, but it ruins our integrity.

No truth that cannot be a guide for intelligent action deserves to be preached as a truth: the absurd is not the ideal. On the other hand, no action that we know for certain to be evil can possibly be wise. I am not advocating a crude and rigid radicalism of the Puritan or Jacobin type: "All or nothing!" I shall be satisfied, not with half a loaf, but with a few crumbs, if the bread is bread indeed, and not poison. I am ready for complexities, fine shadings, delicate adjustments, but not for compromise. Evil may be forced upon us, but we

have no right to call even the lesser evil *good*. The links between belief and action may be multiform and flexible, but
there must be a connection.

America seemed to me, during those years of indecision,
like a large army with an excellent air scouting force. The
planes are sent on a reconnaissance flight, daring and perilous.
When they return, the pilots report: "Exciting trip!"—the
land commanders congratulate: "Marvelous show!" But what
did they learn? Oh, nothing. No one in his senses will connect
the sport of aerobatics with the serious business of plodding
through the mud. Never cross the bridge until you come to
it; if there is no bridge at all, you will find it out pragmatically.
Never fight an enemy until you bump against him. If he out-
numbers and outranges you, you will receive the information
in the school of hard knocks. The oddest thing is that flyers
and land hogs are not of different breeds. They are the same
people, and they know it. But they profess that there should
be no contact whatever between their *Excelsior!* mood and
their practical activities.

This ubiquitous delusion is absolutely contrary to American experience. Every one of our boasted achievements—
our national capital, our great public works, our industrial
empires—had to go through the three stages: vision, blueprints, execution. The San Francisco bridges did not simply
happen as the result of unplanned, unco-ordinated, purely
selfish individual efforts. They had to exist first as a conception
in some daring mind (as a matter of fact, they were ordered
built by mad Emperor Norton). Then those Utopian schemes
were carefully explored in every detail; and now they span
the bay and the Golden Gate in aerial majesty. And other
bridges could be thrown across other chasms, if we dared, between nation and nation, between East and West, between
liberty and social justice. If we dared. If the good and the

wise were not so cravenly afraid of what they know to be right: "We must not be perfectionists."

This conflict, enormous without greatness, absorbing without vitality, was constantly present in my mind. In this land of kindness and good humor, I felt oppressed. Not that my freedom of thought or speech was in any way abridged: between the shameful Mitchell Palmer era, and the present witch hunt or "purge," America enjoyed, under Republicans and Democrats alike, a quarter of a century of true liberalism. I was not silenced. I was allowed to express myself as vigorously as I could, in reputable magazines, and many friends, known and unknown, responded to my voice. Yet, in spite of all tolerance and courtesy, there were invisible bars. We were not alone, but we were isolated. Our challenge was quietly ignored. The worst blows took the form of praises: "Admirable sentiments! What a pity they are so Utopian!" The high-brow reviews were hospitable, but blandly noncommittal: it is unscholarly to have definite views, except about the dating of the Kiersy-sur-Oise Edict. With the Marxians I could have no truck, since their whole doctrine denies freedom of thought and action. The "Liberals" had at any rate one definite advantage: as they were capable of articulate expression, their utter confusion was made manifest.

In 1928, I was asked by a British paper the perfectly inane question: "What do Americans think about life?" I answered: "We are too happy to think at all." A man never thinks about his lungs, his stomach, his heart, until they start bothering him. Thought is a malady. Of course, Adam and Eve did not think until they ate the fatal apple.[7] In October, 1929, came

[7] Prof. Oliver Martin Johnston, of Stanford University, established that *pomum* means fruit, not apple. There could be no apple trees in the zone of Eden. *Pomum* must have been a citrus fruit; in all likelihood, a lemon.

the resounding Stock Exchange crash. Even then, we tried
our hardest not to think. We were told that it was a mere
financial panic—not an unfamiliar experience in American
history—and that it would soon exhaust itself. No drastic
measures were necessary: let the wise and ineluctable economic laws take their course. (To be sure, the same administration was to endorse the Smoot-Hawley tariff, a rude challenge to Manchesterian orthodoxy.) There was no reason to
alter our policy: our natural resources were unimpaired, our
industrial plant intact, and prosperity just around the corner.

Less than twenty years after this crash, we have completely
forgotten its lesson. It is slurred over, as an untoward but
minor incident. Historians, I believe, will restore it to its
sinister eminence. It is a more memorable date than the
delusive Armistice. It afforded a perfect demonstration that
the so-called Capitalistic System was not an eternal and self-
enforcing verity. At the height of its success, in peace and
prosperity, with a Great Engineer as captain and a Great
Financier as his mate, it had hopelessly foundered.

The first method that comes to the mind of an individual in
financial distress is: "I must reduce expenditures." It is not
applicable to the community. For reduced consumption
means reduced production, increasing unemployment: the
infernal descending spiral. The Great Engineer, his eyes
bandaged and his ears stuffed with doctrine, stoutly declined
to be saved by unorthodox means. He was a martyr to a form
of idealism which was undoubtedly narrow, which may have
been misguided, but which, in its austere inflexibility, was
wholly admirable.

The collapse of the Stock Market shook the world. America, unravaged, unthreatened by foreign foe, unshaken by
revolution, could bear such a shock: Europe could not. In
1929, Europe was convalescing, materially and morally. Eng-

land had been pale and languid for years, but Germany and France were definitely improving. What is more, they were drawing closer together. The Locarno Pact, freely agreed to, on a basis of full equality, had become the foundation of peace, instead of the *Diktat* of Versailles. Germany was admitted into the League of Nations, not as a humble probationer, but with the rank and privileges of a great power. But that recovery, although undeniable, was still precarious. The effect of the American crash upon that weakened organism was immediate and disastrous.

It was manifested dramatically. In May, 1928, the Nazis returned twelve members to the Reichstag. In September, 1930, they elected one hundred and seven. What had happened in between? Not the alleged "stab in the back," not the Versailles *Diktat*, not the cruel and humiliating occupation of the Ruhr, but the toppling down of the American boom. The demonstration is irrefutable. In this age, it is impossible for America not to be the leader. This burden of greatness has been thrust upon us: if not through our merits, then through our luck. It is ours, and others, through sinfulness or misfortune, have missed it. No Congressional filibuster against Destiny will enable us to escape it. And when the leader is willfully blind, in home affairs as well as in international affairs, the world is bound to stumble. Hitler was but a symptom (which does not make him any more lovable). The disease was the utter bewilderment and despair so well depicted by Hans Fallada in *Little Man, What Now?* That despair was a chain reaction which started in Wall Street. Washington failed to foresee, to avert or to mitigate the catastrophe. We had a Business administration, and the faith of Business in its own infallibility was unshaken. This doctrinaire aloofness from reality was the second Great Refusal to be scored against us. It was not to be the last.

I am not nonpartisan: I am antipartisan. My party line is accurately defined in the jingle of the British National Anthem:

> Confound their politics,
> Frustrate their knavish tricks!

In this again, I am the disciple of George Washington, in whose eyes parties were but factions. I hope, someday, to challenge our acquiescence in a system which is a manifest and unnecessary evil. We deprecate the party system in the activities of church, school or shop: why tolerate it on the national scale? When it is urged that natural resources, *de facto* monopolies, basic industries, public utilities, should be under the ownership and management of the commonwealth, the inevitable and irrefutable objection is: "But would you entrust such vital interests to *politicians?*" So I followed the 1932 Presidential campaign with my customary skepticism. In the duel of the Machines as such I was not interested in the least. I happened to have great personal regard for the Republican candidate. The Democratic contender enjoyed the somewhat equivocal support of the Hearst papers. And, although I was not a Prohibitionist, I did not believe that we could sail back into prosperity on a flood of booze.

Roosevelt's First Inaugural made me prick up my ears. Campaign banalities and mendacities were transcended. The new Executive promised a policy in which I had believed all my life. I did not have any particular measure in mind: a Presidential election is the choice of a general direction; and it appeared to me that, in spite of the tumult and confusion of the contest, America had chosen wisely. Apart from conventional party labels, the choice is between meanness and generosity. Some regimes are incurably mean. The bourgeois monarchy in France, not inefficient, not dishonest, not ruthless, was congenitally ungenerous. It thought of interest first,

not of men. Its chief concern was to protect the haves against
the have-nots: a police guarding the moneybags. It placed
competition, which even at its best is narrowhearted, above
co-operation, which, even when selfish, is at any rate enlightened. Coolidge had been meanness unashamed; and the
principles of Calvin the Taciturn had not been openly repudi-
ated by his successor.

In order to be effective, generosity, a quality of the heart,
demands a quality of the will, courage. Standpattism is
timidity: we are afraid to move, although it is neither safe
nor sane to stand pat on ground that is crumbling under us.
And courage, in its turn, if it is not to be foolhardiness, needs
an intellectual quality, foresight: the faculty to peer ahead,
to descry new problems as they arise, to meet them by new
methods. I hope to expound someday how, in my opinion,
this progressive, dynamic temper is identical with the historical spirit. It is the sense of creative evolution, of momentum. The standpatter may be an antiquarian, but he
denies history: his dream is to arrest the flow. Generosity,
courage, foresight, mean planning instead of drifting, experi-
menting instead of hoarding. They turn collective life from a
timorous and dwindling investment into a pioneering venture.
They mean initiative, enterprise—inevitably individual in
origin, social in their benefits—instead of routine, conservatism, protection. To me, that triad of dynamic virtues was
the very soul of America.

For the first time, I had at least an adumbration of a leadership that was generous in spirit, definite in direction, and
wholly free from doctrinaire intolerance. Systems are valid
only as working hypotheses, to help us meet, from day to
day, problems that no system can solve. If the system becomes an end in itself, it turns into a prison; or, to vary our
metaphors, a system is a short cut that leads into a blind
alley. The pragmatism of James and Dewey, which Roose-

velt turned into an admirable political tool, has often been degraded into a witless empiricism: "Whatever works, is right." Certainly James, Dewey and Roosevelt never ceased to have worthy ends in view. A plague "works" with marvelous efficiency; but between the plague, and the means of checking the plague, the true pragmatist does not remain neutral: "A shrewd blow, plague!—A good parry, medicine!" Pragmatism is purposive; its purpose is not conspicuous waste, and not the glorification of the system maker, but the dignity of man. The pragmatist is not committed to Adam Smith, Ricardo, Karl Marx or Henry George, because, in the human sphere, he does not believe in eternal and mechanical law. The law is constantly in the making. It is the daily Orders of an army on the march. It translates into terms which are ever inadequate and transitory the increasing purpose found in our hearts.

Roosevelt wanted to build a pioneering road, so as to develop new territory. The road started from our own familiar world, not from A.D. 3000: in this Roosevelt was an unimpeachable realist, in the legitimate sense of the term. He did not promise that the road would reach its unknown goal in a perfectly straight line. He was willing to have alternative routes surveyed: if they proved impracticable, they would be abandoned. He was prepared for emergency crossings long ahead of permanent structures. He was not dismayed by the necessity of detour. A detour—America seems at times to misunderstand this French word—means: "Go around and proceed," not "Give up and turn back." All this was not haphazard opportunism. Feeling one's way is the experimental, the scientific method.

It was also a joy for me to find leadership with a smile. I have little patience with "God's angry men," who have even less patience with me. One of my favorites in the Bible is the Book of Jonah, in which the Lord, gently, humorously, rebukes the fierce prophet of doom. Roosevelt's endeavor was on so grand a scale that he could disregard the accusation of levity. I was not amused by many of his wisecracks: he was "bright" rather than witty. But he enjoyed them: why should we grudge him that simple pleasure? A smile may be the badge and the reward of courage: stricken in body, crushed by formidable responsibilities, hated by men of his own class and even of his own party, Roosevelt had won the right to smile.

That hatred of Roosevelt will seem incredible to future generations—unless it is expunged from the people's memory, like the violent attacks against Washington, Jefferson and Lincoln. I could gauge it: although unworthy, I move among respectable people, and many of my best friends hated Roosevelt throughout their waking hours; I feel sure that some of them must have hated him on in their dreams. Yet he was no alien conqueror, but one of their own race, faith and station. That hatred was too virulent to be merely sordid: the profiteer in his purity does not hate; Laval was noted for his "greasy good nature." The Roosevelt haters were not defending their pocketbooks: they were aware that the New Deal had been far better for Business than the Hoover-Mellon era. Their anger was righteous. Their moral standing was linked in their minds with certain economic doctrines. The plums were sweet in themselves; but sweeter still because they proved the Wall Street Jack Horners to be good boys. Roosevelt, in his smiling way, cast doubt upon that comfortable scheme. People who would not listen to socialistic agitators were lured by his gentle insidious voice: "My friends. . . ." Perhaps luxury was a sin rather than a reward? Perhaps the true name of the Profit Motive was greed? The New Deal threatened to take from the rich, not their pelf, but their self-righteousness, which is infinitely more precious.

Roosevelt came nearer providing generous, farsighted, finely shaded leadership than any man in modern history.

Jaurès and Blum, who had some of his qualities, never had his magnificent chance. Yet there were irremediable flaws in the work and in the man. I followed him with admiration, but not with confidence. My delight in his words and deeds was constantly tinged with irritation.

A progressive, he had to rely upon a party the permanent elements of which were the Solid South and the Machines in the big cities. Both ultimately rebelled against him; but he would never have reached power without them. We may wonder what would have happened if he had rebelled against them first; if, in 1941, he had frankly struck a Progressive alliance with Wendell Willkie. The speculation is idle, however, not because it did not happen, but because it could not happen. He was better able to rise above mere party than Wilson. His use of Stimson, Knox, Vandenberg, was highly to his credit. He was not afraid of shattering precedents. But he could not share power, or even the limelight. He called De Gaulle a prima donna, and he was probably right. But the term applies even more accurately to himself.

His supreme gifts were his limitations. Of course he was ambitious: the Presidency was not thrust upon his reluctant shoulders. Of course he believed that he alone could manage an incredibly complex and perilous situation. The virulent opposition to Wallace must have given him secret satisfaction: he remained indispensable and unique. He could not groom a successor: no "peerless leader" can, without admitting that he is not peerless. It is probably an absurdity to dream of a Leader free from the *Führer* complex. Of course he was clever. He would never have won, with the most incongruous coalition that ever masqueraded as a party, unless he had been endowed with cleverness beyond the reach of men and angels. He knew it, and reveled in it. A virtuoso, he preferred the most subtle moves. He thought a masterly game had to be disconcerting. His paths were involved without being crooked. He used most effectively the method of dramatic personal conferences. I have no doubt that his skill and charm enabled him to work profitably with Churchill and Stalin. But the results were "secret covenants secretly arrived at," a monstrosity in a democracy. Personalism is a dangerous method. When Roosevelt vanished, everything that he had worked for—the New Deal, co-operation with Russia, a world of friendliness and peace—came toppling down. No doubt there was, after a great strain, the natural reaction of the ungenerous. But the utter collapse of the Roosevelt policies was due first of all to the flaw in Roosevelt's character. He trusted his skill more than his principles. He ardently loved peace and justice: but I am afraid he loved Roosevelt even more.

CHAPTER TWELVE

The Shadows Fall

THIS IS THE record of my thought, and not of my pleasant, uneventful career. "What me befell" did not affect the world in the least; and it has colored my opinions only to a very slight extent. All I need to say is that I enjoyed with gratitude the rare privilege which ought to be every man's birthright: my business was not an obstacle, but an incentive, to my thought. How many lawyers, politicians and clergymen are denied that advantage! Freedom, like celibacy, involves a renunciation. Success, even in the academic world, is a snare; authority hampers the man who commands. The popular writer is hemmed in by his own popularity: he may so degenerate that he is no longer conscious of his enslavement. I was spared all these temptations.

So I shall touch but briefly on my worldly moves and concerns. In 1924, I left the Rice Institute. With deep regret: we found the social climate of Houston ideal. But the physical atmosphere did not suit us so well, and we thought the bracing air of California would be more favorable to our growing children. I went to the University of California at Los Angeles, then modestly called the "Southern Branch." It was in the very first year of its existence, an enormous baby; its name, status and permanent habitat were still uncertain. I remember watching a long and patient line of very obvious freshmen by the lily pond in front of Millspaugh Hall. I asked Dean Rieber: "What are they waiting for?"— "Oh! to be ducked. They have just voted to make it a tradition of this University that the seniors should duck the entering class." Men and institutions have an imperious and pathetic desire to feel rooted in the past; no country has so many antique shops as young America. As no suitable pond was provided on the new campus, I suppose this academic baptism was dropped. Many traditions die in infancy.

I never knew the official boundaries of Hollywood; but in 1924, the university, on Vermont Avenue, was supposed to be within the Film Capital. At any rate, there were studios east and west of us; and our very handsome buildings were frequently used for college movies, a genre which has declined in popularity. It was at times difficult to tell bona fide co-eds from professional supers, and the scholastic term "make-up examination" became ambiguous. As far as I know, none of my colleagues was ever picked out to impersonate the stage professor. I am afraid we were not the type.

I acquired a queer, shamefaced affection for the sprawling southern metropolis, "a hundred suburbs in search of a city." Its oddities so wickedly exposed by Aldous Huxley in *After Many a Summer Dies the Swan,* were a constant source of amusement to me. In the dismal era of "normalcy," it was a relief to come across restaurants in the shape of bowler hats, an equestrian statue of Napoleon advertising *The Thief of Bagdad,* and cemeteries so excruciatingly beautiful that they made you cling to this life. On Saturday nights, the announcements of religious services for the morrow provided instructive and delightful reading. Evidently, the pre-Romantic and Romantic eras were not closed. Heirs of Cagliostro and St.

Germain walked abroad in the days of Calvin Coolidge. Aimée Semple McPherson wore an untarnished halo; and there was a "Church of the Divine Secret: Mrs. McGillicuddy, Discoverer of the Secret." I understood at last what the British meant by the "balmy" shores of southern California.

Yes, I could have been happy in that incredible and cheerful chaos—99 per cent humdrum, the rest wicked, or crazy, or both. It was not cohesive enough to be tyrannical—although it tried its feeble best. It was heterogeneous enough, and naïve enough, to be amusing. It obeyed impulses with childlike ingenuousness. Because "the Curse of Tutankhamen" had touched archaeology with melodrama, we had apartment houses and a theater in the purest Egyptian style. Los Angeles confirmed one of my favorite ideas: the notion of *culture*, accepted as a reality by the anthropologists, is a delusion. We may think that the Trobrianders have a "culture," because we do not know them from within. We observe them as we might study the ants—and how an ant would laugh at our interpretation of their curious ways! But I was an Angeleno myself: I knew that our bric-a-brac accumulation of faiths, customs, traditions, tempers and dreams did not form an organic whole. The sole principle which enabled us to live together at peace was tolerance, the fine flower that springs from a deep soil of indifference. The material bonds of union—the English language and traffic regulations, both frequently transgressed—had nothing to do with a philosophy, conscious or unconscious. They simply provided a *modus vivendi*.

Dr. Ernest Carroll Moore, Provost of the Southern Branch, had invited me to spend with him "the evening of my days." I was in no twilight mood, neither was he, but I found that association with him at any hour of the day would be a delight. I never knew a man in whom sheer unadulterated kindness had such a positive quality. In comparison, I, who used

to think of myself as mild and benevolent, became conscious
of my inborn and cultivated wickedness. We are apt to consider gentleness as a lamblike quality, and I have no use for
lamb except as *gigot rôti*. But there was no lack of strength
in Dr. Moore. A philosopher by training and temper, he
was an educator of nation-wide experience and repute, a
shrewd administrator, and, I surmise from the mere fact of
his retaining office, something of a diplomat. In his spare moments, he was a criminologist and a banker. All these things
I took for granted in him. But it was unexpected to meet a
man who, in middle life, had kept intact his faith in human
nature. My friends the Covenanters would say that he lacked
one essential element: the conviction of sin. He made the
doctrine of total depravity a mockery. He proved that it is
not radically impossible for a do-gooder to be keen-sighted
and practical; we all know that it is extremely easy for a
cynic to be a weakling and a fool.

I was prepared to spend the long sunset hours in the widely
advertised climate and the cafeteria culture of Los Angeles
when I was called back to Stanford. The offer was irresistible.
We had never ceased to love our first home, and to believe
in its spirit. We still had many friends on the faculty, including President Ray Lyman Wilbur who, for a brief season,
had been our family physician. Dr. Jordan was still alive and
active. I was to be blissfully free from administrative duties,
and independent from any departmental control; I was to
enjoy as professor of General and Comparative Literature,
that *Lehr- und Lernfreiheit*, that absolute freedom of teaching and learning, which once was the glory of German universities.

So I said farewell to the promising young giant at Los
Angeles. I have lived to see it prosper mightily, housed in an
Italian hill town which, in certain lights, looks almost con-
vincing; at its feet a village which is a realtor's Xanadu, the

perfection of futuristic baroque. It has become a great power in the football field. Incidentally, it has attracted such men as W. A. Nitze, Fernand Baldensperger and Bertrand Russell. I remember my brief sojourn in Los Angeles with unmitigated pleasure.[1]

My twenty-one years at Stanford, until I retired, will be the subject of another work, a purely academic report on the meaning and methods of the Humanities. It would be invidious to pick out for mention a few of my colleagues and students. Stanford deprecates sentimental effusions. When I returned after twelve years, one of my very best friends remarked: "I haven't been seeing you lately. . . ." Dr. Wilbur in particular would receive any tribute of affection with that poker face of his, which covers unfathomable depths of humor. This I may say, for it is common knowledge: I have found him the perfect executive. A born and trained diagnostician, he would see your problem at once, and hand out a decision when you were still fumbling for an approach. This left you speechless, which was exactly what he intended; for, a very effective speaker himself, he has no patience with idle words.

We were both devoted to Dr. Jordan, and this created between us a bond which has grown firmer with the years. Like Jordan, he has kept absolutely true to the spirit of academic freedom. We may have been on different sides of the barricade at times—else we would not be the rugged individualists we are—but I never had the slightest suspicion that such differences might interfere with my academic security or with our mutual esteem. Like Jordan, he believed that the one great aim of a university is the advancement of learning;

[1] I wonder if Miss Agnes de Mille remembers that she once requested to be excused from class, because Pavlova was in town, "and Pavlova is my religion." I assured her it was our policy never to interfere with any one's religious beliefs or practices. This might have been a dangerous principle in Los Angeles.

Stanford, to him, was first of all a community of scholars and scientists, young and old. Finances, administration, pedagogy, public relations, were in his mind necessary "services"; but he never allowed them to usurp a predominant place. Like Jordan, he was a forward-looking pilot. (In spite of a widespread prejudice, looking back is not the safest way to steer.) He was better prepared to consider bold experiments than many of the trustees, faculty or alumni. Like Jordan, he could lift his eyes beyond the cloisters, the state and even the nation, and labor for mutual understanding and peace. But even these few words might seem fulsome to him. I cannot rival his imperial brevity.

Someday, if I reach the years of George Bernard Shaw, I may indulge in personal garrulities. It would be a relief to be human without remorse. Naturally, many more men and incidents than I can mention affected the growth of my thought, even though they did not change its nature. Travel is an education, especially for educators. It is good to check up on our books, once in a while. It was not a matter of indifference that we had relatives and friends both in Great Britain and in France, and visited them repeatedly; that I spent a few weeks in remote Galicia and in Madrid under Primo de Rivera; that we were in Germany at the time of reviving prosperity and apparent sanity, when Hitler was a laughingstock; that we saw the brief heyday of the Front Populaire in Paris; that we visited French North Africa thoroughly, in complete freedom, but, thanks to André Siegfried, with the best assistance from the French authorities. Many of my opinions grew more definite as well as more delicately shaded, not through the printed word, but in the homes of foreign friends and in the streets of foreign cities.

This is true, not only of voyages abroad, but of tours in our own country. Had I not taught for a summer in Honolulu, I would not know, as a personal experience, that it is possible for "Anglo-Saxons" to associate with other stocks without arrogance. The modest and friendly home of the Kahanamokus, has taught me much more than sociological statistics; and my classes—a veritable ethnographic museum—proved to me that East and West could meet. I owe a great deal to a summer session in the Agricultural College of Logan, Utah. There, in a community composed almost solidly of Latter-day Saints, I discovered old-fashioned rural America at its very best: healthy, kindly, God-fearing folk, with a great sense of fun; persuaded that tea and coffee were almost as sinful as smoking; virtuously swilling buttermilk by the gallon, which seemed to enhance the fairness and candor of their Scandinavian countenances.

Above all, I should like to express my gratitude to Cugnot, inventor of the automobile, and to his distant successors, Messrs. Dodge, Ford, Chrysler, Marmon and Buick, who devised for our family marvelous conveyances. From 1923 on, we hardly ever used the railroads for our annual tours. We crossed the country in every direction; twice we circled it, from Stanford to Percé on the Gaspé Peninsula, thence to the tip of Florida, skirting the gulf and the Mexican border on our way back. We stopped at the homes of friends, at village inns, tourists' rooms, camps and Motels. We saw main streets and side streets, and not merely the dingy districts that cluster around railway stations. We were lost, flooded, bogged in mud, sand or snow, and marooned in many delightful manners. We explored the lost Spanish villages in the Sangre de Cristo Mountains, that only the rugged and sure-footed Ford could reach; and, in an Oklahoma cloudburst, we spent the night unexpectedly with most friendly Indians. Pullman and airplane travelers are mere living parcels, efficiently collected and delivered: the man at the steering wheel truly owns America. It is on the highways that I won my final diploma as John Doe. But, as a devotee of

Alfred de Vigny, it rejoiced me to think that the lure of the open road had been so searchingly, so poetically expressed by him a full century before.[2]

Yes, my family and professional paths were all pleasantness and peace. But I was conscious of the darkening sky. Ever since 1917, we had lived, even in the hours of triumph and prosperity, in an ominous atmosphere. The end of the First World War, the fumbling efforts that followed, the rise of Mussolini and Hitler, the Second World War, and the tragic confusion which oppresses us at present, are all part of a single drama. The final catharsis—the intelligent acceptance of destiny, the understanding that would ennoble our suffering—is not yet in sight.

Throughout this thirty-year crisis, I have attempted to follow principles which are at the same time complex and definite. I agree with everybody, with the result that nobody agrees with me. I am the fellow traveler unwelcome in every company. So help me God, I cannot otherwise. These principles I have alluded to in my preceding chapter: they seemed to me to underlie the New Deal at its best. I must state them again and more explicitly now, as we are nearing the end of this record.

First of all, I believe there is a choice before us. Even if predestination, fatalism or determinism is true, we have to act as though they were not. The choice, in simplest terms, is between the high and the low, between generosity and meanness, between the do-gooder and the profiteer. I find it hard to give an abstract definition of "values." I am satisfied with the rule: "Act so that you shall not have to despise yourself, or the common man in you." We may be ludicrously unequal to our faith, and we may strive in vain. But my

---

[2] In *La Maison du Berger* (1844), one of the great poems in the French language; a nostalgic farewell to road travel, then being superseded by the railways.

sympathies, cutting across national, racial, sectarian, political boundaries, go to those who are seeking the nobler way. "Myself, first, last and all the time!" seems to me the epitome of meanness, even though, in different spheres, it may call itself individualism, patriotism, the profit motive or "realism."

The second point is the recognition of change, of growth (I am willing to discard the question-begging term "progress") as the law of life; so that every moment, conditioned by the past, is an adjustment to the onrushing future. There is no stability but in motion. This is the only "eternal verity" I recognize. I happen to be, professionally, a student of history.

The third point is the infinite complexity of human conditions, which makes it impossible to give an irrefutable account of the past, or a rigorous blueprint of the future. We must choose our direction, and plan ahead as far as we can see, but we cannot plan for all men and for all time. We must take the *long* view; we cannot take the *eternal* view. Hence the vanity of all hard and fast systems as keys to the absolute. Systems at their best are guides that may help us over a difficult pass. There usually are other routes; there certainly are other obstacles ahead beyond the ken of our present guides.

The choice of a direction, and long-term planning, would be daydreaming, without *practicality*. Practicality, or pragmatism, experimental and constructive, differs radically from opportunism, which is passive and haphazard: "Meet the issues of the day as they arise, without thought of a general trend." And pragmatism is poles asunder from realism in the usual political sense, which is the deliberate adoption of meanness as an ideal.

In the fourth place, we must recognize that revolutions, like wars, are catastrophes; that they invariably destroy much that deserved to live, if only perhaps for aesthetic reasons; that if they release energies, they also exhaust them; that they must place a premium on fanaticism and brutality; that, after the storm, the world is morally and physically weaker. America would have been better without our War of Secession from England, or without the war for Southern Independence. (I never could bring Dr. Jordan, who hated all *other* wars, to see this particular point.) It is a great calamity that the French Revolution broke out *in 1792*,[3] and the Russian Revolution in 1917; and the world should bend every effort toward the prevention of other revolutions.

But it must never be forgotten that revolutions—as distinct from riots, revolts or sporadic disorders—are caused by those who strive to dam the normal flow of history. The blind leaders first show their inefficiency by failing to recognize the direction and power of a trend. Then they throw haphazard and feeble obstacles in the way—enough to increase the menace of the mounting waters, not enough to stop them for long.

So although I consider a revolution, however "great and glorious," as an evil, I cannot automatically place the blame on the revolutionists. The alleged forces of conservation are guilty: either because they were ungenerous and blind, or because they lacked determination and efficiency, a lack which is the symptom of moral weakness. I cannot think of a single regime destroyed by a revolution, in which the proper verdict would not have been: "Suicide."

A revolution is deplorable only as a method; just as a bombardment is not the most intelligent way of clearing slums. Still, at an exorbitant cost, a revolution may destroy obstacles

---

[3] I said 1792 advertently, because what I have now in mind is violent, destructive revolution. The word has other meanings: either the discovery of a new process, a new thought, the attempting of a new path; or the peaceful acceleration of overdue reforms. In spite of one sensational episode, the symbolical storming of the Bastille, the Revolution of 1789 belonged to that last category. This Burke failed to comprehend.

to normal growth, and it would be exceedingly foolish to restore the obstacles, because they had been removed by violent means. Our legitimate hatred and dread of a revolution does not commit us to the undoing of its work. Both for the prevention of impending evil, and for the cure of evil already done, the one remedy is a generous and farsighted policy. Giving tanks and bombers to a reactionary government is a provocation, not a palliative.

I have no intention of giving here an epitome of world history for the last thirty years. I am interpreting, not the baffled progress of mankind, but my own. What follows is, I repeat, the projection of my principles upon the screen of events; and the principles are myself. The result is not a scientific verdict, but a self-portrait. Certainly these problems were the web of my biography. I had my simple comforts and pleasures, and my minor tribulations. I did my work honestly. But, even in the realm of "General and Comparative Literature," I could not forget the shadows that were engulfing us all. *Preface to World Literature, Literature and Society, Art for Art's Sake,* the half-finished *Criteria,* were not propaganda for a particular policy. They were exercises in method. If a man learns to thread his way through the maze of culture, he should be better able to face the more elementary issues of power, profit, and political freedom. In the dedication of *Art for Art's Sake,* I quote the inevitable words: "For what shall it profit a man, if he shall gain the whole world, and lose his own soul?" This thought is valid in religion, literature, economics and politics.

For thirty years, the Western world has been unable to make up its mind about the Russian Revolution. In that stubborn fight for incomprehension, Clemenceau was the first offender: he blocked Wilson's attempt to treat the Bolshevists otherwise than as mad dogs. He was not a reactionary; and, although a ruthless individualist, not a fanatical anti-Socialist. But the fight against Germany had absorbed his whole soul. The Communists had capitulated, and he viewed them in the same light as De Gaulle did Laval. The Western democracies—need we rehearse the familiar story? —supported every White adventurer they could discover or invent. There were Allied and Associated Forces at Archangel, Murmansk, Odessa, Vladivostok. The West backed the nefarious imperialism of Pilsudsky, and smiled approval when the Turks grabbed Kars.

In those benighted days, the ruling classes were determined on a crusade. They were halted by the articulate protest of a few intellectuals; including—Fate has mischievous ironies—young William Bullitt. They were halted above all by the unorganized, sullen and invincible reluctance of the masses. The people of the West had by no means been converted en bloc to communism, or even to socialism. But they had no desire to fight for a capitalistic ideology. Their barely conscious but steady policy was Wilson's: the scholar and the common man had arrived by totally different processes at similar conclusions. "Obtain for Russia an unhampered and unembarrassed opportunity for the independent determination of her own political development and national policy and assure her of a sincere welcome into the society of free nations under institutions of her own choosing."

So the crusade had to be given up. The West had to be satisfied with a *cordon sanitaire* of anti-Communist, anti-Russian satellite states. Both England and France had liberal velleities, under Ramsay MacDonald and Edouard Herriot. Unfortunately, these statesmen, intelligent, upright, generous, were among the weakest that ever reached nominal power. They headed parties, or coalitions, without any definite foreign policy. In diplomacy, the Tories, both British and French, are alone in possession of a personnel, a tradition, a technique, a doctrine. The "popular" parties, untrained in that field, think first and last of home reforms.[4] So while Europe, in a dazed but steady fashion, was growing more democratic, its governments hardened in their anti-Russian attitude. In such a mood, how could they resolutely oppose Mussolini and Hitler? The dictators were the spearheads of the fight against communism. When Mussolini sent aid to Franco, the British Tories "ran interference" for him. They evolved the cynical farce of neutrality. Mussolini swore that there were no Italian troops in Spain, and solemnly promised that they would be withdrawn on the morrow of victory. Léon Blum, who deserved a better fate, gave up in his turn: France, divided, threatened with Fascist civil war, could not have faced Italy and Germany without British support.

Czechoslovakia next was sacrificed. She had committed the same unpardonable sin as the Spanish Republic: she was not virulently hostile to the Soviets. She could have been saved only with Russian assistance, which was proffered. But the very thought horrified the West, and was vetoed by Poland. At the time of Munich, the situation ought to have been clear. Mussolini, Franco, Hitler, who were protecting Europe from the spread of communism, should have been given a free hand. The central bastion of Russian sympathies, Czechoslovakia, had been reduced. Poland and Rumania, whose governments were anti-Communist and anti-Russian, should have understood that, in the interest of the sacred cause, they had to accept unconditionally the leadership of Germany. The material terms offered by Hitler to Poland, up to the last minute, were extremely reasonable. But they implied a fact which no "realist" could evade: Poland had to fall definitely within the orbit of Germany.

Of course the common people of the West were still averse

---

[4] This is true of the popular parties, not of the people. Repeatedly the masses have shown keen interest in international affairs, and greater foresight than the *bourgeoisie*.

to an anti-Russian crusade; but they had no stomach for a pro-Russian crusade either. They were confused and weary. We now wonder why the conservative *bourgeoisie* of Poland and the West did not see the light, and give their blessing to Hitler's eager hosts. What prevented Hitler from being chosen as the champion of Western civilization was a ghost, the dead hand of the past strangling the present. Hitler himself was to blame. He was still haunted with the defunct treaty of Versailles; in his eagerness to exorcize its shadow, he treated the West with studied arrogance, and made "collaboration" unthinkable except for the craven. He was drunk with his own insolence, and did not realize that it hampered his mission. If he had allowed the Allies to cherish feebly the shreds of their phantom victory, he would have been accepted by them as a Heaven-sent Führer.

But it was not merely the recent past that befogged the present. There were still statesmen in Europe who thought in terms of the old Balance of Power. The rise of Germany to an imperial position among nations hurt their traditional pride, and contravened their immemorial doctrine: *Debellare superbos.* Germany was to be resisted and humbled, although her power was indispensable to the great enterprise. These men were moved neither by economic interests nor by social prejudices: they belonged to an earlier age. Their guiding thought was national prestige, the "greatness" of England and France. With that single end in view, they turned against the dominant power. They were even ready to ally themselves with its enemies. Did not Francis I, His Most Christian Majesty, seek the aid of the Grand Turk against the nominal head of Christendom, the Emperor? Did not Richelieu, a Prince of the Church, support the Protestants against Catholic Austria? Of these statesmen in the grand tradition, the clearest minded were Louis Barthou, Winston Churchill and Vansittart. They were unable to stop Hitler: Barthou was assassinated in 1934, Churchill was in opposition, Vansittart never held a policy-making office. They could only snarl the efforts of the men who were aware of the Red Peril, and who knew that Hitler was their buckler and their sword. The trouble with "the clock of history," to borrow Alvin Johnson's phrase, is that it registers twenty different "times" at once. In 1939, the people should have been thinking of 1939, and, if they had been very wise, of 1950. But the clock kept striking 1648, 1713, 1763, 1815, 1871, 1919. Machiavelli, Richelieu, Talleyrand, Metternich, Palmerston, Bismarck, Disraeli, thronged the council table. But for the confusion they created, dividing the forces of the anti-Communist world, what in 1947 we called the Truman Doctrine could have won a decisive victory in 1939, and the world could have been made safe for private enterprise.

Europe had lost faith both in Clemenceau, "Old Father Victory," and in Wilson. Of this utter bewilderment, Chamberlain and Daladier were the outstanding examples. To the last, they attempted to appease Hitler, to bribe him with offers of a loan; at the same time, they haggled in the most distrustful manner with the Soviets. There was only one way in which their anticommunism and their antinazism could be reconciled: if only Germany and Russia would come to blows, and thoroughly mangle each other! Then the West could safely step in and collect the remains. This wishful thinking was so transparent that Hitler and Stalin could forestall it with great ease. They decided to defer their inevitable quarrel. As soon as the agreement was known, Chamberlain and Daladier understood that they had lost all control of their destinies. The people caught from them a mood of horror-stricken resignation. In 1918, the West had failed to heed Wilson's appeal; the nations had not stood "the acid test." Twenty-one years later, the price of their recreancy had to be paid in full.

Our material situation was infinitely better: we were not immediately threatened. Our moral situation was, if anything, worse. The Great Refusal had left ugly and still aching scars. We could no longer be roused by such a call as Wilson's. It was, as Herbert Agar said, "a time for greatness" (which, by the way, is exactly what General de Gaulle means by *Grandeur*). But America, old and young, radical and reactionary, had but one desire: to make herself so small that Destiny might pass her by. Her watchwords were negative: Strictest neutrality; the Yanks are not coming. Perhaps it was wise. If you refuse to think, it might be safer not to move. War had to be forced upon us.

When Japan made up our minds, our enormous energies were immediately polarized. Everything that we were supposed to stand for—individualism, private enterprise, the profit motive—was cheerfully modified. America, conscripted, rationed, regulated, became to a considerable degree socialistic. The result was an epic of material achievement without precedent and without parallel. If we had a five-year reconstruction plan on the same scale and by the same methods, the face of the country would be changed. We went through the most sweeping technical revolution of modern times. But there was no parallel change in thought. While we were demonstrating to the world the glorious possibilities of collectivism—the whole merchant shipping under co-ordinated management, for instance—we still clung in theory to the preindustrial economics of the Village Blacksmith.

Unthinking became a rigid law. We were too busy winning the war to consider what it was about. "Unconditional surrender" covered everything. It postponed the evil day when it would be necessary to plan for the future of the world. Hitler was an ideal scapegoat: victory came, Hitler was gone, and we faced with dread the void of our own minds. Fortunately, there always is another scapegoat in readiness: communism. So we picked up the good work just where Hitler had to drop it. Communism provides a perfect excuse for not thinking. The Communists do not think, since Marxism is *the* Eternal Verity. Their opponents do not think, since communism is Evil Absolute. On either side, dissenters are denounced and purged away as "disloyal." Blessed are the Many, for their minds are at rest.

In 1942, I happened to have a cumulative six-month vacation. This was no time for idleness. I believe in Art for Art's Sake; but the spirit did not move me to fiddle. I had inherited a Puritan conscience and married another. I was eager to obey their stern voices, but I was too old to fight, and not clever enough to work with my hands. It is easier to convert an industrial plant to war purposes than a professor of General and Comparative Literature.

It did not please me in the least to be above the strife. Fortunately I was acquainted with Lewis Galantière, head of the French Section in the Office of War Information, and to him I offered my technical skill. No novelist or playwright would dare to invent Galantière: a delicate man of letters, a scholar, a Broadway wit, and also that impressive and somewhat sinister character, an "international banker." But Galantière does exist, in the teeth of verisimilitude, and he gave me a job. Altogether, in New York and San Francisco a three-year assignment. The material output was enormous. I have kept rough drafts of my scripts: they form volumes, which I may glance at some day, when I am in a grimly humorous mood. The material results have to be accepted on faith: we won the war, didn't we? and this was part of our global warfare. The experience was novel and exhilarating.

I had always been an isolated worker: I found myself in a factory. But a foundry would be a haunt of claustral peace compared with the pandemonium of the OWI. In a former garage at the corner of Fifty-seventh and Broadway, each floor was a single enormous room, with our desks in serried rows. All the telephones were in use all the time; verbal basketball was played from end to end of the gaunt echoing hall; the highest problems of policy were discussed in shouts over our heads, while a bevy of secretaries and messenger girls filled the rare interstices of silence with their delightful chirping.

We were an incredible Foreign Legion, recruited from all countries, faiths and walks of life. I believe at one time only Galantière and I were American citizens. We had Russians of all shades, Greeks, Turks, a Martinique Negro, a marvelous young Estonian. The OWI was the refuge of all Displaced Persons; a cartoon posted on the bulletin board reminded us that once a milkman had been pressed into service, on the chance, because no one could understand a word he said. Some names could not be pronounced without coughing or sneezing; and if a charming young couple were called Day, it was simply a wise abbreviation for Durakinowsky or some such portentous patronymic. Yet the whole cosmopolitan crew was unbelievably French; and there was a fine *esprit de corps* in that haphazard conglomeration.

We had medical men, actors, opera singers—the fine veteran Rothier, of the Metropolitan, from whom I learnt many a trick of diction—judges, writers, politicians, journalists. André Breton, the Surrealist, walked nobly among us, his leonine head thrown back, with the elaborate distant courtesy of a king in exile. Julian Green had a youthful, kindly, amused smile, totally at variance with the somber and morbid tone of his novels. Once in a while, we saw the willowy figure, the furrowed ascetic face, the waving halo of gray hair of Jacques Maritain. Philippe Barrès, Robert de Saint Jean and Pierre Lazareff represented the summits of journalism.

Lazareff was the animator. Small, bald, wiry, he was of energy all compact. We could see him pacing furiously in his glass cage, his hands behind his back like Felix the Cat, chewing his fountain pen, dictating like a machine gun. He would explode into magnificent rages, and revert as suddenly to his natural, sunny cordiality. An incomparable maestro, a perfect diplomat under his mask of exuberance, this Little Corporal of journalism loved his trade as Napoleon loved his armies. He too could pinch the ear of his *grognards,* and make them feel that they had their share in the common victory. I suppose there were several abysses between us: I do not know. I was too busy working enthusiastically with him to think of any differences.

This unwonted excitement, and the blasts of a very sharp early winter, nearly unhorsed me. I had a severe heart attack, which proved to be a benediction in macabre dress. A couple of weeks after knocking at death's door, I resumed my script writing, and, soon after that, my broadcasting. But I was excused from punching the clock. I came to the office only for the conferences, and for my own "show." I provided desk space at home, without charge to the government: an arrangement so sensible that it passeth bureaucratic understanding. I enjoyed the tumult of the office all the better for taking it in infrequent sips. This severe warning had a deeper effect. It gave me great serenity, which the following years have not destroyed. Because I had been so near departing, I discovered, not without pride, that I was ready to depart. Since then, I have had my share of worries, but not a moment of anguish. In Babu English again, "I have one foot in the grave, and with the other, I hail the dawn of a saner day."

Some of us gave war news, and statistics of our formidable effort, the things our listeners most wanted to hear, the one kind of propaganda in which plain truth was the most effective weapon. Others, and I among them, were detailed to present to the world a portrait of America. We had to do it in self-defense. We had to dispel the horrific picture evoked by the Nazis: America as a ruthless plutocracy, sneering at ideals, spurning principles, animated exclusively by the profit motive, an America whose only business was Business. I had a long series on "Episodes of Franco-American Friendship," and a breath-taking, bird's-eye view of American culture in twelve quarters of an hour. Especially, I had daily comments on current events, for which I was promoted to the dignity of John Doe. What I was appointed to say, I firmly believed; and I came to believe it with ever-increasing cogency. This was my postgraduate course in Citizenship, in which I was both teacher and pupil. Here, in briefest form, is its syllabus. There is not merely an American scene and American folkways, but an American *movement*. It is not all unconscious momentum. It has sense. It makes sense. I accepted the gibe that our theme song was: "I don't know where I am going, but I'm on my way." It meant, in less homely terms: "I have chosen my path. What obstacles lie ahead, I cannot fully foretell; what delights, I can only surmise. But I never expect to stop and turn back. For the way and the life are one."

I confess that my colleagues in Broadcast Control frowned once in a while when I quoted too liberally from Washington, Jefferson, Lincoln and Franklin Roosevelt. They had not realized how radical, how Revolutionary, is the American tradition. They had to make sure that the Declaration of Independence, the Preamble to the Constitution and the Gettysburg Address were not contrary to the latest Directives. I must admit that my absolute sincerity did not preclude at times a tinge of irony. There is a wholesome pleasure in agreeing with people better than they agree with themselves.

I do not know how many listeners I reached; at any rate, I fully persuaded myself. So I closed a cycle of forty years with the same conviction I had at the beginning, only more deeply rooted and better documented. Many Americans had tried to shake my faith, but I still believed in America. And I had as good a right as the next fellow to speak in the name of our country. No doubt I had my personal equation. I was born in Paris, France, and not in Paris, Texas. But I felt at least 99 per cent human. I was Man, the Common Man. I had taken to heart my assigned role as John Doe.

During the San Francisco Conference, I was invited to give twelve radio addresses. My sponsor was Mr. Paul Verdier, President of the city of Paris, and the model of a useful citizen. My freedom was unlimited. If I had to present the French aspect of world problems, it was not as a propagandist, but as a student of history. It would have been impossible for me to be a retained advocate in any case: there was no French policy to defend. The French delegation was circumspect to the vanishing point. It faded away with dignity, with elegance: no one could be silent, or abstain from voting on vital issues, in a more masterly fashion. In an atmosphere of equivocation, it is proper for French logic to wear a mask; and no mask could have been more bland than that of M. Bidault. I had hoped that France would take the lead of the minor nations against the autocracy of the Big Three. But, a Great Power by courtesy, her position ill defined, with a barely recognized provisional government, France found it advisable to leave that honor to Australia.

My central thought remained the one which had guided

my teaching, my writing, and my activities with the OWI. America and France, alone among major nations, are founded upon the same principles. And because they are principles, not historical compromises of the British type, these are applicable to the whole human race. The burden of President Roosevelt's speech on the Four Freedoms was: "Everywhere in the world." We should all strive to be, in the words of George Washington, "citizens of the great Republic of Humanity at large."

I had hoped that the San Francisco Conference would be the constitutional assembly of such a commonwealth, not the elaborate poker game so dear to traditional diplomacy. It soon became apparent that the delegates were the representatives of the states, not of the people, and that they were unable to learn the one essential lesson. The principles proclaimed were lofty enough: not more so than at Vienna, at the Hague, at Paris in 1919. They were, according to custom, on the *Excelsior!* level. After this perfunctory genuflection before an empty shrine, the conference proceeded to business. And "business" meant the denial of everything for which we had fought.

Nearly a century and a half ago, a small knot of Parisians were gaping at the Constitution of the Consulate, just placarded on the walls. A workingman asked his neighbor: "Do you understand all this stuff?"— "Perfectly. There are only two words in it: Napoleon Bonaparte." Let us be "realistic," and strip off all the pious or juridical verbiage. The San Francisco Charter has 111 articles, which may be summed up in three words: "Might is Right," or, more tersely still, in one: "Power." And Power means war.

Power is the right to bully. When Cordell Hull said that there was no dream of coercion on the part of the Big Three, the right lobe of his brain did not know what the left lobe was thinking. For if you abandon the thought of coercion ("Do

as you are told, or else. ، . .") the very idea of the Big Three
dissolves into thin air. The Big Three happen to be the World
Directorate because they are big, and, coincidentally, because they are right. But the Big Stick is the ultimate argument. Only willful blindness can deny that the privilege of
the Great Powers is the very essence of power politics. If
we do renounce war as an instrument of policy, if we give
up the thought of placing force at the service of injustice,
then we are not more assured of having our own way than,
say, Uruguay or Sweden.

"Placing force at the service of injustice! What blasphemy!
Is it not plain that we, and Great Britain, and Russia (remember, we are in the Spring of 1945), desire to rule only
in the interests of righteousness?" And who shall judge of
righteousness? If it is we alone, we shall have the classical
argument betwen the Wolf and the Lamb: *"La raison du plus
fort est toujours la meilleure," ergo* Hong Kong, the guerdon
of the Opium War, must have been assigned to Great Britain
by Divine Providence. If, on the contrary, we are ready to
submit our case to an impartial tribunal which cannot be
coerced, then we give up the "realistic" notion of Great
Powers; we revert to plain honesty, that is to say, I surmise,
to Utopia.

In those days, writers of all shades, from Walter Lipp-
mann's lily white to Freda Kirchwey's most becoming pink,
agreed that "realistically," the domination of the New Axis
was a necessity. When I pleaded for world democracy ("No
liberty without equality of status"), Frederick Schuman,
proudly tough-minded, smiled at my "delusion." Yet I did
not live in a dream world. I knew that the moral law is not
self-enforcing. I did not proclaim in the same breath the
World Community and "the sovereign equality of all peace-
loving states," an accumulation of antinomies hard to match
outside of a theological treatise. I never believed that "squir-

rels were elephants" or that "minnows were whales," to use
the quaint phraseology of Messrs. Fox and Schuman,[5] any
more than I imagined I was the equal of Joe Louis in the ring
or John D. Rockefeller, Jr., in the auction room. But, in a
civilized state, the law is not in the hands of the prize fighter
or the billionaire. I, the merest minnow, have my rights. I
can freely differ with them without being told: "Want to
fight? Where is your atomic bomb?" The government has
not abdicated into the hands of the gangsters, although they
have "power" and the peaceable citizen has none. All this
may be exceedingly "unrealistic," but, thank the Lord, it is
the American way of life.

We had made—we were still making—a titanic collective
effort. We were never told: "Not so fast! Let us not be *perfectionists*. Of course, we cannot hope to crush the Nazis altogether. That is a radical, a Utopian dream. One step at a
time. Let's rap their knuckles, and call it a day. Next time,
we shall rap them a little harder. Eventually, they will learn
their lesson." No: we were taught that the principle of brute
force, of terrorism, as incarnated in the Nazis, was evil, and
was to be rooted out. It was this conviction that nerved our
effort. The momentum that had carried us through those
three years of struggle was not exhausted. It could have lasted
awhile longer, to establish a civilized peace. Foresight, discipline, co-operation, self-sacrifice do not turn from stern
dynamic virtues into "starry-eyed delusions" as soon as the
roar of the guns is stilled. But at San Francisco, the magnificent momentum was stopped with the magic words: "We
must be realistic."

Of course, realities have to be faced; and many of them are

[5] To be sure, I doubted the most unnatural history that would sharply
divide the world into three whales and fifty minnows. There are quite a few
other species of assorted sizes. And the giant that is cowardly, dull-witted, or
divided in purpose, may be no match for a much smaller opponent. Power
is not sheer weight, but will power.

hideous, in this "the best of all possible worlds." Such realities cannot be exorcized by prayer. But they can be met in two ways: resistance and capitulation. Gangsterism among nations, that is to say power politics, is an evil which we must refuse to condone, even when it seeks refuge in our own hearts. No surrender to the Hitler within us.

To have placed *power*, stark and unashamed, at the core of the World Charter was another "Great Refusal." For this moral catastrophe, the common people were not to blame. In so far as they thought at all, they were "realistic" enough to want peace; and if they had been frankly told that the price of peace was the acceptance of world law, they would have paid it without haggling. Neither were the cliques wholly responsible—the military, the career diplomats, the merchants of death. Wrong principles would do little harm if they were held only by the selfish few, or by the illiterate: the former are easily discounted, the latter do not count. There is in the modern world a genuine democracy, an enormous class which cannot originate thought, but is capable of understanding it. That class means well, and is responsive to guidance. It followed Wilson and Roosevelt with enthusiasm; it bought Willkie's book by the million. But it is self-diffident; it grows discouraged if experts haughtily affirm that its desire for justice and peace is foolishly Utopian. When narrowness of heart and mind finds talented, plausible advocates, then the masses lose faith in their own generosity. This degradation of the many by their leaders is what Julien Benda called "the treason of the intellectuals."

Now the American intellectual, the man whose trade is thought—journalist, essayist, book writer, political orator, professor—is, for all his smartness and toughness, a Timid Soul. He lend-leases his talent to the vested interests, at times simply because he is for hire; at times because he hopes

to join the ranks of the privileged, were it only as a retainer;
at times because his education in literature, religion and
politics has been conformist and conservative; at times because he dreads appearing naïve and crude. So the elite
deserts its proper post, which is the vanguard. It kills the
hope of the common man, instead of serving it.

In 1944–1945, many leaders of the Left, including Mr.
Wallace himself, clung to the unholy idea of the Big Three
as the most efficient means of preserving Soviet-American
friendship. It was easy to prophesy then that a "friendship"
based on power would inevitably turn sour. The only way in
which we could have remained friends with Russia was
within the framework of universal law. Power—that which
Denmark lacks, and which Hitler once possessed in a high
degree—means brutality and selfishness. It breeds jealousy
and diffidence. The Three Giants began worrying lest one
of them should become a Superpower. Marshal Smuts urged
Britain to seek allies, so as to keep level with the Bigger Two.
We and Russia started rounding up "satellites." A time was
bound to come when our expanding "orbits" would interfere. To divide the world is to spoil for a fight. So it was with
Napoleon and Alexander of Russia. So it was with Hitler and
Stalin. This inevitable strife is inherent in power politics.

We are at present at war with "communism," and undoubtedly the clash of ideologies embitters the tussle for
power. It looked at one time as though Russia would emerge
mortally wounded from the conflict with Hitler; if such had
been the case, and if Churchill's Empire had come out with
renewed resources and energies, then it is with England that
we should now be engaged in desperate rivalry. Power is an
end unto itself, and contemns ideologies, which after all are
ideals. In its purity, Power cannot be "reasonable." If it were,
it would abdicate its usurped supremacy, and place itself at

the service of justice. So long as we say: "Peace, peace," and add: "But Power is the sole reality," there shall be no peace.[6]

With the destruction of Hiroshima and Nagasaki, I felt as though the heavens had rolled up like a scroll. What struck me with awe was not the formidable efficacy of the new weapon. This was but another step—a very long step, it is true—in a direction already too familiar. We knew the effect of rockets, blockbusters, saturation raids. We were aware that bacteriological and chemical methods of warfare were held in leash only through the fear of retaliation. It had long been manifest that man's capacity for evil had far outstripped his social intelligence, and that rugged individualism was no panacea against wholesale slaughter. Such alternatives as *Utopia or Hell, One World or None*, were offered to us before as well as after August, 1945. Ironically, the professionals of war, fighters and diplomats, were least affected by this revolution. They became fossils overnight, but have not yet wakened to realize it. Two years after Hiroshima, conscription was still advocated, old-fashioned armaments were still piled up, moves and countermoves were still made on the futile old chessboard. We are still averting the next war by the approved method of preparing for it. You cannot expect men in the full flush of their martial glory to confess that they are superseded.

To me, the atomic revolution heralded, in the material world, the full vindication, the complete triumph, of the scientific method. It is a paradox that the victory should have been delayed so long. But, throughout the nineteenth cen-

[6] Power corrupts the home scene as well as the international atmosphere. As singleness of purpose is the most essential element in power, a nation bent upon being mighty cannot tolerate dissent. Freedom is branded as disloyalty. The military state without is of necessity a police state within.

tury, especially in England, many were still sneering at abstract research. The steam engine, we were told, had been invented and slowly perfected, "from precedent to precedent," by practical men who worried little about the laws of thermodynamics. Edison, the Wright Brothers, were not theorists. Although the Germans had brought science and industry closer together, the old tradition still lingered: the rule of thumb, the hunch, trial and error. The pure scientist was shrugged away as an unworldly character, almost as quaint, harmless and useless as the scholar.

Now theory in its most abstract form had its revenge. The whole development started with problems far beyond the ken of common sense and everyday experience, with daring hypotheses, with abstruse formulas. Practical men were needed to turn thought into explosives; but they were hirelings; the primacy of thought was beyond dispute. Nothing could be more radical, nothing more revolutionary, than this stupendous experiment. It is the flowering of a long process; but it is not guided by mere precedent. It reveals vistas which the scientists themselves cannot fathom. Empiricism is not dead, but it is reduced to a subordinate position. And so is the profit motive. The men who won this most decisive of all battles in world history deserve to be millionaires, far more than the manufacturers of chewing gum or the operators of slot machines. But they returned quietly to their laboratories, and the world hardly knows their names. The whole perspective is changed. The mighty of yesterday appear absurdly small.

This triumph of human intelligence brought to me an exhilaration which, for a moment, obliterated the horror of the actual deed (our conscience is still numb) and the dread of a new barbarism armed with irresistible power. It filled me with the solemn joy of a new Renaissance. I could intone the exultant words of Raoul Glaber: "The earth hath shaken off the rags of its antiquity," or sing with Rabelais: "At last we are out of Gothic night!" Or best of all, I could stand "with a wild surmise, Silent, upon a peak in Darien." What counted was not the achievement merely, but the method. The victory won in nuclear physics foreshadowed advances in every field —in organic chemistry, in agriculture, in physiology and medicine, in psychology, in sociology. Man, if willing to take thought, has the power to eliminate disease and want.

My internationalism assumed a new form. I ceased to be interested in federating the relics of the past: here was a new departure. The world could unite on the basis of that which obviously had nothing to do with race, caste, class, sect or nation: scientific research. Let the many paths of tradition meander as they will: this is the common road. Scientific research, on that unexampled scale, is not a new factor in an old society: it is the living nucleus of a new commonwealth. At present, we are thinking in negative terms: how to harness the new power to the ancient values; how to protect our secrets, how to foil our rivals, how to prohibit new efforts which might upset our precarious advantage. We should be looking ahead. If we threw our whole energy into promotion, prevention would lose most of its significance. We are attempting to save our contending civilizations and regimes: but they were, every one, conditioned by a technique which is brushed aside under our very eyes. The problem at present is not Imperialism, the Balance of Power, individual profit vs. the Commonwealth: it is the organization of a universal Scientific Research Board.

But the forces of the past still have life enough in them to grab the new power and turn it into a curse. A wild beast is most dangerous when wounded to death. Nationalism, a brief and tragic phenomenon in the history of mankind, was not killed with Hitler. It must be curbed, and the United Nations, each still nominally sovereign, cannot rise above their source. That is why I gladly joined the Committee to Frame a World Constitution: I can see no other assurance of peace. A World State per se is not the millennium: but its essential purpose will be to hold in check hatred, fanaticism, anarchy. We need the World State as the receiver of our bankrupt civilization. That task accomplished, the Scientific Community will be able to grow, in ways which we cannot forecast.

I, who am not a scientist, hail this conquest of the world by the scientific spirit without humility and without jealousy. What I expect of science is that it will free mankind from ancestral fear. Then man will be able to address himself to problems which physical science cannot even define. Science is the deliverer: but what shall we do with our liberty?